PHILOSOPHY IN A TIME OF LOST SPIRIT:

ESSAYS ON CONTEMPORARY THEORY

In the last two centuries, our world would have been a safer place if philosophers such as Rousseau, Marx, and Nietzche had not given intellectual encouragement to the radical ideologies of Jacobins, Stalinists, and fascists. Maybe the world would have been better off, from the standpoint of sound practice, if philosophers had engaged in only modest, decent theory, as did John Stuart Mill. Yet, as Ronald Beiner contends, the point of theory is not to think safe thoughts; the point is to open intellectual horizons.

In *Philosophy in a Time of Lost Spirit,* Beiner reflects on the dualism of theory and practice. The purpose of the theorist is not to offer sensible guidance on the conduct of social life but to test the boundaries of our vision of social order. Whereas the liberal citizen should embody the practical virtues of prudence and moderation, the theorist should be radical, probing, and immoderate. Looking back at the liberal–communitarian debate of the 1980s, Beiner recognizes that the antidote to our spiritless times lies neither in the embrace of community over individualism nor of individualism over community: both individual and community need to be submitted to radical questioning. It is by exposing ourselves to the challenge of fearless thinking encountered at the philosophical extremities that we are most likely to understand our own world at a deeper level.

In this collection of essays and reviews, Ronald Beiner helps us to think critically about the thought-worlds of our foremost contemporary thinkers, including Hannah Arendt, Allan Bloom, Michel Foucault, Hans-Georg Gadamer, Jürgen Habermas, Will Kymlicka, Christopher Lasch, Richard Rorty, Judith Shklar, Leo Strauss, Charles Taylor, and Michael Walzer.

RONALD BEINER is professor of political science at the University of Toronto. His book *What's the Matter with Liberalism?* was awarded the Macpherson Prize in 1994 by the Canadian Political Science Association and the University of Toronto Press.

RONALD BEINER

Philosophy in a Time of Lost Spirit: Essays on Contemporary Theory

UNIVERSITY OF TORONTO PRESS
Toronto Buffalo London

© University of Toronto Press Incorporated 1997
Toronto Buffalo London
Printed in Canada

ISBN 0-8020-4210-4 (cloth)
ISBN 0-8020-8067-7 (paper)

Printed on acid-free paper

Canadian Cataloguing in Publication Data

Beiner, Ronald, 1953–
 Philosophy in a time of lost spirit : essays on
 contemporary theory

 Includes bibliographical references and index.
 ISBN 0-8020-4210-4 (bound)   ISBN 0-8020-8067-7 (pbk.)

 1. Liberalism.   I. Title.

 JC574.B44 1997   320.51   C97-930851-8

University of Toronto Press acknowledges the financial assistance to its
publishing program of the Canada Council for the Arts and the Ontario Arts
Council.

For Zimra

Contents

III: Political Judgment Revisited   173

Preface: The Theorist as Critic

But philosophy must beware of the wish to be edifying.

Hegel

Let me first hasten to make clear that the cross-hairs I refer to in the lead essay of this collection are not those of a gunsight, as if my purpose were to wage war on liberalism. What I actually have in mind are the instruments of optical inquiry: the ocular of a telescope or microscope. Hence the aim is an enhancement of vision.

I suspect that this is not the only misapprehension to which readers of these essays will find themselves subject. Indeed, running through these essays – and perhaps through my entire work – is a conception of theory that many readers will likely find paradoxical. For this reason, it would probably be sensible of me to begin this preface with a brief discussion of the problem of theory in general, if only to show that I am aware that many will find my core conception of theory paradoxical. If there is one idea that is at the heart of all my efforts as a theorist of social life, it is the notion that radically different existential demands are made by civic life on the one hand and by the life of theory on the other. This is a theme that runs from the opening chapter to the closing chapter of this book; in Chapter 19 I refer to it as the 'dualism' of theory and practice. The purpose of the theorist, at least as I see it, is not to offer sensible guidance on the conduct of social life, but rather to probe the normative adequacy of a given vision of social order by pushing that particular vision as far as it will go: hence the 'intellectual extremism' that is, as it were, built into the whole enterprise of theory (as enacted by its most ambitious practitioners). The exemplary theorists are what J.S. Mill referred to (and celebrated) as 'one-eyed men' whose 'one eye is a penetrating one' precisely because it does not see the whole truth: 'if they saw more, they probably would not see so keenly, nor so eagerly pursue one course of inquiry.' The practice of citizenship should be sober, sensible, prudential, moderate, and (in the best sense of the word) 'liberal,' whereas theory should be radical, extravagant, probing, biting, and immoderate. That is why one should never presume that exemplars of the adventure of theory will also be exemplars of civic praxis (Plato was hardly the last philosopher to go astray in Syracuse).

As one example of the competing imperatives of theory and citizenship, consider the political problem of nationalism. As a matter of prudential citizenship, it may make perfectly good sense to try to strike a reasonable compromise between liberalism and nationalism. Yet it is in the interests of good theory to drive them apart, in order to clarify the pure demands that each makes upon the human being *qua* human being: the liberal's demand for universal dignity versus the nationalist's demand for communal belonging. This is not to deny that having submitted liberalism and nationalism to the exercise of radical theoretical scrutiny, one may be left with insights into the essence of each that can be profitably applied to the world of practice. My point, rather, is that the vocation of theory must be animated by imperatives of its own that are distinct from our need, as citizens, for salubrious maxims of political practice. In civic life it is often desirable to fudge sharp differences and to seek pragmatic compromises: to try, if possible, to have our cake and eat it too. In the life of theory, on the other hand, splitting the difference between opposing theoretical alternatives is always intolerable and violates the very meaning of the enterprise: to think through in a fully coherent way what it means to interpret the ultimate nature of social life according to one set of philosophical categories rather than another.

This issue of the utter radicalism of the theoretical enterprise comes out as well in Chapter 16, where I contrast Charles Taylor's 'rhetoric of understanding' with my own 'rhetoric of criticism.' The simple fact is that there would have been no grand tradition of political philosophy at all if, say, Plato's aim had been to 'understand' the Greek polis, or if Rousseau had sought to 'understand' the world of the Parisian salon, or if Marx had sought to 'understand' the bourgeoisie, or if Nietzsche's enterprise had been to 'understand' the culture of nineteenth-century Europe. Our experience of the present is enlivened and enlarged by these grand philosophies precisely because their aim, in each case, was a project of root-

and-branch criticism. Contrary to the contemporary injunction to eschew foundations, each of the great theorists just mentioned made such an exemplary contribution to the enterprise of theory precisely *because* each was determined to search for an ultimate ground. In the case of Plato the idea of a rational ordering of the soul provides an ultimate normative standard for the judging of politics. In Rousseau's case, the ultimate normative standard is the idea of self-legislation – of the free determination, whether individually or collectively, of a law for the self. For Marx, the ultimate normative standard is the idea of human self-mastery attained through the rational provision for human needs. And in Nietzsche the ultimate normative standard is the maximum creativity of the human will, and the joy that comes in reordering or reshaping the world in conformity with the strength and vitality of one's own volition.

Now I certainly do not wish to deny that liberal political theorists from Mill to Rawls offer salutary and sensible guidance concerning the business of being a good, decent, sensible citizen of the liberal polity; and citizenship in a decent, sensible, liberal polity is not a negligible good. However, a theorist like myself shrinks back in horror at the thought of a tradition of political philosophy composed exclusively of decent liberals like Mill and Rawls, without the intellectual extremists like Plato and Rousseau and Nietzsche. In fact, there is something absurdly self-emasculating in the reproach commonly directed by liberals against Rousseau, Marx, and Nietzsche for having composed a body of work that was ripe for ideological misuse by Jacobins, Stalinists, and fascists respectively. To be sure, one has little reason to doubt that our political world of the last two centuries would have been a decidedly safer place if Rousseau, Marx, and Nietzsche had practiced theory in more or less the way that John Stuart Mill practiced theory. Yet the point of theory isn't to think safe thoughts; rather, the point is to open intellectual horizons, which one is hardly likely to do with much effectiveness unless one hazards dangerous thoughts. Without Rousseau, Marx, and Nietzsche, our political world might well be a safer world; but unquestionably, our *intellectual* world would be radically impoverished if the great critics within the tradition had been merely Swiss and German clones of John Stuart Mill (think of Wilhelm von Humboldt! – perhaps the most soporific political philosopher who ever lived). The greatest theorists are always dangerous precisely because they practice theory in a way that doesn't betray the essential mission of the theorist.

If I am right, the great virtue of theory in its contribution to social experience is not the 'connectedness' of the theorist-critic (as a leading contemporary account would have it), but the possibility of tremendous distance from the prevailing norms of social experience. This may help to clarify a statement in Chapter 16 that will again likely strike many readers as paradoxical. There I present myself as both antiliberal and anticommunitarian. How can this be? Needless to say, many of the essays in this collection (especially those in Part I) arose out of the 'liberal–communitarian debate' that gripped political theory in the 1980s. It was a staple of that debate that to be a critic of liberalism was to be a partisan of something called 'community.' In response, liberals rightly protested the folly of giving a blank cheque to the claims of community as such (as if there were something equally elevating about communal experience of whatever description). But as an avowed critic of liberalism, I have no desire simply to replace the liberal's principle of rational autonomy with a principle of communal identity, nor to see the latter principle spared the same degree of theoretical scrutiny to which liberal ideals ought to be submitted. As I see the matter, the problem with liberal theory is not that it leaves community out of account but that it fails to offer a sufficiently robust challenge to the individualistic self-understanding of contemporary social life. If 'communitarianism' requires that one yield up a blanket affirmation of community, regardless of content, then communitarian theory becomes subject to precisely the same objection – namely, that it falls short of the calling of theory, which is to issue fearlessly radical challenges to existing self-understandings.

We live in spiritless times. But this would be a blander assertion than it is intended to be if it sufficed, as a remedy to this spiritlessness, to come to a richer awareness of our communal attachments and historical identity. This is why the communitarian 'alternative' fails. It should also help explain why I am of the view that the whole liberal–communitarian debate falls short of the mark. To hit the mark, we have to begin by acknowledging just how much in contemporary life is sordid, empty, mechanical, and dispiriting. Or, alternatively, we need an account of why this grim picture is untrue, of the ways in which the social reality of contemporary life is in fact rich with meaning and purpose – an account that, so far as I am aware, no one has yet supplied. The real problem with liberalism as a political philosophy is that it refuses to take up this challenge, on the grounds that individuals, as self-directing centres of moral agency, must come to their own verdicts concerning the lives they live; ambitious judgments on the part of the theorist with respect to meaningful substance in contemporary life, or the lack of it, illegitimately impinge on the right of individuals to judge these things for themselves. Now, is it the case that this abdication on the part of liberal social philosophers is remedied by communitarianism? Not necessarily. By itself, the communitarian thesis concerning the social constitution of the self tells us nothing about the richness or banality, dignity or degradation, of the selves thus constituted. It all depends, of course, on the substantive character of the communities that are doing the constituting of selfhood. Indeed, it is sometimes the case that individuals react against the emptiness and spiritlessness of contemporary experience by embracing bonds of community and religion in their most tribal, zealous, and illiberal incarnations. This is not an alternative to the liberal predicament, but a reconfirmation, in mirror image, of the very ill that one means to flee. Again, a blanket affirmation of community in general seems to entail a theoretical abdication that exactly matches the one with which I tax liberal theorists. The solution is not to embrace community over against individualism, or to embrace individualism over against the sometimes oppressive demands of the community, but rather to subject both the individual *and* the community to a more searching interrogation in a fully ambitious theoretical dimension – that is, with respect to judgments about the *substance* of a satisfying life.

What these essays, I hope, teach (and the concluding chapters on judgment are intended to underscore this lesson) is that it is possible to combine a taste for the most exalted theory with a respect for the most down-to-earth practical prudence: that one can be a high-flying Platonist in one's conception of theory without losing sight of the fact that practical decisions should be governed by experience and historically informed prudence. Indeed, if prudence possesses an autonomous integrity of its own, and can therefore be trusted to look after itself, then the theorist need not be merely a handmaiden to prudence, and theory is liberated to pursue a higher calling. As a citizen, I am committed to many or most of the same policies and political goals as are professed by leading liberal philosophers of our day; but as a theorist, I nonetheless insist on presenting myself as a critic of liberalism because I am convinced that theoretical understanding of our own social world (namely, the galaxy of liberal experience as I define it in Chapter 1) requires exertions of self-questioning that test the boundaries of that world. In this sense, we are likely to understand ourselves at a deeper fathom by exposing ourselves to the challenge of the alien thought-worlds of (for instance) Augustine, Rousseau, de Maistre, Marx, and Heidegger than by contenting ourselves with the familiar verities of the contemporary descendants of Locke and Mill.

Most of the essays and reviews in this collection were written because various editors and organizers of conferences solicited them, so I have them to thank for this book; among my editors, Philippa Ingram of the *T.H.E.S.* and Jeffrey Friedman of *Critical Review* deserve special thanks. Thanks are also due to the journals and publishers that gave permission for republication. This seems a good opportunity to express my gratitude for the generous assistance that I have received from two sources: the Social Sciences and Humanities Research Council of Canada, which provided a general research grant; and the University of Toronto, which provided a Connaught Research Fellowship during the spring of 1996. I would also like to express my deep thanks to friends and colleagues – in particular, Edward Andrew, Alkis Kontos, and Stephen Newman – who have helped make the Toronto chapter of the Conference for the Study of Political Thought such an important forum for the practice of political theory in Toronto. This gathering has been a continuous source of valuable stimulation; several of the essays in this collection were presented to the CSPT group, which provided me with very helpful friendly criticism. Finally, I'd like to thank two other colleagues: Thomas Pangle, both for his extremely thoughtful critical response to Chapter 13 and for kindly agreeing to allow his letter to be published here; and Jennifer Nedelsky, for presenting me with an equally thoughtful and challenging critical response to Chapter 20.

I LIBERALISM AND HYPER-LIBERALISM

1

Liberalism in the Cross-Hairs of Theory

Nietzsche is the one, I suppose, who has expressed what it is about modernity that makes life impossible.

Hans-Georg Gadamer[1]

My purpose in this essay is to give an account of the kind of robust social criticism that I associate with the very enterprise of theory and to explain why the liberal philosophy that prevails in the contemporary academy is averse to this sort of social criticism. My aim is both to explore a certain conception of radical social theory and to defend this conception against familiar objections posed by those who represent the dominant liberal political philosophy.

The so-called liberal–communitarian debate of the 1980s seems a good starting point, since this debate gave prominent focus to anxieties about the theoretical sufficiency of liberalism, and helped to keep alive theoretical challenges to the hegemony of liberalism that might not otherwise have survived the demise of Marxism. 'Communitarian' critics of liberalism such as Charles Taylor, Michael Walzer, Alasdair MacIntyre, Michael Sandel, Robert Bellah, and Christopher Lasch put the problem of community on the theoretical agenda by addressing questions both to liberalism as a social philosophy and to the kind of society we think of as a liberal society.[2] These critics asked whether liberalism as a basically individualistic creed could do justice to the richly textured narrative histories

Originally published as 'What Liberalism Means,' *Social Philosophy and Policy* 13, no. 1 (Winter 1996). Reprinted with the permission of Cambridge University Press.

and socially constituted practices by which individuals in any society come to acquire meaningful selves. And they asked, quite properly, whether liberal societies, which basically define and understand themselves within a framework of individualistic categories, can offer the rich experiences of co-involvement that make for a meaningful human life. In order to assess whether these communitarian concerns pose a sufficiently radical challenge to liberal theory and the social reality it justifies, we need to probe the term 'liberalism' more deeply.

What is the basic character of the social order in which we live? From what source may we draw theoretically illuminating categories to make sense of our experience within this social order? Within what horizon of theoretical understanding can we become fully reflective about the shared way of life in which we participate? Questions of this sort are, surely, central to the enterprise of theory. Yet when we take our bearings by the dominant liberal philosophy of our day, we will discover, to our surprise, that such questions are almost impossible to formulate. For leading liberal theorists such as John Rawls, Ronald Dworkin, Bruce Ackerman, Charles Larmore, and Will Kymlicka, liberalism does not name a pervasive social order;[3] on the contrary, liberalism refers to a principle of political organization that accords individuals the freedom to navigate a course of their own design – a course constituted by self-elected plans and purposes. In the view of right liberals (such as F.A. Hayek, Robert Nozick, and Michael Oakeshott), this vision of individual self-government requires that the state intervene as little as possible in the social and economic life of the society;[4] for left liberals (all the defenders of liberalism cited in the previous sentence are left liberals), considerable state intervention is required so that all individuals receive an equitable share of the total aggregate of social resources, and so that all individuals have a fair opportunity to give play to their unique conception of their own personal good. But all of these liberals, whether right or left, agree that there is no overarching social order to which it would be reasonable to apply the term 'liberalism.' Rather, liberalism for them denotes an officially agnostic or 'neutral' grid that allows self-governing individuals to co-ordinate their reciprocal relations in ways that maximize the attainment of their own individual purposes.[5]

The kinds of social phenomena that are of concern to critics of liberalism include the following: anemic citizenship, a brutalizing mass culture, the resort to hyperindividualistic fantasy and escapism, the increasing brittleness of basic social institutions such as the family, the overwhelming of civic confidence by problems of scale and technological complexity in contemporary life, the mindless frenzy of modern consumerism, and the world of therapy and self-preoccupation associated with Lasch's 'culture of narcissism' – to say nothing of the attenuation, by market-based individualism, of that degree of civic solidarity needed to sustain even a minimally decent welfare state (for example, one that provides universal health care). Liberals will maintain that these cultural–political concerns actually have very little to do with liberalism in a strict sense; even if they grant that these are real problems in contemporary society, liberals will want to contest the use of the term 'liberalism' as an appropriate designation for the social order that tends to generate such problems. The complaints about liberal society that I share with other critics of liberalism – liberal society's disorientation, and its tendency toward anomie, civic pathologies, and widespread soullessness – are, liberals will say, a function of many things that strictly speaking are entirely distinct from liberalism: namely, capitalism, mass society, secularization, and so on. Liberalism, defined strictly, has to do with delimiting the moral authority of the state in order to shield individuals from having what are for them indigestible moral beliefs and practices coercively thrust upon them. Or so will insist those liberals made indignant by efforts to blame all the ills of the modern world on them and no one but them. I certainly accept that people describe themselves as liberals in a wide variety of ways and for a wide variety of reasons, and I am aware of the peril of getting too hung up on quarrels over labels. Nonetheless, I feel an urge to defend my nomenclature, and to demonstrate to the liberal that what strikes him or her as a merely eccentric or perverse overenlargement of the scope of the term 'liberal' actually does help to pinpoint a common core of moral commitments, reasonably described as liberal, that do in fact connect up with the range of supposedly distinct social pathologies that concern me.

One may distinguish three broad senses of the term 'liberalism': (1) liberalism as a political doctrine, referring to the liberal urge to circumscribe the authority of the state as a legislator of morality; (2) liberalism as a social order, which I have elsewhere labelled 'the regime of the modern bourgeoisie';[6] and (3) liberalism as a philosophical ranking of priorities, according to which intellectuals ought to be focusing more on the achievements than the debilities of modern liberal societies. A liberal in this last sense typically disdains antibourgeois, antimodernist cultural critique for its political irresponsibility. If it turns out that of these three definitions, only the first is legitimate, one will be obliged to conclude that this essay is incorrectly titled, and that much of what I want to subsume under the critique of liberalism is directed at a target that doesn't actually exist. Many of those who feel comfortable being philosophically classified as liberal will no doubt come to this very conclusion. Therefore, if I am to uphold my enterprise as a critique of *liberalism* (rather than a critique of something else about which I am fundamentally confused) I must elaborate on and defend my threefold definition.

Let me start with the question of *why* liberals everywhere are so pre-·occupied with resisting threats posed by the state to the independence of individuals. As we pursue this most basic element of liberal conviction, we will be drawn inescapably toward larger, more encompassing moral commitments which, I hope, will show that my use of the term 'liberal' is less eccentric, less perverse, and perhaps even reasonably plausible.

What I want to maintain is that *depoliticizing moral life*, ejecting the state from the business of tampering with the soul, is but one aspect of a larger moral vision. The basic liberal idea is to give the individual the space in which to make something of his or her life, and to allow the individual to exercise ultimate moral responsibility. According to liberalism, the state in effect says to the individual, 'Okay, Bud, it's your life. Do something with it.' (This vision is not necessarily biased towards individualism, since if individuals freely opt for communalist commitments, this is certainly fine with the liberal. But nothing in liberal philosophy *requires* individuals to embrace such commitments.)

The fundamental anxiety underlying all my critical reflections on liberalism is this: Having given individuals this moral space, suppose they then proceed to unfold a shared way of life that is spiritually empty, with only a minimum of humanly meaningful moral substance? The question then will be whether liberal political philosophy will have left itself the intellectual resources with which to pass judgment on this outcome.

The basic liberal idea I have described is captured quite nicely in MacIntyre's helpful phrase, 'the privatization of good.'[7] To this, liberals will object that rather than 'privatizing' the good, liberal politics seeks to 'socialize' it, as opposed to 'politicizing' it.[8] While it is illegitimate for the *state* to shape moral character, it is perfectly okay for character to be shaped within the moral agencies of civil society: family, church, neighbourhood, and so on. I certainly agree that liberals by and large are more sympathetic to civil society as a locus of moral life than they are to the idea of the state as a moral authority. But I don't think this formulation fully captures the moral thrust of liberalism. Why should the liberal be any more comfortable with citizens being morally bullied by preachers from the pulpit or by community leaders within the neighbourhood than with bullying by politicians holding public office at the level of the state? (Admittedly, the state possesses powers of coercion that are unavailable to civil society, but there are other ways of orchestrating people's lives than by applying direct coercion.) Liberals want individuals to think for themselves, to choose for themselves. From the point of view of this ideal of moral self-government, *social* pressure that locks individuals into preappointed roles and expectations is as objectionable as political pressure. As Mill's *On Liberty* makes clear, if liberals want to fortify individuals against pressures to conform, civil society can be just as oppressive as the state.[9]

If the basic liberal goal is to ensure that individuals are not imposed upon as they go about forming moral convictions and moral commitments – and this, after all, is the *point* of liberal anxiety about the state – then the moral ideal here is indeed 'the privatization of good.' And this brings me back to my bedrock objection: Having privatized the good, are we still able to render critical judgments on the global way of life in which these putatively 'self-governing' individuals nonetheless participate? The basic question, as I see it, is this: Are we as theorists willing to be bold enough, *illiberal* enough, to admit that taken as a whole, the moral civilization that defines contemporary liberal society is not terribly impressive? My claim is that you can tell a liberal every time by his or her aversion to being so presumptuous.

I know what the liberal will say to all this. The liberal will say that this insistence on passing judgment on the moral substance of a way of life violates the overwhelming 'fact of pluralism' that surrounds us.[10] For liberals, pluralism – the condition whereby individuals are committed to irreconcilably different moral ideals, personal aspirations, visions of the good life – is a sociological given in all modern societies. My response is that, once again, we require the moral and intellectual resources to distinguish phony pluralism from real pluralism – resources that are missing in contemporary liberal philosophy. One has less true pluralism in a hundred different trashy tabloids than one has in one or two quality newspapers; but in order to say this, one has to be prepared to offer substantive judgments – judgments that theorists of a liberal disposition are reluctant to make available.

Here, as elsewhere, we may take Isaiah Berlin as a paradigmatic liberal. For Berlin, the liberal tradition is defined by its recognition of the absoluteness of rights and the idea that 'there are frontiers ... within which men should be inviolable.'[11] Presumably, it is impermissible for these frontiers to be violated by civil society any more than by the state. My *main* point here is that liberals are averse to any very penetrating social criticism for fear of impugning or casting into question this inviolability of frontiers. This comes out very well in the following statement of principle by Berlin:

Most modern liberals, at their most consistent, want a situation in which as many individuals as possible can realize as many of their ends as possible, without assessment of the value of these ends as such, save in so far as they may frustrate the purposes of others. They wish the frontiers between individuals or groups of men to be drawn solely with a view to preventing collisions between human purposes, all of which must be considered to be equally ultimate, uncriticizable ends in themselves.[12]

Once again, the concern with the state's power over individuals appears as merely derivative; what is primary is a certain moral vision. Liberals are fearful of state power on account of a certain understanding of what it is to respect individuals, not vice versa.

Some may think that what I am actually criticizing is 'capitalism,' not 'liberalism.' I don't think so. Capitalism is the label applied to an economic system for the relatively efficient production of commodities and services involving the free disposal of capital. Liberalism – at least according to the broader definition that I am trying to render plausible – is a philosophy of life that seeks to liberate individuals from the shackles of predefined social roles and stations in life. Let us be clear about which of these two categories has logical priority. Morally speaking, it can be presumed that one opts for a capitalist economic system with a view to securing a wider play for individual liberty; one does not embrace liberalism in order to serve an antecedent commitment to capitalism. It is true enough that a given society (say China) might be induced to liberalize itself over time in pursuit of the material benefits dangled in front of it by a free market economy. But I don't think this affects my point here, which is this: if political philosophy is concerned with the grounds for embracing one moral-political world rather than another, then the question of liberalism 'trumps' the question of capitalism. Capitalism denotes merely an *economic* alternative to feudalism; liberalism denotes a *moral* alternative to feudalism. I am not suggesting that political philosophy shouldn't concern itself with choosing among alternative economic systems. Nor am I suggesting that the choice of an economic system is unrelated to a comprehensive choice of a way of life – quite the contrary! What I'm suggesting is that the choice of one economic system rather than another is logically subordinate to the choice among alternative visions of moral order.[13]

I have discussed the relationship between capitalism and liberalism; let me now discuss briefly the relationship between democracy and liberalism. Some will charge that to criticize liberalism in the context of a liberal democratic society is really to criticize democracy, or to use criticism of liberalism as a cloak for criticizing democracy. In response, I would say that my own inclination would be to criticize liberal democracy from the perspective that it is not democratic enough, not that it is *too* democratic. My intention as a critic of liberalism would be to criticize liberalism in the name of democracy, but at the same time to elevate democracy to a rather demanding standard. My criticism of liberal democracy is that it neither encourages nor requires citizens to be more active or more knowledgeable in their command of public affairs. However, there is an opposed conception of democracy which consists in deferring to whatever happen to be the current standards of public participation, be they high or low (more likely low, or extremely low). According to this conception, talk about elevating the standards of democratic participation is itself antidemocratic. Invoking the banner of democracy simply as a way of legitimizing an acceptance of a descent to the lowest common denominator with respect to standards of cultural and political life is another way of formulating precisely what I understand by liberalism.

Thus far, I have tried to suggest some reasons for preferring a broader rather than a narrower definition of what it means to be a liberal. Another advantage of the broader definition is that the narrower definitions fail to cover adequately the full range of contemporary liberal thought. According to the narrowest definition, a liberal is someone whose central anxiety is the possible abuse of state power, and who is preoccupied with devising institutional means for dealing with this anxiety. Yet when we look at the huge span of opinion among self-defined liberals with respect to the legitimate exercise of state power – the gulf between, say, the welfare liberalism of Rawls and the antiwelfare liberalism of Nozick – we realize that this is not a terribly helpful way of pinpointing what a commitment to liberalism entails. But even when we consider less narrow definitions, we encounter similar problems. Suppose we define the liberal as someone who believes that society exists in order to furnish individuals with the best possible opportunity to develop their own unique personalities. Without question, this is what defined the political vision of certain nineteenth-century liberals, including John Stuart Mill. But again, this definition is betrayed by what leading liberals are professing today. For some of the most influential contemporary formulations of liberal philosophy (those of Rawls and Larmore, to name two) consider individual autonomy as

merely one moral view among a plurality of competing moral conceptions, and think it would be morally and politically illegitimate to privilege
the ideal of individual self-development; rather, this ideal should be per-
mitted its place among other ideals in a larger 'overlapping consensus,' or
alternatively, in a *modus vivendi* among moral views.[14]

These definitions therefore fail the test of all-inclusiveness. This gives
us a reason to opt for my much more encompassing definition, which is
this: a liberal is someone who sees nothing *fundamentally* questionable,
morally or metaphysically, in the kind of social order that has currently
been developed in the United States of America, a society devoted to
guarding the rights, freedoms, and well-being of individuals, and who
finds nothing questionable in applying this social order as a standard for
judging social progress in other parts of the world. According to this definition, the liberal restricts the function of social theory to suggesting
piecemeal reforms – perhaps in order to render such a society somewhat
fairer, more open, more democratic, and more generous than it presently is. I take the ameliorative liberalism defended by Richard Rorty
(notwithstanding certain idiosyncrasies bound up with his own philosophical project) as representative of what I understand by liberalism in
this very broad sense.[15] I think that my definition captures what is distinctive about contemporary proponents of liberal philosophy better and
more inclusively than other, narrower alternative definitions. A liberal is
someone who feels quite comfortable, metaphysically speaking, with the
kind of social order made available by contemporary American society,
and whose moral and philosophical concerns are exhausted by an urge to
make such societies incrementally less unjust. For Canadians, the vision
of liberalism that I'm trying to sketch gains clarity through a contrast
between the unbridled social dynamism at work south of the border and
the residual preliberal traditions that we see being swallowed up in contemporary Canada; and therefore my sense of the term liberalism should
be reasonably familiar to readers of George Grant's *Lament for a Nation*
(particularly Chapter 5).[16] As well, in all those countries around the world
where the struggle between modernity and premodernity is still being
fought out, the stakes involved in cultural liberalism ought to be pretty
clear, both positively and negatively. (To mention examples: positively, it
means an end, thankfully, to practices such as female circumcision in the
Sudan; negatively, it means the growing hegemony of certain imperialistic languages – notably English – that serve as the agents of the liberal way
of life, and correspondingly, the tragic withering of languages that are
marginal to the liberal empire.)[17]

Many liberals will deny that liberalism has anything to do with cultural judgments about modernity; they will assert that liberalism has to do with the extent to which the state does or does not impinge upon the citizen. But liberalism has everything to do with cultural judgments about modernity. A liberal is someone who celebrates modernity wholeheartedly as emancipatory. An antiliberal is someone who is at least somewhat anxious about the quality of this emancipation, and who worries about the price we have to pay for being culturally 'emancipated.' Let me offer an illustration that goes to the heart of the *Kulturkampf* being waged by liberals. On 14 February 1989, to the horror of liberals throughout the West (a horror I certainly share to the fullest), Ayatollah Ruhollah Khomeini issued a *fatwa* against Salman Rushdie for having written *The Satanic Verses*. But in his 1990 Herbert Read Memorial Lecture, Rushdie himself told us that this same Islamic culture that ultimately condemned him as an author instilled in him a capacity to *cherish* books – to treat *all* books as holy – that is not unrelated, I think, to the *fatwa*. His Islamic upbringing taught him to kiss any book that had been dropped in order to repair the disrespect shown to the book, whatever it happened to be (whether a novel or a comic book).[18] In such a nonliberal culture, books *matter*, and because they matter, one either kisses them or burns them.[19] A liberal society is one that does not take books seriously enough either to kiss them *or* to burn them. A liberal celebrates this; an antiliberal, as I mentioned earlier, worries about it. And it seems to me that an analogous point applies across a wide swath of cultural experience (including sexual life).[20]

In order to penetrate to what liberalism means, we must look not just to the mechanical politics of the liberal state, but to the spiritual politics of the liberal soul. We must, as Plato in *The Republic* insisted, draw the connection between the polis and the psyche, and see that a liberal political order does not guard the individual against governance by larger forces, but rather, shapes that governance in a particular fashion. Here, it is well to observe the paradoxical character of MacIntyre's definition of liberalism in terms of its attempt to privatize the good. While it is indeed true that liberalism aspires to privatize the good, it really can't be done, because this very attempt at privatization already expresses a larger, global conception of what the good is (for instance, the conception of the good as something that admits of private stipulation – which is itself a global, not a private, conception).

Saying that we inhabit a *liberal* civilization is therefore different from saying that we inhabit a capitalist civilization, a democratic civilization, a civilization of mass culture or mass society, and so on. The most discerning liberals have been able to appreciate this very well. Let me cite three liberals on this point:

(1) Stephen Macedo has written that 'liberalism holds out the promise, or the threat, of making all the world like California.'[21]
(2) According to John Gray, 'liberalism ... is the political theory of modernity.'[22]
(3) And finally, Richard Rorty acknowledges that the liberal order is not neutral on the question of how human beings should live, but on the contrary, embodies a decision that human beings be 'bland, calculating, petty and unheroic' because this is the necessary price one pays for a society that cherishes individual liberty.[23]

These three liberals here give expression to an insight about the relationship between the individual and society that has eluded most contemporary liberal philosophers. What distinguishes most liberal theorists today is the philosophical assumption that we start with individuals and then ask how we can design social institutions that allow these individuals, in a fashion that best suits them without prejudicing the welfare of others, to define and redefine their own needs, wants, interests, and preferences. This runs directly counter to the philosophical assumption shared by almost all the great political philosophers running from Plato to Nietzsche (and shared even by nineteenth-century *liberals* like Tocqueville and Mill), which is that we rightly start with a social order and then ask how that social order shapes individuals of a particular cast. In accordance with the tradition stretching from Plato to Nietzsche, we interrogate liberal society by first of all asking what kinds of human beings it characteristically churns out.[24]

Does it make sense to speak of modern, individualistic societies as animated by a shared way of life? And is it fair to emphasize the term 'liberal' when characterizing the global ordering principle at work in contemporary liberal societies? To address these difficult questions, I want to make a short detour into art criticism. It might seem odd (to the liberal it will seem *very* odd) that I would conceptualize my understanding of liberalism by offering a commentary on a cultural artefact, instead of inquiring into structures of government or institutional power; however, it should already be clear that the questions I want to pose require cultural exploration. In thinking of what liberalism means, the image that comes to my mind is an exceptionally striking painting by David Hockney titled *Mr.*

David Hockney, *Mr. and Mrs. Clark and Percy*, 1970/71. Acrylic, 84" × 120",
©David Hockney. Tate Gallery, London / Art Resource, NY.

and Mrs. Clark and Percy, from 1970–71. Anyone who has seen the painting
hanging in the Tate Gallery in London would, I think, have trouble for-
getting it. It is a portrait of two nearly life-size figures – a man seated and
a woman standing – in a typically barren sixties domestic landscape. *Mr.
and Mrs. Clark and Percy* portrays two close friends of Hockney – Ossie
Clark and Celia Birtwell, both successful and quite well-known London
fashion designers, who were married in 1969. The painting was intended
as a marriage portrait and is set in the living room of their flat in Notting
Hill Gate, London. Everything in the painting bespeaks emptiness: the
insipid pastel colours throughout; the soulless sixties furniture; the blank
walls, adorned only by a Hockney print off to the left side; the white cat
on Ossie's lap (Percy refers to the cat); the tasteless sixties carpet into
which Ossie's bare feet are sunk; the sterile white lilies on a sterile white
coffee table; and the telephone and lamp deposited forlornly on the floor
to the right. Clark and Birtwell look on as if deposited in a spiritual void:
utterly lost, uncomfortable, and ill at ease with themselves, and in some
strange way separated by an immeasurable distance. It seems entirely fit-

ting that the marriage celebrated in this strange painting was to end in divorce.[25]

How is this painting relevant to an understanding of liberalism? Let me try to translate my commentary into more theoretical terms. Liberalism as I understand it does not merely refer to a particular relationship between the state and the individual; rather, it expresses an encompassing view of human life, one that aspires to leave individuals as free as possible to shape their lives according to their own notions, with society offering no official guidance on how people are to conduct their lives in a meaningful direction. What Hockney's painting conveys is that this vision of things has the consequence that the *furniture* of our world, as it were, is reduced to the bare minimum. In short, I think the painting offers a visual answer to the question that concerns me here – that answer being that the liberal preoccupation with formal freedoms obscures the issue of the political–moral–spiritual matter or substance of a particular way of life.

At this point the philosophical liberal is bound to leap up and cry, 'Aha! Just as I suspected! Cultural criticism masquerading as political analysis!' What is my rejoinder? Well, to be honest, I have real trouble seeing why political philosophers should be required to abstain from cultural criticism, and I find considerable comfort in the fact that the most ambitious theorists of the tradition – Plato, Rousseau, Tocqueville, Nietzsche – showed no reluctance in placing cultural critique at the heart of their enterprise. Indeed, my chief complaint against contemporary liberal political philosophers (as opposed to the nineteenth-century liberals, who did *not* feel obliged to observe maxims of intellectual parsimony) is that they have abandoned this essential critical dimension of theory, and in so doing have limited themselves to pursuing, at most, a modest reformist agenda. When seen in juxtaposition to the great tradition of theory from Plato to Nietzsche, this amounts to chopping political philosophy off at the knees.

Contemporary theorists should strenuously resist this constricted agenda. For instance, in order to reflect properly on the character of liberalism as a regime devoted to comfortable bourgeois existence, one must give some account of why so many individuals in modern society feel driven to experience life through the mediation of opiates and hallucinogens. This would be less difficult to do if drug use were confined to a deprived underclass, since it could then be interpreted as an intelligible response to the hopelessness of their social condition. However, it is clearly much more difficult to explain, say, how cocaine use by lawyers, doctors, teachers, and civil servants (that is, by the privileged middle class) can become commonplace. To characterize it philosophically, I would say that widespread drug use is a symptom of nihilism as diagnosed by Nietzsche – that is, the drying up of the narrative possibilities of our civilization, of our capacity to project civilizational purposes in which we ourselves still believe, to sustain narratives that make these purposes credible to ourselves. A public void is then compensated for by a retreat to hypersubjectivity. Yet if the liberal parameters of theorizing prevail, this never even arises as a topic for philosophic reflection.

A liberal society is a society chiefly dedicated to the protection of individual rights and liberties. A liberal theorist is an intellectual who is reluctant to cause liberal society to feel uneasy with itself by posing radical (that is, tactless) questions about the real worth of the activities to which individuals within such societies devote their main energies.[26] If my reading of Hockney's painting is more or less on the mark, what it communicates is that a liberal world is a world without furniture.[27] We purge our dwelling-place of furniture because its presence would derogate from the moral imperative resting upon individuals to create every bit of spiritual furniture from out of themselves. (In this sense, liberalism begins with the Protestant Reformation.) The liberal impulse is an adventure in spiritual self-creation, and it transfers what the greatest poets and artists have been able to accomplish onto the shoulders of 'Everyman.' This is liberalism's most primal egalitarianism.

A liberal is someone who says that the present social order in contemporary Western, democratic, individualistic, and pluralistic societies is basically okay, apart from a need for improvements in equality of opportunity and for more equitable social distribution. A critic of liberalism like myself will say this is nonsense. To this, the liberal will reply, 'Okay, this isn't good enough. So what's your alternative?' It is both necessary and legitimate for me to claim that I don't need to answer this question. I don't see myself in the business of designing an alternative social order. People who do that always end up making fools of themselves. That's not my job. My job as a theorist is to criticize the prevailing social order, and to draw upon the great traditions of Western political philosophy in order to puncture liberal complacency. The rhetorical trademark of the liberal, by contrast, is the readiness to denounce as 'romantic nostalgia' any effort at a more ambitious social criticism.

Relative to this standard of a more ambitious social criticism, I fear that exactly the wrong lessons have been drawn from the so-called liberal–communitarian debate, and that communitarianism, rather than inducing contemporary liberalism to become more robustly self-critical, has actually done the opposite. Rorty, for instance, thinks that the postcommunitarian Rawls is preferable to the precommunitarian Rawls because communitarianism teaches liberals to historicize and relativize their liberalism. This means that liberalism meets the communitarian standard simply by relating liberal principles to the existing practices and self-understanding of liberal societies as they have unfolded historically. In my opinion, this is exactly the wrong influence for communitarianism to have had upon liberalism, because what was welcome about the communitarian challenge was that it was a *challenge*: it made necessary another look at fundamental issues concerning the adequacy of liberal society in satisfying radical human needs for rootedness, common purpose, and meaningful traditions. But what's happened, unfortunately, is that this challenge has been turned around so that it functions as a rationale for greater complacency with our own historically evolved liberal way of life. The communitarians demand appeals to tradition and historically rooted practices; to meet this challenge liberals need only point out liberal society's own rootedness in a historical community of self-interpretation.[28] So the net effect of the liberal–communitarian encounter is not a more probing examination of liberal practice, but one that is, precisely because it has been 'communitarianized' and therefore historicized, *less* probing, less radical. The consequence of the debate is therefore the opposite of what, I think, theorists like MacIntyre, Taylor, and Sandel had intended. It's as if one thought one could accommodate Simone Weil's analysis of our 'need for roots' by asking people who are products of modern suburbia to appreciate the communal constitution of their selfhood by embarking on an exploration of their suburban roots! (I take this to be a *reductio ad absurdum* of the communitarian liberalism celebrated by Rorty.)[29]

Let me sum up my position regarding liberalism, in order to make my standpoint as clear as it can be made: First of all, philosophical antiliberalism doesn't require that one embrace some militantly illiberal or antiliberal creed. For myself, I'm sure that my politics differ hardly at all from those of the left liberals I criticize. As I have discussed elsewhere, liberals and their critics commonly embrace identical policy commitments in practice.[30] What the debate concerns, rather, is the underlying philosophic visions that furnish the *grounds* for convergent policy commitments (since opposing theoretical premises can yield the same practical conclusions);[31] it also concerns the enveloping cultural attitudes that are often the chief mark of liberal/antiliberal sympathies. Liberals typically regard these cultural attitudes as politically irrelevant; the critics hold that if a people is culturally anomic, rootless, and dislocated, this will inevitably give rise, sooner or later, to political pathologies such as civic apathy and alienation from the state, and contribute to what has come to be called a 'legitimation crisis.'[32]

Second, if we are to consider ourselves heirs of a Socratic tradition, as members of a liberal civilization we owe it to that tradition to be as self-critical as we can about liberal assumptions about social life. My problem here is that I find it hard to see how a theorist committed simply to articulating liberal principles can be much of a gadfly in the context of a liberal society. To be sure, I fully recognize that such a liberal theorist can be a most effective gadfly in the context of *il*liberal societies, and of course I don't dispute that in illiberal societies, liberal gadflies are not merely desirable but indispensable. (Indeed, I'm really not sure whether Socrates counts as a liberal gadfly in an illiberal society, or as an illiberal gadfly in a liberal society. It seems likely that in some respects he was each of these things.)

Finally, and perhaps most importantly, we owe it to ourselves as intellectuals to make sure we don't bore ourselves to death by reducing the grand tradition of Western theory to ridiculously modest proportions – that is, by merely tinkering with the economic and political details of the liberal order in a way that leaves unquestioned its most fundamental assumptions. If we convince ourselves that our sole task as theorists is to write uplifting treatises explaining why liberal citizens should be decent and tolerant toward each other, the whole enterprise of theory is sure to become a big yawn; lunatics like Nietzsche and Heidegger, on the other hand, remain genuinely challenging and profound precisely *because* they conceive the task of philosophy far more ambitiously. But again, one can find one's philosophical reflection richly stimulated by a thinker like Heidegger without being obliged to embrace his odiously illiberal politics. It must be conceded to liberals that as good citizens, we have an obligation to be sensible enough not to be Stalinists, nostalgic conservatives, evangelical moral-majoritarians, or Islamic fundamentalists. But as intellectuals, we also have an obligation to keep the space of intellectual life as rich and open as possible, and in practice we can only fulfil this duty by blasting away at liberal orthodoxy.

2

The Proper Bounds of Self

Within the sprawling Rawls industry, Michael Sandel with *Liberalism and the Limits of Justice* has written a genuinely important and philosophical book on the nature and limits of Rawlsian liberalism. Sandel is able to identify the limits and deficiencies of the contemporary liberal vision because he possesses a penetrating understanding of the moral and intellectual force of that vision. Sandel's work is written with style and precision, making it equally valuable for both student and specialist.

Sandel's argument concentrates on two defining features of Rawls's version of liberalism: the priority of the right over the good (deontology); and the priority of the self over its ends (the deontological self). Sandel seeks to demonstrate that contemporary liberalism is based on a certain conception of the moral self and the knowing subject that derives from Kant. His undertaking is then to expose the contradictions in this conception of the subject, and to show why it is, ultimately, untenable. If the argument succeeds, the liberal understanding of morals and politics is shown to be founded on a contradictory and incoherent theory of the self.

What are the proper bounds of the self, and how does one secure the integrity of the moral subject? According to Kant, unless one can locate a basis for the autonomy of the self completely detachable from the contingent factors and circumstances that empirically condition experience, both knowledge and morality are reduced to incoherence. Rawls takes this as the starting point for his basic definition of the liberal self: a disem-

Review of Michael J. Sandel, *Liberalism and the Limits of Justice* (Cambridge: Cambridge University Press, 1982); originally published in *The Times Higher Education Supplement*, 14 January 1983. Reprinted with the permission of The Times Supplements Ltd.

bodied or situationless subject whose essential identity is constituted apart from any empirical attributes or desires it may possess and independent of any ends it may choose for itself. Justice is the primary social virtue because it relates to original selves who construct principles of social life in a state of complete autonomy in respect of empirical conditions and circumstances.

Rawls wishes to secure the autonomy of the self by asserting its priority to its ends and attributes. The problem raised by Sandel is that without *some* effort to situate the self and to define what empirical conditions are essential to it, the moral subject is in danger either of shrinking to vanishing point, in which case it becomes impossible to see why it is so important for its dignity and autonomy to be upheld, or of expanding into a universal subject, thereby negating the primacy of plurality – a primacy that Rawls takes to be fundamental to his theory and the lack of which he roundly condemns in utilitarianism. A minimal self radically distinguished from what it possesses and what it chooses turns out to be incoherent both in its relations with its own ends and attributes and in its relations with other selves.

One major problem with Rawls's theory is that he assumes that the assets and resources that are shown not to be essential to the identity of the moral and political self should automatically devolve to a 'social pool' so that society can distribute shares and benefits without any injury to the individual's rights and entitlements. However, Rawls is incapable of giving an account of community that is rich enough to explain why this should be so. Therefore, Sandel concludes by arguing for a 'constitutive' understanding of community that would be capable of providing an account of why unattached assets might be thought of as common assets. This involves appeal to an intersubjective concept of the self: 'As the independent self finds its limits in those aims and attachments from which it cannot stand apart, so justice finds its limits in those forms of community that engage the identity as well as the interests of the participants.'

Another important contradiction exposed by Sandel is that whereas Rawls's theory presents itself as a contract theory, placing its emphasis on volition and choice, the voluntarist interpretation of the original position ultimately gives way to a cognitive one: 'what begins as an ethic of choice and consent ends, however unwittingly, as an ethic of insight and self-understanding'; 'the language of choosing and willing is displaced by the language of seeing and perceiving.' Just as it is difficult to see how there could be distinct parties to the contract, since all occupy the same position and all reason identically, so it is equally difficult to understand how the act of choice adds anything to what is rationally apprehended in the original position. Rawls's Archimedean point is arrived at by discovery, not decision.

Sandel's account of friendship and self-knowledge in the concluding section of his book is luminous. The entire Rawlsian project depends on defining the integrity of the self apart from supposedly contingent attachments and commitments, and its ethical reflection, if it is to have any depth, must proceed within a history, identity, and self-understanding constituted by them. To extricate oneself from these constitutive attachments or to consider the self as prior to them would remove the very possibility of ethical character or moral identity. This in turn would mean that the pursuit of self-knowledge could never get underway at all, for the latter presupposes a 'thickly constituted self' that guides reflection on the coherence between the ends that I choose and the person that I am.

The fact that our moral identity is not secured in advance, but develops subject to a process of self-reflection, is very well illustrated by the experience of friendship. It is not the case that our understanding of who we are and what we want is established antecedent to entry into relationships with others. Rather, these constitutive attachments help us define more adequately our own identity and purposes. Friendship is therefore a matter not only of feeling (liking the person) but also of knowing (understanding oneself better), a way of 'mutual insight as well as sentiment.' In other words, the experience of friendship refutes 'the ultimate privacy of self-knowledge.' It follows from this that 'we are neither as transparent to ourselves nor as opaque to others as Rawls's moral epistemology requires.'

3

Reconciling Liberty and Equality

John Rawls is generally acknowledged as having launched the contemporary regeneration of liberalism as a philosophy of society through a thoroughgoing reflection on first principles. Rawls did this by placing the question of distributive justice at the centre of liberal philosophy. A great many writers have followed in his train, the most recent of whom is Michael Walzer with his important new book, *Spheres of Justice*.

Before stating my criticisms, I should declare my admiration for the book. Walzer writes with enviable lucidity (and wit) and also with a marvellous command of historical and sociological detail. His substantive discussions contain abundant insight and good sense. He understands what is involved in the life of a community in a way that eludes the capacities of a great many social scientists. Among my favourite passages are his discussion (on p. 87) of how we have substituted the cure of bodies for the cure of souls, and thereby traded longevity for eternity; and the brilliant contrast he draws between (public) holidays and (private) vacations (pp. 192–6). The book is brimming with ideas, and should be read by everyone who is seriously concerned with social theory as a guide to contemporary social policy.

Walzer seeks a solution to the old problem of how to promote both equality and liberty – that is, without advancing one at the expense of the other. He thinks he has found a solution to the problem in what he calls 'pluralism.' This, according to one formulation, is the principle that 'social meanings call for the autonomy, or the relative autonomy, of dis-

Review of Michael Walzer, *Spheres of Justice: A Defense of Pluralism and Equality* (New York: Basic Books, 1983); originally published in *The Times Higher Education Supplement*, 13 January 1984. Reprinted with the permission of The Times Supplements Ltd.

tributive spheres.' Thus, for example, the sphere of security and welfare is autonomously governed by the distributive principle of need, the sphere of reward and punishment is autonomously governed by the distributive principle of desert, and so on. (This recalls Plato's conception, according to which justice is 'minding one's own business,' where each social function is isolated from the rest, and none violates the jurisdiction of another.)

The idea here is a stunningly simple one. It is that no person should be dominant in one sphere of the human good (say, wealth or opportunity) simply because he or she is foremost in another sphere (say, political power or intelligence). Each social good prescribes *its own* norms of distributive justice, and the society in which these various norms do not encroach upon or trespass into other domains will be a just society. Walzer himself credits Pascal and Marx with having inspired this conception of 'complex equality,' or the principle that we should respect the autonomy of the different spheres of justice.

Substantively, what Walzer is after – a society free of domination and that is committed to broadly egalitarian social distribution – is pretty similar to what Rawls is after; philosophically, however, they proceed in quite opposite directions. Rawls wishes to abstract as much as possible from the particular forms of social life tainted by familiarity in pursuit of a universalist standpoint, while Walzer's standpoint is avowedly particularist ('I mean to stand in the cave'). Walzer has no desire to depart from the particular and the familiar; rather, his ambition is to make clear those social practices and ways of arranging our shared collective life to which we are already committed.

To my mind, both procedures are theoretically defective. Walzer takes up his standpoint too close to the standards and perspectives of a given society, Rawls takes up his too far away. In the latter case, philosophy threatens to turn into abstract economics (with its rational choice model-building), in the former, it threatens to turn into descriptive sociology. In both cases, political philosophy is in danger of losing its proper location, and with it, its autonomy. (Ronald Dworkin has recently challenged Walzer's attempt to reorient political philosophy more toward the empirical, the concrete, and the historical, concluding that 'we cannot leave justice to convention and anecdote.')

Walzer also reverses Rawls's procedure by shifting the centre of theoretical attention from a theory of rights to a theory of goods (comprising not only material goods, such as wealth, security, office, and power, but also cultural and spiritual goods, such as membership in a community, leisure, education, love, kinship, and self-esteem). Rawls offers a theory of goods, but it plays a secondary role within his theory of justice, and indeed his theory is for all intents and purposes complete before he even embarks on his discussion of goods. For Walzer, by contrast, the theory of distributive justice is wholly based on an account of the goods being distributed. Accordingly, the whole of his book is occupied with the theory of goods (though not with a theory of *the* good: justice, says Walzer, is not controlled by the idea of the good as a singular conception). In explicit counterpoint to Rawls, Walzer emphasizes that he will make no use of the idea of rights in formulating his theory of justice. He thus opposes his own 'pluralist conception of goods' to Rawls's 'universalist conception of persons.'

For Walzer, a theory of distributive justice coincides with a theory of goods, for where there is distribution, there are goods to be distributed (implying that we must be apprised of the nature of those goods), and, conversely, where there are goods, there is the need for distributive principles. The question of distributive justice presupposes the question, 'What are we distributing?' (that is, 'What do we take to be the range of social goods?'), and this in turn presupposes the deeper theoretical question, 'According to what shared meanings and communal understandings do we take these to be goods?' (that is, goods *worth* distributing). For instance, we decide how much affection and respect is due to husbands by asking, relative to a given society, 'What are husbands for?' Walzer thereby gives to the theory of distributive justice an unprecedented scope.

Walzer seems to derive the norms of political life from what Oakeshott called 'the pursuit of intimations.' Competing policies (regarding reverse discrimination, for instance) are embraced or rejected according to whether they are in line with, or inconsistent with, our historical traditions and the bent of our institutionalized practices. Walzer wishes to inquire into what citizens owe to one another *given the community they actually inhabit.* Social policy should proceed in accordance with commitments already entered into. The community should 'live up to the logic of its own institutions.' It becomes the task of the philosopher to enjoin us to follow through the implicit logic of our own social attitudes as these have developed in history (say, our attitudes to medical care in the history of medical practice).

Let us consider one of Walzer's examples. He rejects the claim of American advocates of restricted immigration (around 1920) on the grounds that they were mistaken in thinking that they were defending a homogeneous white and Protestant country: 'Earlier Americans, seeking the benefits of economic and geographic expansion, had created a pluralist society; and the moral realities of that society ought to have guided the legislators of the 1920s.' But what if the earlier Americans *had* in fact created a club of WASPs? Would it then have been legitimate to exclude non-WASPs from membership in the state? Walzer introduces various qualifications, but his answer seems to be that in questions of membership, community as a social good normally takes precedence over other considerations (which means that the community retains the prerogative to define its own identity, however restrictively). A less historicist answer might be that a multiracial society is an inherent good, even if members of a given community have not seen fit to incorporate it in their collective vision of themselves.

It is true that we take our bearings by shared goods. But is sharing, by itself, enough to make our shared goods, and shared conceptions of the good, ultimately desirable? It is easy to imagine shared understandings for which it would be impossible to produce any rational justification as soon as one stepped outside of that particular social world. Walzer comes perilously close to robbing us of the independent standpoint from which we can draw back and critically judge cultures, assuming that they have satisfied the criterion of internal coherence – for social criticism, according to Walzer's conception, is always a form of immanent critique. To provide such an independent standpoint – to probe whether shared beliefs and conventions are in fact rationally justifiable, irrespective of the fact that they appear compelling within the cave – has always been the function of political philosophy. Walzer fears that this provision of a privileged standpoint by theory imposes a coerced unity upon the wonderful plurality of goods that are actually cherished and sought after in society.

At the beginning of his book, Walzer proclaims that his theory of justice 'proceeds without foundational commitments' (such as Aristotelianism or utilitarianism). But if the foundations are not provided by philosophical inquiry, can they really be left to the contingencies of cultural self-understandings as these evolve through history? Walzer is right to emphasize the theory of goods the way he does, for it is true that we cannot sensibly determine just distributions if we do not know what we are distributing. It is more questionable, though, whether Walzer can bring his theory to fruition without confronting the basic question of political philosophy: Are individuals and communities in history the supreme arbiters of what is good?

4

Cruelty First

In her book *Ordinary Vices*, Judith Shklar has set out to offer a defence of liberalism. The vehicle of this defence is a moral psychology of the vices. This is appropriate, for liberalism is often interpreted as the turning of a blind eye to private vice, on the proviso that all adhere to a common minimum standard of public legality. It might be inferred from this, as some critics allege, that liberalism lacks a moral vision. Shklar challenges this interpretation head-on. Her aim is to show that sufferance of vice does not imply lack of awareness or indifference. Quite the contrary: liberalism, she says, rests upon a definite and deliberate ranking of the vices, and displays a realistic understanding of 'the common ills we inflict upon one another every day.' Liberalism, on this view, is vindicated by a moral psychology that owes more to novelists and dramatists than to philosophers; the latter, she claims, have failed on the whole to give rich or complex enough treatment to the table of vices.

Many have attempted to defend liberalism by claiming that it postulates no substantive 'liberal character.' As Ronald Dworkin puts it, 'liberalism does not rest on any special theory of personality'; it 'requires official neutrality amongst theories of what is valuable in life.' Shklar stakes out the theoretically more rewarding position that one *can* delineate a substantive liberal character, and that liberalism itself is justifiable on account of the particular virtues embodied in the liberal character. Therefore, liberalism is 'difficult and constraining,' not a blank cheque for any moral or political disposition one cares to inscribe. (In fact,

Review of Judith N. Shklar, *Ordinary Vices* (Cambridge: Harvard University Press, 1984); originally published in *The Times Higher Education Supplement*, 9 November 1984. Reprinted with the permission of The Times Supplements Ltd.

Shklar demonstrates that even Kant, who is the philosophical inspiration of Dworkin's version of liberalism, was vitally concerned with the cultivation of character; Kantian liberalism – at least in its original version – therefore *does* rely on a particular 'theory of personality.') The liberalism advocated by Shklar is a liberalism defined not by Bentham or by Kant but by Montesquieu – it is a liberalism defined not in terms of the happiness of mankind or the dignity of persons, but in terms of the fear of cruelty and the hatred of inhumanity ('the liberalism of fear,' as opposed to 'the liberalism of rights').

Aristotle's ethics began the tradition that places a consideration of the virtues and vices at the centre of moral reflection. But Shklar's book contains an implicit repudiation of the Aristotelian tradition. According to Shklar, Aristotelian ethics is preoccupied with analysis of the virtues, to the neglect of the vices. For a redress of the balance, one must turn to the sceptical tradition, exemplified best of all by Montaigne, who never lets hope for virtue get the better of fear of vice.

Montaigne and Montesquieu are the heroes of her book because, Shklar explains, they 'put cruelty first' among the assortment of human vices. Moreover, each was able to see beyond the illusions of the other. Montaigne, unlike Montesquieu, knew that the spread of commerce would not cure cruelty. Similarly, Montesquieu, unlike Montaigne, realized that a more secular understanding of death would do little to make men less cruel. Together, they contribute an understanding of this foremost vice that in Shklar's view is unsurpassed: 'We have not really improved upon Montaigne and Montesquieu.'

Shklar casts a hard and unyielding eye at political reality. Hers is what she refers to at one point as 'an eye for darkness.' She writes as a stern critic of a politically naïve and psychologically shallow contemporary culture. It is on account of their distance from this culture that Dickens and Benjamin Franklin are praised, in particular for their ability to see hypocrisy as a lesser vice, if a vice at all. This tough-minded stance sometimes produces an impatience with moralistic reactions to the vices. At times, she is harder on the antihypocrites than on the hypocrites, harder on 'antisnobbery' than on snobbery itself. As a rule, she sees the vices – leaving aside cruelty – as less of a danger than the misanthropy and despair that go with hyper-reaction to the vices. It is therefore the function of 'the skeptical intelligence' to preserve a 'measured' response to the vices by restraining such a hyper-reaction, and it is in this 'moral balance' that Shklar sees the genius of liberalism.

The argument is both intricate and elegant. Every ranking of the vices involves 'paradoxes and puzzles.' For instance, hatred of cruelty, which Shklar associates with the humane liberal consciousness, may entail misanthropy, or may require that one abide moral cruelty in order to abate physical cruelty. Alternatively, if one opts for hypocrisy as the prime vice, one may be led (as Nietzsche was) to tolerate vices that humanitarianism keeps in check. Every moral stance implies a ranking of the vices, and every such ranking implies a trade-off: liberalism abhors cruelty but may involve embracing hypocrisy – or rather, may embrace hypocrisy precisely out of its abhorrence of cruelty. Thus constitutional government, in accordance with Montesquieu's liberalism, is 'set up by and for people who could do no better than to indulge in lesser vices in order to avoid worse ones.' The conclusion is that liberalism alone puts misanthropy to good purpose.

Whatever one's remaining doubts concerning the adequacy of liberalism as a political philosophy, one cannot help but admire Shklar's skill in setting forth the moral basis of liberal society. Above all, the book is a delight to read. At every turn of the argument it spurs one to think; and gives added pleasure with each new perplexity it raises. Shklar's purpose is not to resolve any moral predicaments, but simply to lay them bare. The essays express a joy in reflection and a joy in coming to insights, and readers who relish thinking for its own sake will be happy to join in the sheer exuberance of it.

5

Liberalism as Neutralism

Toleration and the Constitution is a book that, very encouragingly, promises to cure the typical 'lawyer's disease' of insular narrowness with a good dose of robust theory. It abounds with references to Augustinian theology, Lockean political philosophy, and contemporary American jurisprudence. The basic thesis of the book is that at the heart of the American Constitution is a tradition of 'metainterpretive diversity' (p. 128), the appreciation of which requires a narrative retelling of the historical sources of the theology, political philosophy, and legal embodiments of this tradition. The intention is emphatically holistic and cross-disciplinary, in pursuit of a genuinely philosophical jurisprudence. This ambition is unquestionably a noble one; however, the suspicion arises that all this history, philosophy, and theology is serving to make our proud liberalism look a good deal grander than it really is.

One of the key strategies of the book is to give as exalted a reading as possible to the liberal discourse of contractarianism. One means of doing this is by tying it in with the biblical idea of covenant. In itself, it is not implausible that the language of biblical covenant added power to the characteristic tropes of American political consciousness. But the plausibility is diminished on a closer examination of the terms of Richards's reading. It is hard to fathom how anyone can interpret God's covenant with Abraham in Chapter 17 of *Genesis*, as the act of 'a just God, who limits His power on terms of our free and rational consent' (p. 101).

One might easily assume that the more natural home of contractarian

Review of David A.J. Richards, *Toleration and the Constitution* (New York and Oxford: Oxford University Press, 1986); originally published in the *University of Toronto Law Journal* 38, no. 1 (Winter 1988). Reprinted with the permission of the University of Toronto Press.

discourse is the legal-commercial world of business contracts drawn up between freely consenting parties who desire minimal constraints upon their entrepreneurial endeavours. Is this not a rather more plausible source of the rhetorical attraction of the language of contract, consent, and autonomy that has shaped the tradition of liberalism? But to make note of this defeats Richards's strategy, which is, once again, to give as sublime and morally uplifting a rendering as he can to the language of liberalism.

Richards is not content to claim that liberal diversity is politically salutary – he is resolved to confer theological sanction upon it: 'The patterns of secularization in Western culture ... make possible a distinctive kind of religious concern, namely ... respect for persons' (p. 120). This conception, as articulated by the liberal tradition of Locke, Jefferson, and Madison, expresses 'our experience of equal respect for the moral powers that are an ethical God's image in us' (ibid.). While there may be historical warrant for this genealogy of liberalism, it is quite jarring to think of the modern cult of individuality as a contemporary version of the biblical doctrine that we are made in the image of God! Putting to one side what Locke or Jefferson actually believed, can anyone today seriously imagine that God's presence is manifest in the practices of liberal pluralism? And if not, it is difficult to see the enduring relevance of the possibility that this odd theology might have been believed by the American Founders or by their philosophical heroes.

Again and again, Richards attempts to demonstrate that liberal constitutionalism instantiates a religious–ethical vision of free conscience that transcends politics itself. It is a bit of an irony here that Richards's leashing of religion to liberal–republican politics is in turn a function of a certain understanding – one with a discernably Protestant character – of the requirements of authentic religion. Part of the irony is that political neutralism toward religion (and 'values' in general) is dictated by a notion of the inviolability of conscience that is identifiably associated with, in fact derived from, one *particular* religious tradition (just as Kantian moral ideals, for all their apparent universalism, are of a piece with Kant's Protestantism).

The spuriousness of this recurrent appeal to the sacredness of conscience is very clearly displayed in the discussion of pornography. How can this possibly be a matter of *conscience*? What is at issue here, surely, is the sacredness of consumer preferences. The individual's sovereign prerogative to purchase magazines like *Penthouse* and *Hustler* has little to do with free *speech* (let alone rights of conscience); the only liberty at stake is that of unhindered consumption. The truth is that it pertains not to the marketplace of ideas but to the marketplace of commodities.

Richards's attack on the 'invidious nonneutrality' of restrictions on 'pornographic communications' (!) offers a dramatic illustration of the follies to which rights-based liberalism can lead. Richards ventures to dignify the buyer/seller of *Hustler* with high-minded talk of free speech, independent moral powers, and rights of conscience – and this in the very midst of a highly moralistic doctrine of 'equal respect'! (One cannot help thinking that the cause of equal respect would be better served by protecting women from being exploited by the likes of Bob Guccione and Larry Flynt.) Or again, consider the following passage: 'The right to drug use, if it is a right, is a right associated with the control of consciousness and thus with the right of conscience itself' (p. 281). By this contorted reasoning, the decision to snort cocaine constitutes an act of conscience.

At times, Richards seems a bit too hasty to read the 'equal respect' doctrine of Dworkin and Rawls back into the thought of classical liberal thinkers such as Milton, Locke, and Kant. For instance, Richards refers to the 'democratic theory' of Locke's *Second Treatise*, suggesting a premature conflation of liberalism and democracy. In the case of Kant, there is a tension between Kant's political philosophy and his moral philosophy that Richards omits to address. Kant's political writings do indeed affirm that republican government observes respect for its citizens by not seeking to impose morality; his moral teaching, by contrast, makes it clear that the real foundation of respect is the exercise of strict autonomy, which rational beings experience solely in the observance of the moral law. What Richards comprehends within the notion of conscientious belief is, from that point of view, closer to what Kant, in *Religion within the Limits of Reason Alone*, slightingly refers to as *Willkür* – mere free choice (which may or may not embrace full moral freedom). Furthermore, Richards endorses a procedural conception of moral rationality that he identifies with Kant (p. 134). But Kant assumed that even merely procedural conditions yield a determinate moral content – a moral law that is binding on all rational beings. One gets the distinct impression that Kantian rigorism is being relaxed to suit the looser sensibilities of contemporary mores.

Richards writes of 'our need for a common ethical basis in the face of radical metainterpretive diversity, that is, for an ethics of equal respect centering on all-purpose general goods' (p. 128). In other words, since we modern liberals disagree radically on matters of ethical substance, we situate the essence of ethical experience in our capacity to choose autonomously what to make of our lives. The function of civil society is to make available the 'all-purpose goods' (in Rawlsian terminology: 'primary goods'), and it is presumed that all conscientious individuals will make use of these primary goods in ways that are equally worthy of respect. A cynic might say that since virtue has dissolved into irreparable diversity, diversity itself is turned into a virtue – indeed, into the highest of virtues.

According to Richards, the free exercise and anti-establishment clauses of the First Amendment both derive from the principle that the state should observe strict neutrality as between diverse 'conceptions of a life well and humanely lived.' As he puts it: 'The state should show no concern with the content of conscientious belief expressive of our moral powers, for such judgments suggest the kind of content-bias that is not consistent with respect for the right to conscience,' although 'the state may appropriately regulate and protect general [i.e., noncontroversial] goods.' Therefore, 'the state may not pursue religious purposes, but only secular ones' (pp. 139–40). Is this ideal of neutrality really feasible, or even coherent? Isn't even the choice between a secular state and a theocratic state already the embodiment of a substantive judgment about how we ought to live? How can the secular state observe neutrality toward the theocrat whose religious aspirations will be necessarily frustrated unless the political community as a whole is directed toward the realization of God's purpose? Here Richards's dichotomy between 'substantive conceptions' and 'all-purpose goods' – or between *ends* that are at the discretion of autonomous moral agents and *means* that can be utilized for any set of ends – inevitably breaks down. It is, to pursue our example, highly questionable that the all-purpose goods sought after by the liberal will coincide with those preferred by the theocrat, since the latter will be indifferent to secular goods relative to his or her overriding interest in salvation. Thus, neutrality is a myth. What is hidden by the means/ends dichotomy is the reality that 'all-purpose goods' are already predefined according to the 'substantive conceptions' embraced by the liberal. What one identifies as primary goods will certainly depend on one's substantive judgment of the proper ends of the state – which can hardly be neutral among 'conceptions of a life well and humanely lived.'

The illusoriness of liberal neutrality is visible in Richards's description of scientific method as 'a neutral educational good' (p. 153) that in no way violates the moral impartiality of the state. But clearly, the exalting of modern natural science as the privileged mode of epistemic rationality is not a neutral instrumentality; rather, it implies an entire way of life that excludes alternative ways of life. Surely, the reciprocity of liberalism and scientism within the way of life of modern societies cannot pretend to evaluative neutrality. To embrace science as the authoritative mode of cognition is precisely to endorse a determinate conception of the preferred way of life. The civilization that has come to prevail since the seventeenth century has quite evidently unfolded the content of this way of life.

Needless to say, the above is not an argument that it is unjustifiable (on grounds of nonneutrality) for the state to be educating its young citizens in principles of scientific method rather than, say, fundamentalist doctrines of creationism. The argument merely shows that the pursuit of neutrality with respect to competing ideals of life is chimerical. A liberal–secular education, no less than any other, will be vindicated by the content of the way of life it circumscribes, not on account of its presumed neutrality.

If the claim regarding the liberal state's evaluative neutrality with respect to substantive political beliefs cannot be sustained, much of Richards's case for a rights-based, contractarian political theory collapses. For instance, Richards upholds the classical liberal view that the state ought not to intervene in cases of racial or ethnic defamation (as in the famous Skokie affair), for to do so would be to violate the sovereignty of individual conscience that is at the heart of liberal constitutionalism. The ideal of equal respect requires a jurisprudence of 'content-neutrality.'

There appears to be a central incoherence in this whole vision of the state as a neutral guarantor of equal respect. The notion that moral independence is inviolable, that the chosen purposes of persons are prior to the responsibilities of the political community, that the state can judge only the procedural aspects, and not the substance, of the beliefs of its citizens – all of this circumscribes a *substantive* conception of what is a proper life within political society, and therefore itself fails to meet the content-neutrality precept. Richards himself seems to concede this when he notes that the First Amendment was prompted by 'background substantive values' (p. 295) – namely, the abhorrence felt by Madison and the other Founders toward the political evil of faction. This is emphasized most explicitly at the end of the book, when he insists that the theory of toleration is a substantive, not a procedural, theory (p. 296). Yet at the same time he is compelled to say that these substantive values express 'a deeper procedural conception' (p. 297). This equivocation as to whether procedure defines substance or substance underlies procedure defines liberalism's basic conundrum.

One would certainly be hard put to make sense of how the state could be substantively neutral on the question of whether constitutional neutrality itself is or is not a good way for a society to organize its affairs. But this judgment in turn has 'content-biased' implications for the personal beliefs and practices of individual citizens. Imagine for a moment a society composed of individuals craving paternalistic governance. Richards's contractarian account implies that the liberal state must in effect tell them that they have misconceived the purpose of their own lives, which is to become autonomously self-directing (since any attempt to answer their pleas for moral direction would grossly violate the state's own legitimacy). This may be sound counsel, but it is not evaluatively neutral. At this point, the required distinction between form and substance begins to dissolve (the one fades off into the other), for even a formal or procedural notion of the state's responsibilities invokes at some level (and cannot help invoking) a substantive conception of what are to count as proper ends of the person.

The virtues of Richards's book are manifest: it is clearly and vigorously argued, richly illustrated, and goes straight to the heart of issues that are of deep concern to the contemporary liberal. All the standard favourites of doctrinal liberalism are here: privacy, free speech, pornography, acts of consenting adults, and so on. Here we have a pure articulation of rights-based liberalism at its best: a sincere vision of what it is to be a choice-making person and why autonomous personality confers equal moral dignity on all, regardless of the dubiousness or imperfection of the actual choices made.

What this vision presupposes, however, is that citizens of the liberal republic are already active in the deliberate design of their autonomous ways of life. But as Richards recognizes in the most incisive section of the book, where he considers how contemporary mass media degrade the public culture of a democratic citizenry (pp. 219–26), this can hardly be assumed, especially in the context of a mass society. The question that must be raised is whether the liberal philosophy of toleration makes available suitably rich theoretical resources to uncover the social and political sources of ethical deficiency. If believing X rather than Y or preferring Y to Z is considered a sufficient entitlement to the majesty of conscience, if attention to the content of our beliefs and choices is thought somehow to diminish our sense of moral equality, it is hard to see how liberal theory can yield much in the way of critical reflection on the quality of the exercise of our moral powers. In his eagerness to apply theory to legal practice, Richards sees only the theoretical strengths, not the theoretical weaknesses, of rights-based liberalism and contractarian political theory. Notwithstanding Richards's celebration of theory, his book suffers not from too much theory but from too little.

The ambitious intention of this book is to engage, sometimes at the risk of undue eclecticism, in a genuinely cross-disciplinary inquiry that seeks to illuminate constitutional theory by means of the light cast by philosophy, political theory, history, and even theology. None of my criticisms ought to be read as a repudiation of this worthy aspiration. Nor should my reservations about Richards's project of a historico-theological repackaging of liberalism be taken as expressing complacency about the need to keep a fresh supply of arguments to defend secularism against theocracy. In an age when the separation of church and state is under increasing threat from the New Right, it is quite understandable that one would desire a renewed appreciation of the historical and philosophical grounds of religious toleration. At the very least, we want to be assured that there is a good case ready to be argued should Pat Robertson win the Republican nomination for president. One wishes, though, that the job could be done without either exaggerating the theoretical coherence of rights-based liberalism, or inventing for it a mythic neutrality.

6

Revising the Self

With *Liberalism, Community, and Culture* (Oxford: Clarendon Press, 1989), Will Kymlicka has written a penetrating, highly illuminating, and exceptionally lucid book in which he sets out a systematic liberal doctrine of the relation between the individual and the community with respect to the kinds of cultural membership that one finds in pluralistic societies. He defends the egalitarian liberalism of Rawls and Dworkin, reformulates this liberalism in places to render it more coherent in the face of challenges from critics of liberalism, and extends this liberalism in new directions. It is a book that deserves to be taken seriously by both liberals and their critics.

Kymlickian Liberalism

Kymlicka's first aim is to rebut what he considers the communitarian's caricature of liberalism. According to this caricature, liberalism is a radically individualistic and subjectivistic philosophy that is blind to the social formation of character and individual purpose, and that subordinates practical reason to the caprices of individual desire. Kymlicka's response is that no intelligent person would affirm these premises, and that certainly no intelligent liberal would, or does, affirm them.

Kymlicka draws from his favourite liberals, or imputes to them, his own vision of what it is to be a liberal. Kymlicka's vision of liberalism centres on what one might call the revisability of the self. Individual freedom is not cherished for its own sake; rather, it is cherished because it allows us

Originally published in *Critical Review* 8, no. 2 (Spring 1994). Reprinted with the permission of the Critical Review Foundation.

to reflect without constraint on whether the choices and commitments that we presently assume, or hitherto have assumed, to define our best interest really do secure what's best for us. If we are too tightly locked into cultural commitments, or if the state applies pressure to point us in one particular direction or another, this process of reflective self-examination and possible revision of the self will be stymied. State neutrality is crucial not because the proper ends of life are in principle unknowable, but because it is a necessary condition of this process of reflective self-revision. 'Since lives have to be led from the inside, someone's essential interest in leading a life that is in fact good is not advanced when society penalizes, or discriminates against, the projects that she, on reflection, believes are most valuable for her' (34).

On Kymlicka's rendering of liberalism, the liberal agrees with Alasdair MacIntyre that 'the good life is one spent in search of the good life' (56). The liberal disagrees with MacIntyre as well as other critics of liberalism when it comes to the conditions necessary for the effective pursuit of this quest for the good life. For the Kymlickian liberal, the crucial condition is restriction of the state's function to upholding the traditional liberal set of personal liberties. For MacIntyre and the communitarians, the basic necessary condition is embeddedness or situatedness in a communal tradition, historical identity, or set of social practices that give structure, direction, and coherence to what would otherwise be an aimless and disoriented quest for the good life. Kymlicka is perhaps right to suggest that if both the communitarian and the liberal can be taken as defining the good life as quest for the good life, then either the communitarians are more liberal than they have presented themselves, or liberalism leaves sufficient room within its theoretical space for communitarian insights. Yet even if MacIntyre and the other antiliberals accept Kymlicka's revisability doctrine, it might still constitute a significant difference of principle for MacIntyre to insist that for the process of self-examination to be a meaningful one, the practical agent weighing alternative conceptions of the good life must have a clear sense of where he or she is coming from and of the basis on which he or she is deciding to carry forward or repudiate a concretely established historical identity – that merely negative liberties guaranteed by state agnosticism do not suffice. By what criterion can we test whether the self has substituted a new identity for its old one simply on the basis of whim, or out of boredom with its old identity? The liberal emphasis on negative liberties and noninterference by the state makes it difficult to probe too closely here; whereas MacIntyre's emphasis on character formation, and on the historical and cultural conditions of an identity that is not phony or shallow, is capable of making this question of the meaningfulness of self-examination and self-revision a central one. Kymlicka's relentless interrogation of what precisely in liberalism is being repudiated by the antiliberals – or what it is they *appear* to be repudiating without really repudiating – renders the dividing line between liberals and their critics an exceedingly subtle one; but this is not to say that subtle differences cannot nonetheless be decisive ones.

In an important section of the argument, Kymlicka says that while the basic calling of the self, according to communitarian critics of liberalism, is to discover and reflect on what is already given in its historical identity, the calling of the self for the liberal is to *judge and evaluate* these givens of historical identity. But the critic may reply that the liberal has too narrowly circumscribed what is subject to judgment. It is true that I may have chosen at some point in my life to pursue material comfort through the life of an accountant, and that on reflection I now see this life as pointless, and give it all up for the more authentic existence of a free-spirited wandering minstrel. Yet why should this exhaust the scope of judgment? What about judging a social order that encourages me in the first place to want what the accountant wants – or indeed, that induces me to rebel against social roles as such in pursuit of individual authenticity? Doesn't the liberal horizon of questioning impede questioning and judgment of a broader kind?

Perfectionism

For Kymlicka, it is ultimately for *individuals* to weigh competing conceptions of the good, and, as adverted to above, it is central to this vision of liberalism that the state butt out of this process of self-deliberation and adopt an attitude of political *laissez-faire*. What is it for the state to be involved in the process of weighing conceptions of the good? A nonliberal answer to this question might run something like this: Every social order instantiates collective determinations of what is good, shared ends of a global character, patterns of moral and political order that run through the whole fabric of social life and that are more or less binding. So it is *not* simply a matter of the individual deciding on 'projects that she, on reflection, believes are most valuable for her' (34) – nor are the collective determinations reducible to such judgments. Furthermore, the state cannot help but be involved in rendering such collective determinations authoritative. Consider, for example, transportation policy – say, the provision or nonprovision of a subway system in Los Angeles. There is no possibility of neutrality here: either the state provides such a service or it doesn't (or provides more expansive or less expansive versions of the service). Not to provide it is not to abstain from involvement in civil society, for a policy of minimal public transportation tends to subvert or impugn modes of life premised on alternative policies. The existence of public transportation favours certain modes of life, while nonexistence of such facilities favours alternative modes of life. Either way, the state is implicated in a collective decision. To insist that the state safeguard maximal personal liberty so that individuals can decide these things for themselves is thus to participate in the propagation of a liberal myth.

The problem is that talk of advancement of particular conceptions of the good by the agency of the state immediately conjures up images of Stalinist gulags, Nazi eugenics, and Khomeiniist theocracy. But it is not so clear why one should be so quick to rule out much more modest and even prosaic and familiar varieties of state-promoted non-neutrality. Consider fiscal policy. The state discriminates against cigarette smokers through punitively high taxes on tobacco consumption. This is not a case of allowing individuals to investigate for themselves whether they have made right or wrong judgments about their best interests. Yet social-democratic liberals of the Rawlsian type are not likely to get terribly worked up about such violations of state neutrality. To be sure, questions of demands on social resources come into play here when cigarette smokers turn into lung cancer patients. But this simply shows that there is also a collective good to be considered here, which itself challenges the liberal model of the individual who deliberates on his or her own best interests, in the privacy of his or her own psyche. Nonlibertarian liberals don't get too worked up about such things because the policy, non-neutral as it is, is perfectly reasonable and defensible. And so are countless other non-neutral policies of the state – in fact, it's difficult to think of *any* policies of the state, good or bad, that don't in some way privilege certain aims and aspirations and discourage or hinder other aims and aspirations. If I'm an uncompromising pacifist, tax dollars spent on defence are prejudicial to my view of what's good. If I'm adamantly opposed to the work ethic in all its forms, state policies designed to boost productivity and to render the national economy more competitive prove that the state officially rejects my hippie philosophy. If I'm a child-hating misanthrope (or simply a libertarian bachelor who believes that all services should be financed exclusively by user fees), state policies to improve education and child welfare condemn my vision of the good. And so on. (According to the neutralist principle, governments are not supposed to make judgments about the relative worth of alternative ways of life. But all liberal governments *have* made the judgment that these ideas of how to live are less worthy, and have put these judgments into practice.) These examples of non-neutralism do not strike us as offensively illiberal; but the fact that they seem so benign relative to what we tend to associate with the political imposition of conceptions of the good does not prove that they don't also contravene the liberal principle of state neutrality. Rather, it proves that a strict enforcement of this principle would preclude the state from doing most of the things it typically now does.

Communitarian Liberalism

Just as in the first half of the book Kymlicka tries to show that there are larger doses of liberalism in communitarian arguments than communitarians sometimes pretend, so in the second half of the book he tries to show that there is a greater scope within liberalism for communitarian commitments than liberals generally assume. Thus, the second main aim of the book is to show in practice how a reformulated liberalism could justify the sort of communal identity and collective self-definition that the critics say it can never accommodate.

Kymlicka begins by addressing the Trudeau liberalism of the late 1960s that sought to undo the special constitutional status of native people in Canada. White liberals had sought to promote individual equality *on behalf of* Indians; yet the native people perceived the policy as an intolerable assault against the collective preconditions necessary for the defence of their way of life. No doubt with considerable bewilderment, the liberals retreated when faced with the violent resistance of those they were attempting to 'liberate' according to the model of liberal equality. Kymlicka tries to render intelligible the hostile reaction of the native people as well as what was so misguided about the proposed liberal policy.

The standard liberal response, embodied in the moral impulse behind the Trudeau government's native policy of 1969, is to say that in a conflict between the claims of the group and the claims of the individual, the claims of the individual must prevail, even if this means that the group dissolves and cultural membership goes by the board. This liberal response does violence to communitarian intuitions, which Kymlicka seeks to rescue, not by jettisoning liberalism but by redefining liberal principles with greater subtlety. Kymlicka's treatment of the theoretical issues raised by the predicament of minority cultures is extremely fine, and he articulates the conflicting intuitions of a nondoctrinaire liberal with sensitivity and insight. In fact, the discussion of the moral complexities of according respect to native people in a majority white culture, and of how liberals must modify their individualism and egalitarianism in this case, is one of the real highlights of the book.

Kymlicka's efforts to construct a *liberal* argument on behalf of minority rights contain something of a paradox, however. The argument, basically, is that in order for the Indian or Inuit to make a reflective choice between the aboriginal way of life and the modern mainstream white way of life, the aboriginal way of life must exist as an option, and it cannot do so without special help and protection. Therefore, liberal society must make special provisions to preserve this way of life, even at the cost of modifying or abridging certain basic liberties that it would otherwise guarantee to all citizens. However, the object is to broaden the choices of individuals (in this case, broaden the choices of certain disadvantaged individuals at the expense of other individuals), not to perpetuate the culture as an end in itself: 'Liberalism should be concerned with the fate of cultural structures, not because they have some moral status of their own, but because it's only through having a rich and secure cultural structure that people can become aware, in a vivid way, of the options available to them' (165). The paradox here is the use of the term 'options' in this context, for the only realistic way to protect the aboriginal cultures is by insulating them from the pressures of the mainstream culture, which offers a false seduction and then destroys the lives of those it seduces. Kymlicka's paradoxical liberal argument is that options are enlarged through the restriction of options: he does not fully face up to the fact that what he is advocating as an entailment of liberalism is assistance for a community to fend off the liberalization of its way of life. Kymlicka presents some dubious distinctions in Chapter 8 in an effort to pretend that this is really not what he is doing. For instance, he tries to insist that in coming to the aid of an aboriginal way of life, the state is not promoting a substantive choice, but merely sustaining a 'context of choice'; this distinction seems obscure, however, since the aboriginal culture can only function as a context of choice to the extent that it has a definite content which embodies certain substantive choices and excludes others. Kymlicka tries to elaborate an analogy between Indian and French-Canadian culture according to which French Canadians retained their French-Canadian identity as a context of choice even after Quebec society had undergone a liberalizing revolution in the 1960s. Yet this analogy seems to defeat Kymlicka's purpose, for if Indians retain their Indian identity no matter how radically their culture evolves, what is the point of government helping them to defend a *particular* way of life? Here one can indeed begin to appreciate why liberals have thought it better to stay off this tricky terrain. Yet it is to Kymlicka's credit that he explores ground that is bound to be uncomfortable for liberals.

Kymlicka is right to demand that liberals stand up for the preservation, as a collective goal of the society, of aboriginal cultures threatened with extinction (and he is equally right to suggest that legitimizing aboriginal claims doesn't automatically legitimize all minority claims everywhere, independently of context). However, Kymlicka's idea of neutral concern and the provision of a sufficiently broad range of options in the liberal choice of a preferred way of life seems an implausibly roundabout way of defending government support for the aboriginal way of life. It seems much more plausible to say that these ways of life are simply *valuable* – that they are ways of life worth cherishing, and that it would be a crying shame if society (or government acting for society) were indifferent to their fate and allowed these forms of life to die out or (more accurately) to be snuffed out by the erosive individualism and irresistible dynamism of a bourgeois civilization. But even if it offers a less awkward defence of minority cultures, this is not something that *liberals* can permit themselves to say.

Shopping for an Identity

If Kymlicka's venture succeeds, then liberalism's critics on the left will be silenced. Kymlicka wants liberalism to incorporate everything that communitarians can tell us about the communal constitution of the self, while remaining recognizably liberal – that is, upholding the individual's ultimate prerogative to opt out of fixed roles and heteronomously determined ends. And Kymlicka wants liberals to take to heart Dworkin's dictum that liberal egalitarianism 'cannot be denied in the name of any more radical concept of equality, because none exists' (95). (He intimates that Dworkin himself does not fully put into practice his own dictum.) Kymlicka's preferred liberalism is one that may still be objectionable to conservatives but that will have satisfied all the radical egalitarian aspirations of communitarians, feminists, and Marxists. Kymlicka more or less says what Rawls and Dworkin never say, although Kymlicka thinks their principles oblige them to say it: that liberalism put into practice is socialism.

Does Kymlicka's venture succeed? His appreciation of how communal attachments enter into the fabric of a human life is admirable. Yet lurking behind Kymlicka's quasi-communitarian liberal pluralism is the consumer paradigm. The state recognizes a common interest of all citizens in a sufficient range of choice in the selection of a given way of life. Therefore, some ways of life that would otherwise perish are subsidized (or accorded constitutional privileges) to keep them open as living options. The state can do this without compromising consumer freedom, since its function is to enlarge the inventory of cultural goods, not to determine the choice of this product rather than that one. However, once cultural identity becomes merely a commodity in the supermarket of life, it loses that which had promised to elevate Kymlicka's political philosophy into a less impoverished rendering of liberal theory. Although Kymlicka claims to find Sandel's critique of liberalism either trivial or implausible, it is just this point that Sandel intended to make with his idea of constitutive community.

In Chapter 5, Kymlicka responds to the argument that government promotion of worthy conceptions of the good is inescapable. He replies that notwithstanding differing conceptions of the good life, public support of the mainstream cultural structure does not violate neutrality 'because everyone has an interest in having an adequate range of options when forming their aims and ambitions,' even if they ultimately decide to rebel against the majority culture. Following Dworkin, Kymlicka offers the suggestion that we could reconcile this with the principle of neutral concern not by opting for direct government support of ways of life judged to be valuable 'but by providing tax incentives for private citizens to contribute to the ways of life they find valuable' (81). But how can the rich account of cultural membership in Chapters 7–13 be squared with this proposal of tax incentives to enlarge consumer choice, and with the reversion to narrow liberal political devices that it implies? It is when Kymlicka feels himself compelled to uphold Dworkinian neutralism that he reveals the underlying tension between his liberalism and the more expansive vision of social life unfolded in the second half of his book.

For Kymlicka, as for most other contemporary liberal philosophers, what defines liberalism is not just absence of state coercion but state neutrality vis-à-vis the competing ways of life on offer within a modern pluralistic society. (The latter conception places a much more stringent restriction on state action than the former, because when the state endeavours to persuade or educate the citizenry, it violates the neutrality principle without violating the ban on the resort to coercion. In this respect, J.S. Mill was not a neutralist liberal.) However, this question arises: Why would the state go to the effort of encouraging the viability of a particular way of life unless it was thought that that way of life was worth-while enough to warrant support? If it is simply a question of maximizing consumer choice among a variety of possible ways of life, why not subsidize the way of life of transvestites (if we allow that such individuals participate in a larger transvestite culture)? A strict neutralist liberal should demand the same share of state resources to maintain the transvestite way of life as to protect from extinction a threatened aboriginal culture. (Note here that the transvestite minority, in common with Indians and Inuit, is culturally disadvantaged relative to the majority mainstream culture.) In other words, to the extent that Kymlicka enriches his liberalism with his insistence on the preciousness of cultural identity, he undermines the principle by which he defines his liberalism.

Kymlicka acknowledges that not every liberal theory defines liberal equality in terms of neutral concern – that is, the idea that 'governments cannot use as their justification for any action the fact that one person's way of life is more or less worthy than another's' (96–7 n.2). Some liberals do (Rawls, Dworkin, Nozick, Ackerman, Larmore, and Kymlicka himself); and some liberals don't (Raz and Galston, notably). Throughout this review I have been arguing that in many ways Kymlicka's reformulated liberalism is morally richer and less vulnerable to critique than other brands of liberalism (in part, perhaps, because he draws to some extent on the sources of an older liberal tradition that predates the current Kantian vogue). However, in this one rather major respect I think that Kymlicka's own liberalism would be strengthened and enhanced if it were recognized that as a description of liberal society, liberal neutrality is a misdescription, and that as a political ideal it is an unrealizable phantom.

7

Liberalism, Pluralism, and Religion

The reflections that follow were occasioned by three excellent papers that were delivered at a panel on liberalism and pluralism at the 1995 American Political Science Association meetings. The papers were by Alan Ryan, Stephen Macedo, and Pratap Mehta. I'll begin with a brief review of the arguments presented by each of them; after that, I'll follow with some thoughts of my own.

In a very fine discussion of the 'uneasy alliance' between liberalism and pluralism, Ryan contends that before one can say something intelligent about the relationship between liberalism and pluralism, one must first be aware of the pluralism *within* liberalism, and attend not only to the tensions between the various versions of liberalism but also to the complexities and tensions *within* each of these liberalisms.

To illustrate this central thesis, Ryan lays out three important varieties of liberalism: (1) *Millian liberalism,* which is committed to a particular vision of an attractive human life – namely, the life of a fully reflective individual, trying to think through for himself or herself what his or her life is about, and prepared to engage in robust dialogue with other individuals who think differently about the ends of life. This view is in some ways favourable to pluralism and in some ways not. For this requirement to live a robustly reflective 'examined life' is subversive of ways of life (those of monks in Tibet, Mormons in Utah, Hassidim in Jerusalem) that don't go well with Socratic self-examination; and a world that was universally converted to this Millian vision of robust individuality would be subversive of a pluralism that left room for these nonliberal ways of life.

This is a revised version of my contribution to the APSA panel at which Ryan, Macedo, and Mehta presented their papers.

Naturally, Mill had no desire for liberalism to be coercively enforced on these illiberal communities, but he doesn't see why they shouldn't be challenged by a bit of verbal haranguing from the liberal; and, Ryan points out, a world where liberalism eventually triumphed over pluralism so conceived would seem to Mill not such a bad outcome.

(2) *Rawlsian liberalism*, which is obviously a much more modest version of liberalism than Mill's. It doesn't offer anything so ambitious as a full-fledged view of life, but merely a political framework for accommodating difference. The chief thing is to satisfy a minimal standard of 'reasonableness.' Those ways of life or views of the good that fail to pass this threshold of public reason (Rawls's phrase is 'run afoul of public reason'[1]) are excluded from the liberal consensus; whereas those views that do pass this threshold are subject to no further badgering from what Ryan calls the 'gung-ho liberal.' For instance, to cite the example that Rawls himself uses in his book *Political Liberalism*, the Rawlsian liberal need offer no moral or intellectual challenge to the views of right-to-lifers, provided that the latter respect the 'overlapping consensus' that protects abortion rights within a liberal society.[2] Citizens don't have to be liberals in their private convictions or in the way they live their own lives; they are only obliged not to let these illiberal commitments impinge on the shared norms of a liberal constitutional order. This, Ryan suggests, lets the illiberal groups off a bit too easily.

(3) *Berlinian liberalism*, which Ryan labels 'a more simply aestheticist view.' The idea here seems to be diversity for diversity's sake. This version of liberalism is actually parasitic on varieties of illiberalism: in a world in which everyone was a good liberal individualist, we would fall into the Berlinian hell of boring monism. So the Berlinian liberal *needs* lots of illiberal cultural possibilities to keep the world an interestingly pluralistic bazaar of different cultures. Thus, by Ryan's account, when push comes to shove and the tension between liberalism and pluralism requires that a choice be made between them, Mill leans strongly in the direction of unmitigated liberalism, whereas Berlin leans toward pluralism, forgoing a more consistent partisanship on behalf of liberalism (although Berlin, ever faithful to Archilochus's fox, realizes that sometimes the pluralism goes too far, so that one has to lean back in the other direction). It seems rather paradoxical that it should be the case that *any* version of liberalism would cherish the continued existence of pockets of illiberalism to prevent the tapestry of cultural diversity from fading into monochrome, but Ryan is persuasive that this is exactly what defines Berlin's liberalism.

Ryan's conclusion, in a nutshell, is that we should prefer a liberalism that (unlike Rawls's liberalism) is prepared to do some preaching on its own behalf, but that (unlike Mill's liberalism in its most militant version) isn't so militant that it begins to trample on pluralism. Moreover, we are more likely to achieve this desirable balance between self-neutered liberalism, on the one side, and crusading liberal militancy, on the other, by remaining fully conscious of the enduring *tension* between liberalism and pluralism. This strikes me as a very sensible suggestion, and one that offers a helpful way of approaching some extremely difficult and puzzling dilemmas of contemporary life.

Stephen Macedo, in a very illuminating paper titled 'Transformative Constitutionalism and the Case of Religion,' is clearly wrestling with similar dilemmas. How far should liberals go in trying to enforce a liberal view of the world within their political community (as embodied in the constitutional order of the state)? How far should they be willing to accommodate forces of illiberalism within the liberal political community?

Macedo is concerned with what he calls 'the transformative dimension of liberal constitutionalism,' by which he means the need for a liberal political order to shape its citizenry, through intermediate associations such as schools and churches, in such a way that habits and sentiments conducive to the sustainability of the regime are favoured, and that microcultures that run counter to the spirit of the regime, such as religious sects, will be unobtrusively liberalized, or absorbed into the liberal mainstream (one needn't do this in every case, but one needs to do it enough to keep the regime in healthy running order). As this affects policy toward religion, Macedo's thesis seems to me absolutely right: Liberalism is supposed to be committed to a strict separation of church and state – that is, to the utter neutrality of the state vis-à-vis the full range of possible religious commitments. But in fact this official neutralism is just a façade: what the liberal state really needs is for its citizens to let go of robust religious sectarianism, in favour of a shared ecumenical disposition that looks a lot like 'wishy-washy Protestantism'; and an important part of the hidden agenda of the common school movement was to bring about this surreptitious outcome (just as its parochial-school critics charged). But if the neutralist claim of separating church and state is just an ideological façade, then so is the claim to be fostering pluralism. Here, again, we have the same dilemma as discussed above – namely, the *tension* between liberalism and pluralism. Yet what are liberals to do? If they want *liberal* citizens, they have to ensure that they get the kind of socialization that cultivates liberal virtues and discourages illiberal ones.[3]

Liberalism pretends to be theologically neutral; but in fact, whether one draws one's liberalism from Locke or draws it from Kant, it should be evident that liberalism and Protestantism are in a suspiciously intimate alliance. (For a nominal Catholic like Montesquieu to embrace liberalism was enough to get himself put on the Index!) Macedo brilliantly exposes the neutralist myth of the liberal doctrine of segregating church and state: 'Liberal politics cannot in fact leave religion to one side: it cannot altogether leave the soul alone and care only for the body, for the soul and religion need to be shaped in accordance with political imperatives.' To sustain liberalism, one needs a global liberalization, or Protestantization, of all religions. When we look at the contemporary scene in the United States, we see – as Macedo notes – that, paradoxically, American Catholicism has been more thoroughly 'Protestantized' than the fundamentalist *Protestant* sects have! – with the latter still militantly challenging the segregation of religion and politics. There is a great irony here that runs implicitly through Macedo's presentation: in 1990s America, unlike nineteenth-century America, the religious community that still awaits a salubrious liberalization is not the Catholic Church, but rather, evangelical Protestantism.

Like Ryan and Macedo, Pratap Mehta is concerned with exploring the tension between liberalism and pluralism. In an interesting paper titled 'Liberalism, Pluralism and Diversity: Some Reflections,' he too wants to challenge the hasty assumption that liberalism especially recommends itself to us on account of its superior capacities to accomodate pluralism; and like Ryan and Macedo, he challenges the familiar dogma that liberalism and pluralism are a happy couple – so that what's good for one is automatically good for the other. In one place he offers a nice formulation of how this coupling of liberalism and pluralism goes in, for instance, Berlin's work: 'from the plausible fact that monism can lead to illiberalism [Berlin infers] that therefore pluralism should lead to liberalism.' To suggest a way of decoupling them, Mehta asks us to imagine a political community composed of a plurality of illiberal subcommunities, and he rightly asks what the accommodation of such a pluralism has to do with liberalism. What defines liberalism is not an embrace of difference per se, but rather, he says, an 'exacting standard of justice' based on the idea that individuals are free and equal. Obviously, this thought experiment of a community of illiberal subcommunities has something to do with liberalism *if* the subgroups try to accommodate one another's cultural differences by seeking a Rawlsian common ground of public reason. But what if they don't? Suppose they simply settle for a set of ad hoc trade-offs that allows each subgroup to maintain unrepentantly illiberal relations among its own members? But – and this is Mehta's point – such an expedient may actually do more for pluralism than the quest for a Rawlsian common ground.

In the second half of his paper, Mehta turns to a different target: the recent vogue for 'the politics of difference.' Mehta wishes to challenge identity politics as a meaningful supplement to, or improvement on, liberal politics; and moreover, he thinks that appeals to 'identity' trivialize what is really at stake in the attempts by different cultures to articulate profoundly divergent conceptions of human need and human good. If the real strength of liberalism lies in its insistence on addressing problems of justice, then the preoccupation with questions of identity is a step in the wrong direction. Even worse, the politics of identity involves, as he puts it, 'mere valorization of the markers of difference and particularity,' and in that sense fails to take seriously the claim a genuine culture makes to apprehend and embody what's good for human beings. In fact, contemporary life is becoming increasingly homogenized (I'll never forget the experience I once had of watching, to my great astonishment, a large family of traditionally attired Mennonites trooping into a McDonald's in downtown Toronto – like a vision of premodernity being sucked into the vacuum cleaner of modernity!); and the eager yet shallowly conceived celebrations of difference and identity have the effect of masking how difficult it is in the contemporary world to sustain cultures that really matter. The politics of difference, because it extols cultures without sufficient pondering of their substance, therefore tends to mirror rather than challenge the hollowness of our cultural reality today. These are hugely important questions, and further reflection on them promises to deepen our understanding of our current predicaments.

Let me now add a few observations of my own that carry us back to some of the points made by Alan Ryan. Liberals commonly present themselves as possessing a unique insight into 'the fact of pluralism' – or as John Rawls now says, 'the fact of *reasonable* pluralism' (to indicate that the pluralism to which he is willing to defer is not unlimited in its scope). But as Ryan makes clear, there is a big problem here: *real* pluralism entails a confrontation with real otherness. Yet liberals are not likely to find this real otherness in the company of fellow liberals, for liberalism represents one relatively narrow band of experience within the panorama of human possibilities. The liberal horizon of experience involves caring more about civil liberties and the comforts of life, the rule of law and the unconstrained choices of individuals, than, for instance, about grand questions of individual salvation or national destiny. Liberals therefore tend to welcome the liberalizing power of commerce, and the cosmopolitanism of the market. But these are at the same time powerfully *homogenizing* forces. (Ryan rightly asks: What happens if liberals eventually *win* the global fight for liberalism? They will find themselves inhabiting a world composed universally, and boringly, of liberals like themselves; in this context Ryan refers, aptly, to Francis Fukuyama.) So genuine pluralism requires keeping the world safe for (at least some) illiberalism. The case of *Wisconsin v. Yoder*, which rightly preoccupies liberal political philosophers in the United States, offers a powerful illustration of this: William Galston, in a recent essay, quotes the dissent of Justice Douglas in the *Yoder* judgment, according to which, if liberal society defers to the educational preferences of the parents of Amish children, 'the child will be forever barred from entry into the new and amazing world of diversity that we have today.'⁴ Justice Douglas looks at liberal society and perceives 'amazing diversity.' However amazing one finds this diversity, it is a diversity that is articulated within liberal boundaries – that is, a diversity that excludes the Amish way of life as a tenable existential possibility.

I can offer another handy illustration drawn from my own neck of the woods. It is beyond dispute that Quebec society has made enormous strides in transforming itself into a liberal society, relative to the kind of society it was when I was born there, in the early 1950s. In important ways, this triumph of liberal ideals surely opened up a greater space for pluralism, but it did so by driving out the clericalist and theocratic elements that had previously ruled Quebec – that is, it secured one kind of pluralism by eliminating another, perhaps more profoundly pluralistic, range of possibilities. The consequence is clear: Quebec became much more like the rest of North America – like the rest of North America, a society of businessmen and lawyers rather than of farmers and priests. In becoming more liberal, it became less distinctively (because illiberally) Québécois. I have no doubt that there are lots of good reasons to celebrate the liberalization of Quebec since 1960. But I don't think it implies any nostalgia for pre-1960 Quebec to acknowledge that for this liberalization, one must pay a price; and to speak of diminished pluralism is one way of labelling this price. (Even for a radical secularist like myself, it is rather shocking how thoroughly Quebec has been de-Catholicized in the last three-and-a-half decades!) As Berlin or someone inspired by Berlin might put it, there comes to be one less stall at the human bazaar. Again, as discussed earlier, this leaves the liberal in an uncomfortable bind: If respect for pluralism requires a global embrace of all cultural possibilities, however illiberal, then a commitment to liberalism means nothing in particular, and dissolves into nothingness. On the other hand, for liberals to crusade against illiberalism bespeaks a kind of imperialistic urge, which itself appears in that respect illiberal – turning the liberal, paradoxically, into an enemy of pluralism. I share with Alan Ryan the feeling that there is no easy way out of this bind.

To reduce extremely complex issues to a massive simplicity, I would say that the human condition seems to present us with two sets of opposing alternatives: forms of an experience of life that are 'thick' but dangerous, and forms of an experience of life that are safe but 'thin.' The latter are liberal cultures; the former, illiberal cultures. Perhaps not surprisingly, neither are entirely satisfying to the human spirit. I think I'm capable of being as sensitive as any liberal to what makes the 'thick' cultures so dangerous; but I also think that perhaps I'm a little more concerned than certain 'gung-ho liberals' (again, Ryan's term) about the opposing danger: namely, the price we pay when we domesticate nonliberal cultures so as to pacify them, when we 'thin them out' so as to liberalize them. I don't claim to have a solution to these dilemmas. Whether these are new insights or merely very old dilemmas of the human condition, I cannot say. Either way, it seems to me that they are questions very much worth continuing to ask.

8

Richard Rorty's Liberalism

The two leading *enfants terribles* of Anglo-American philosophy in the last ten years or so have been Richard Rorty and Alasdair MacIntyre. In recent years, Rorty and MacIntyre have come under sharp attack from a wide range of critics for being what philosophers are supposed to be – namely gadflies, stinging us into wakeful criticism of long-dormant intellectual dogmas and cultural pieties. The notable difference between MacIntyre and Rorty, of course, is that MacIntyre has emerged as a leading critic of contemporary liberalism whereas Rorty presents himself as a defender – albeit an unconventional defender – of liberalism. However, paradoxically, it is precisely Rorty's intellectual radicalism that clarifies what is at stake in contemporary liberal philosophy and helps us see why this philosophy is committed to a moral vision that is bereft of radicalism. After reviewing those features of Rorty's theorizing that make his liberalism appear so unconventional, we shall see that Rorty's thought is in fact paradigmatic of those cultural, political, and philosophical impulses that incline contemporary liberalism more toward an affirmation of the existing social order than toward thoroughgoing criticism of it.

Thirty-odd years ago, Henry Kariel published a peculiar article arguing that an important source of liberal constitutionalism could be found in Nietzsche.[1] Now Rorty offers us the notion that American liberalism can enhance its self-understanding by locating its source in, among other things, faddish French intellectuals such as Jacques Derrida and J.-F. Lyotard. The publication of Rorty's two volumes of *Philosophical Papers* (volume 1, *Objectivity, Relativism, and Truth* [Cambridge: Cambridge Uni-

Originally published in *Critical Review* 7, no. 1 (Winter 1993). Reprinted with the permission of the Critical Review Foundation.

versity Press, 1991], hereafter *ORT*; and volume 2, *Essays on Heidegger and Others* [Cambridge: Cambridge University Press, 1991], hereafter *EOH*) affords an opportune occasion to evaluate the success of Rorty's project to reconceptualize American liberalism with the aid of some unlikely devices, namely French Nietzscheanism and French Heideggerianism. Rorty, with his tendency to shock, to provoke, and to seize on Continental fashions, might be thought an unlikely liberal. But as I want to suggest in this essay, he illustrates very well some of the characteristic weaknesses of contemporary liberalism. To the extent that he draws upon postmodern and deconstructionist sources, he highlights, and radicalizes, the liberal urge to break out of frozen identities, to destabilize static roles and fixed stations in life. His distinctive version of pragmatism yields a novel way of drawing (liberal) boundaries between private and public, culture and justice. And his antifoundationalism helps legitimize a typical liberal reluctance to engage in any very ambitious social criticism. What distinguishes Rorty's liberalism is its higher degree of candour, which at least acknowledges that a liberal vision of things, far from being 'neutral' toward rival ideas of the good, is implicated in the defence of a particular way of life.

Metatheoretical Debates

Starting with a celebrated book published in 1979 and continuing with an ever-increasing flow of work thereafter, Richard Rorty won for himself a large measure of fame and acclaim by arguing that after a couple of millennia of Western philosophy, philosophers should finally forgo the quest for a divinized (uppercase) Truth and instead content themselves with a set of dedivinized (lowercase) truths. However, Rorty commonly seemed to carry his deconstructive enterprise far enough that he seemed to have abandoned even the lowercase truths, in favour of mere cultural conventions, shared prejudices, or even contingently acquired jargons; in this way he seemed to skirt a relativist quagmire, breeding forms of incoherence to which a host of critics then drew attention.[2] While it may be easier to show that the road from Aristotle to Einstein represents an epistemic progress bearing a relation to a real world out there, the forms of incoherence that the critics detect in Rorty's relativism – if that is what it is (or at least his quasi-relativism)[3] – also have their counterparts in corresponding forms of incoherence in Rorty's social and political thought. Here too, critics have not been lacking. In this essay, after I briefly review the general critique of Rorty's antirealism, I will focus mainly on criticisms of the social-political variety.

What the critics' complaint comes to is that, just as is the case with individuals, the story a culture tells itself – either scientifically, in its picture of the universe, or politically, in its assumptions about the society's own moral properties – is often a false story, and that Rorty's account of truth fails to do justice to why the false story is false.[4] Rorty's account fails because the problem is not that the story 'doesn't work,'[5] or is out of step with the society's cultural evolution, or that it has exhausted its possibilities for furthering the society's cultural or political needs,[6] since the story might indeed 'work' very well for certain purposes (such as helping to bolster the culture's current delusions), and might have a lot of mileage left in it for certain cultural purposes. Rather, the untrue story is untrue because it falsifies – is untrue to – what the story is about;[7] for without reference to a reality that is independent of our stories, how can talk of stories that are obtuse, self-deluding, or merely rationalizing get a purchase at all? On this view, the critics, in holding out for a more robust conception of truth, are not assumed to be in possession of some magic route to the truth, either by a privileged set of natural-scientific procedures or by a privileged mode of metaphysical cognition. The point, quite simply, is that the distinction between a true story and a false story that either an individual or a society tells itself implies *something* in virtue of which the true story is true, and *something* on behalf of which one exerts oneself, in dialogue with an interlocutor, to show that one's own story is truer than one's interlocutor's. If, on the other hand, the ultimate aim is simply to spawn as many redescriptions as possible (*EOH*, 154–5), we seem to be left with no normative constraints on the stories we can get away with.

An important question that will arise even for a sympathetic reader of Rorty is this: What actually hangs upon the distinction between the uppercase and the lowercase, between Reason and reason, or between Truth and truth?[8] For as Rorty himself readily acknowledges, most of the contemporary addressees of his antimetaphysical rhetoric take themselves to have abandoned the old-style foundationalism, the quest for an absolute Archimedean point, no less than Rorty has.[9] After all, in the debates about realism and antirealism that are relevant here, Rorty's interlocutors have not been Descartes and Plato but enlightened representatives of late twentieth-century intellectual life such as Habermas, Charles Taylor, and Bernard Williams. Rorty's antifoundationalist and anti-universalist rhetoric might be entirely reasonable if the only targets *had* been thinkers like Descartes and Plato; but since his targets are also anti-Cartesians and anti-Platonists, the suspicion grows that Rorty is mounting an assault not only upon Reason and Truth, but also upon reason and truth (as is certainly the case with thinkers such as Derrida and Lyotard); the danger lurking here is that he will eventually find himself firmly in the company not only of engaging postmodernist radicals but also of irrationalists and nihilists.

In some of his essays, Rorty challenges those philosophers who have sought to argue that cognitive realism is philosophically mandated in the domain of natural science in a way that it isn't in the domain of ethical life. Rorty's response is to undermine the science/ethics distinction, and to infer that if realism (the correspondence of validity claims to a subject-independent reality) is dispensable in the latter domain, so it is in the former.[10] I would be inclined to argue in the opposite direction: that to the extent that the physics/ethics dichotomy is subverted, a realist meta-theory is warranted in both domains rather than in neither[11] – for reasons that have been given a classic statement in Iris Murdoch's book, *The Sovereignty of Good*. Rorty thinks that pragmatism is what has liberated him from the albatross of Western metaphysics, with all its bogus problems and misspent energy, whereas if my analysis is correct, Rorty's pragmatism is itself an albatross. If Rorty weren't prevented by his pragmatism from giving a more straightforward justification of his moral and political views, he wouldn't have to waste half his energies in defending himself against criticisms of what is widely perceived to be his relativism. So, paradoxically, a realist metatheory, whether for natural science or ethics, is to be preferred even by Rorty's *pragmatist* standard! – a kind of mirror image of the paradox noted by the critics, that in order for Rorty to vindicate his pragmatism he must make the *realist* claim that he has grasped an insight, twigged something about the world and our relation to it, that has eluded his opponents.[12] As soon as he starts to make his pitch for pragmatism, he is forced onto the realist's turf; and even if he manages to stay on his own turf, it turns out that the game is easier to play, more 'expedient' and more free of hassles, in a realist than in a pragmatist vocabulary. Therefore, our conclusion, parallel to the conclusion that Rorty's epistemological critics have come to with respect to his rejection of natural-scientific realism, is that Rorty's rejection of moral realism is *not* a liberation; rather, it places him in a political and intellectual cul-de-sac.

A New Kind of Liberalism

The kind of liberalism developed in *Contingency, Irony, and Solidarity* rested upon Rorty's attempt to segregate how intellectuals relate to their own selves (namely, striving to perfect themselves, or to make of their lives a work of art) from how citizens relate to other selves (namely, striving for greater social justice).[13] Rorty's liberal bifurcation of public and private, politics and culture, has generated evident paradoxes, as more than one critic has noted. Tom Sorell, for instance, refers to Rorty's intention to substitute a poetic culture in the West for the reigning scientific culture, and then asks, 'Can the politics of a poetic culture really be as staid as liberal politics?'[14] It is as if the glamorous cultural superman conjured up by the postmodernist side of Rorty's vision of intellectual life (Rorty's 'strong poet') ineluctably reverted to a demure, Clark Kent-ish political stance when required to enter back into dealings with the public world.[15] This embrace of audacious 'postphilosophy' paired with an all-too-familiar political liberalism may have the appearance of a kind of cultural schizophrenia – a radical split between Rorty's pragmatic 'let's get the job done' self and his aesthetic 'let's play with new vocabularies' self. But if so, Rorty regards this as a salutary schizophrenia; for what are virtues in the sphere of intellectual life – radical vocabulary switches, bold challenges to existing idioms, wild leaps of poetic imagination – may turn out to be not only nonvirtues but in fact serious vices in the sphere of political relationships. One does not have to be a cautious or timid liberal in order to grant that Rorty has a point here in emphasizing the contrast between the demands of intellectual life and those of political life.

So I am inclined to agree with Rorty that if one is swayed by postmodernist (Nietzschean or Heideggerian) cultural impulses, one should at least have the political good sense to confine these impulses to the privacy of the academy. But the question still remains, whether Rorty's own postmodernist proclivities contribute in a helpful way to the political vision that he urges upon us. That is, is it perhaps the case that even after they have been safely 'privatized,' these trendy cultural impulses impinge on a sane and sensible politics?

Rorty's postmodernism (notwithstanding his attempt to 'privatize' it as the cultural stance of a bourgeois aesthete) encourages him to accentuate what is already an unfortunate tendency of liberal theory – namely, liberal theorists' reluctance to engage with the kind of large and ambitious claims about human nature and the essence of our social situation that alone furnish a critical foothold for bedrock judgments about the global adequacy or deficiency of a given mode of life. Rorty criticizes the kind of liberal philosophy that generates universalistic and foundationalist claims, as if this kind of liberalism approaches too closely to the cosmic ambitions of Platonism. So he likes Sandel's critique of Rawls when Rawls had thought he was striving after universalistic claims on behalf of liberalism (*ORT*, 30 n.12, 199–200), and he likes Rawls when Rawls is brought around to disavowing his universalistic claims in favour of a more historicist self-interpretation (*ORT*, 30 n.12, 175–96). But even Rawls *at his most ambitious* falls well short of the dimension of theorizing encountered in the great traditions of preliberal theorizing stretching from Aristotle to Machiavelli and antiliberal theorizing from Rousseau to Nietzsche. Matters are only made worse when even Rawls is theoretically cut down to size (or when Rawls cuts *himself* down to size in order to appease communitarian critics). Rorty's expressly historicist and quasi-relativist rhetoric suggests that the post-Nietzschean theorists he admires are *more* radical – whereas in actual fact they are *less* radical – than the kinds of thinkers whose theorizing generates bedrock judgments as to whether the substance of a mode of life fulfils the most worthy aptitudes of human beings, and therefore whether the way of life to which one commits oneself is rationally deserving of that commitment. Is the fidelity yielded by liberals to the system of social practices that define a liberal society theoretically warranted? In employing a rhetoric which emphasizes that he is addressing a community restricted to those ('we liberals') already committed to liberalism – that is, committed in advance of theoretical scrutiny – Rorty makes it a point of pride that now one is engaged in a postphilosophical intellectual activity where these questions never even arise! Should we really celebrate the end of the epoch of philosophy if the philosopher's successor, the postphilosopher, is conceived as one who only undertakes to preach to the converted?

What's Wrong with Liberal Complacency?

In *Contingency, Irony, and Solidarity*, Rorty relies heavily on Judith Shklar's articulation of the liberal ideal.[16] If the supreme philosophical standard is the avoidance of evil, there is little to criticize in liberalism; the avoidance of evil is indeed, as Shklar believes, what defines the liberal impulse in politics. Relative to the barbarities of fascism, Stalinism, racism, and so on, liberal complacency (the antiliberal's standard complaint) may even appear entirely justifiable as a theoretical stance. The problem with such complacency is that it severely constricts the horizon of theoretical reflection by which we allow ourselves to be challenged. All we can say as theorists is that a society that makes available civil liberties and a reasonable degree of equity in the distribution of material resources is preferable to a society that denies civil liberties and maintains blatant inequalities. This proposition is not readily contestable; but when considered as *exhaustive* of what should concern the contemporary political philosopher, it manifestly leaves out a good deal of what theorists might otherwise undertake to submit to critical reflection.

What's my beef with liberalism? Rorty is a social democrat and I am a social democrat. Rorty believes that Western societies are fairly decent relative to the going alternatives, and I believe that Western societies are fairly decent relative to the going alternatives. So where do we differ? Largely, we differ in our conceptions of the proper dimensions of theory. If the only legitimate standards for assessing liberal society are (1) whether it has civil rights, and (2) whether it has a welfare state, then we must say, yes it has these things, but then there is little else for a theorist to say; the only space left for theory reposes on questions of social justice in the distribution of material resources. These are not negligible concerns, but what about all the other things we might interrogate? Do members of these societies live lives that are, on the whole, satisfying? Consider for starters our society's divorce rates, its rates of drug use, the widespread reliance on psychotherapists, political apathy, and the kind of banal and empty popular culture that pervades the Western world. It doesn't require a very penetrating cultural analysis to conclude that what we have is a society whose members seem to be very seriously screwed up with respect to what they want out of life, and seem unable to understand or express in any focused way a relationship between their private anxieties and social possibilities that might be available to them at the political level. (Needless to say, in addition to the issues I have picked out, there is a great deal one might say about the massive inequalities of wealth and power in liberal societies, but I am assuming that on these topics, liberal theory allows itself to pass judgment.) Now, one might challenge this account as one-sidedly pessimistic, and say that it fails to do justice to the positive aspects of contemporary life. Fine. But the point I'm trying to make about the adequacy or inadequacy of liberal theorizing is that even if one entirely accepts my account in its grimmest version, these features of modern life are nonetheless fully compatible with meeting the egalitarian and civil-libertarian standards of liberal theory – that is to say, the *only* theoretical standards that liberal theory permits itself to apply to social life. One may quarrel as one pleases with my cultural sermonizing; but what is *not* controversial, I think, is the suggestion that a social theory that exempts itself in principle from having anything to say about such phenomena of modern social existence is not a social theory that will have much critical bite to it.

Several years ago a public opinion poll conducted in what was then the

Soviet Union showed that 65 per cent of the respondents would choose the 'American lifestyle' from among a range of other possibilities. (The 'Asian-Japanese lifestyle' came in second, at 23 per cent.) What kind of world are we living in, where *everyone* wants to be an American and live the American lifestyle? And what kind of political philosophy do we have today, when philosophers feel in no way obliged to offer reflections suggesting that there might be anything problematical in this? Of one thing we may be certain: it is not the kind of political philosophy made available to us by philosophers from Plato onwards. But Rorty tells us that the 'old-time philosophy'[17] associated with Plato and his successors is precisely what we don't need; indeed, he goes farther, saying in effect that if inhabitants of a liberal society, materially comfortable in their private life and behaving decently toward one another in their public life, tend to become complacent when they cease to be haunted by philosophical anxieties, well, what's wrong with complacency?[18]

Liberalism and Postmodernity

In labelling the new kind of liberalism that Rorty promises 'postmodernist bourgeois liberalism' (*ORT*, 197–202), the emphasis cannot be on the adjective 'bourgeois,' since this is intrinsic to liberalism as we understand it today and as we have understood it since the seventeenth century; therefore, the emphasis must fall on the tag 'postmodernist.' Rorty helped very notably to get the postmodern bandwagon going, both directly, through his own work, and indirectly, by helping popularize Gallic fashions for an Anglo-American audience.[19] One may well ask, did he do us a service in helping us to think of ourselves as contingent selves whose self-definitions are never immune from redefinition and recomposition, forever in flux? Does the postmodern movement contribute to our liberation, or does it do the opposite of liberate us? J.G.A. Pocock has recently suggested that postmodern thinking makes us less free by denying to us the possibility of the integrative experience of citizenship:

A community or a sovereign that demands the whole of one's allegiance may be foreclosing one's freedom of choice to be this or that kind of person; that was the early modern and modern danger. A plurality of communities or sovereignties that take turns in demanding one's allegiance, while conceding that each and every allocation of allegiance is partial, contingent, and provisional, is denying one the freedom to make a final commitment which determines one's identity, and that is plainly the post-modern danger. I recall reading, a couple of months ago, an article in the *Economist* forecasting that Canada might become the first post-modern democracy, and wondering whether this was an encouraging prospect. It is one thing to decide that being a Canadian – or, like me, a New Zealander – offers one an open range of identities, and that freedom consists in retaining one's mobility in choosing between them. It is quite another when the sovereign or quasi-sovereign powers of this world get together to inform one that there is no choice of an identity, no commitment of an allegiance, no determination of one's citizenship that they regard as other than provisional (or may not require one at any moment to unmake). Under post-modern conditions we do confront these alliances of unmakers, deconstructors, and decenterers, and our citizenship may have to be our means of telling them where they get off ... We may have to resist [the post-modern world], and say that we have decided and declared who we are, that our words have gone forth and cannot be recalled, unspoken or deconstructed.[20]

Can political theorists today, as we approach the threshold of the twenty-first century, bring themselves to entertain the thought that in this respect we were freer in the modern world of Rousseau and Hegel, or even in the premodern world of Plato and Aristotle, when stable citizenship was still a possibility, than we are in the radically unstable world of Derrida, where, in Pocock's words, 'the languages, constantly producing themselves, are more real than the persons speaking them?'[21] If Rorty's deconstructionist liberalism implies the rule of absolute contingency, where our selfhood is both groundless and indefinitely revisable and redefinable, then perhaps such a philosophy offers not a promise of emancipation but the prospect of a postmodernist nightmare of confused roles and incoherent identities. When one observes that everything in modern life militates against settled patterns of social order, that family and occupational norms, no less than economic and political structures, are subject to ubiquitous and ever-increasing turbulence, and that mobility is the universal law of contemporary social life, one might begin to suspect that the postmodern psyche is unliveable. Pastiche is what defines the postmodernist approach to art and culture. The anxiety naturally arises that pastiche will also define the postmodernist approach to shaping identity and constituting one's selfhood – that is, the self as a cut-and-paste job.

Rorty's interest in *la mode française* allows him to present his liberalism in flashy packaging that conventional liberal doctrines typically lack, but this fancy wrapping comes at a price. Rorty's penchant for paradox-generating vocabularies lands him in the following dilemma: *either* absolute irony, where every seemingly serious political commitment is dissolved in Derridean playfulness, *or* relatively sober and more or less irrevocable validity claims on behalf of one's social-political commitments. The problem is that Rorty wants to have it both ways: no restraints in casting all fixed identities into the deconstructionist vortex, *and* the prerogative to engage in serious-sounding polemics on behalf of his preferred version of liberalism. The result is, predictably enough, a kind of pragmatic contradiction – an incoherence in the relations between his intellectual commitments and his political commitments – that matches the incoherence that critics have located in his critique of epistemology (see note 2). Now, needless to say, Rorty is very good at being a slippery fish to grab; nonetheless, at the end of the day either one is serious about not being serious about anything, or one isn't. Either one really means it when one says that all of the self's vocabularies – which are in turn the source of its practical allegiances – are revocable, playfully ironic, and experimentally tentative, or this claim too is just more fooling around. Is Rorty's postmodernist notion of selves without centres (*ORT*, 185 n. 24, 188, 191–3; *EOH*, 1, 197)[22] one that a committed liberal can comfortably embrace?

It is Rorty's slipperiness, not so much in standing by his commitments as in explaining *why* he stands by his commitments, that provokes more traditional theorists to feel exasperated – never entirely sure what, if anything, in this new world of ubiquitous irony, they are being asked to take seriously. As Rorty puts it in one place, in his ideal 'poeticizing' culture, intellectuals like himself will 'desire to be as polymorphous ... as possible,' to dream up new cultural contexts 'for the hell of it' (*ORT*, 110). It is this appearance of frivolity that prompts Thomas Pangle, for instance, to dub Rorty's political position a 'peculiarly apolitical or uncivic liberalism'[23] – that is, a liberalism for aesthetes, where politics itself is aestheticized.[24] If the only binding determinant of cultural and political allegiances is whether it so happens that a culture still gets a thrill out of its old vocabularies, or instead begins to find these boring and decides to try for something new,[25] how do we know that liberalism too won't be tossed into the cultural rubbish bin tomorrow morning, along with all the other discarded vocabularies that we have come to feel were inhibiting us from the practice of free self-creation? If the reply comes that liberalism is what mandates and protects the creativity of the centreless self, is this a sufficient guarantee that Rorty's own political preferences (for he hardly allows them to have a more exalted status than this)[26] are immune from the postmodernist vortex?[27]

As noted above, Rorty's thinking is frankly historicist. This invites the question, why does he think *we* need his new pluralizing, deconstructive, identity-undermining vocabulary? Given the conditions of modern social life, one wonders whether philosophers should be opting for a radical-sounding rhetoric that, as it were, spins the dials all the more; one wonders whether it doesn't make more sense, instead, to opt for a rhetoric that accentuates patterns of coherence in what is already a highly fragmented, precarious, and easily destabilized mode of existence. Living as we do a postmodern *life*, it might be thought that we need least of all a postmodern *philosophy* that can only help to destabilize further the often chaotic jumble of contemporary social relations.[28]

If what we mean, then, by life in a postmodern age is not simply that certain philosophers newly endeavour to reshuffle their disjointed vocabularies, but rather, that members of a liberal social order are obliged to reshuffle their disjointed selves, and are as a result considerably confused about their purposes, postmodernity comes to seem not a marvellous handmaiden to liberalism but the revelation of liberalism's fundamental conundrum. Now many liberals will refuse to allow that liberalism has anything to do with all this. They will insist that liberalism has absolutely nothing to do with cultural confusions and incoherent identities, but is concerned strictly with the self-moderating political institutions that mediate between the state and the citizen. However, this is not, I think, an adequate reply. As even some defenders of liberalism will readily admit, liberalism is a product, and functions as a theoretical articulation, of the inexorable process of modernization whereby individuals more and more rely upon their own resources (however attenuated) in defining their own place in the world. As one of these defenders of liberalism points out (in a formulation that critics of liberalism *cannot* refuse): 'Liberalism holds out the promise, or the threat, of making all the world like California.'[29] It is a measure of Rorty's value as a social theorist that he is aware that this 'promise or threat' is what is at stake in his defence of a liberal public culture, and aware also that this has global implications for how a society defines itself. Rorty's big mistake, however, is to think that this question concerning the worth of liberalism's contribution to the human good has already arrived at its outcome (by virtue of the historical development of a particular political community, a particular 'we') in advance of theoretical contestation. In short, he thinks that history, by shaping a particular community until a cultural consensus evolves, decides issues that philosophers would never be able to settle by the exercise of plain reason. Liberalism is worthy of our allegiance, not because the insights of philosophers assure us of its superiority, but because 'we' have had the sort of shared history, shaped by contingencies, that makes it attractive to us. I hope that what I have said above concerning Rorty's misjudgment in repudiating the 'old-time philosophy' serves to make clear enough why I consider this conception a big mistake.

The Virtues and Vices of a Liberal Ironist

I began by reviewing some objections that have been made to Rorty's anti-realist critique of epistemology, and by trying to show that his antirealism has consequences that are no less troubling in the domain of political theory. Rorty's philosophical sources are American pragmatism and French postmodernism, and from these sources he wishes to draw support for a political project of his own: an antifoundationalist defence of liberalism. While an alliance of pragmatism and liberalism is hardly novel, the alliance between postmodernism and liberalism is something rather new and unexpected. And yet, I want to suggest, this latter alliance is not as surprising as one might think. Postmodernism offers a kind of 'hyper-liberalism.' Thus Rorty, as a postmodern liberal, helps to draw out and hence clarify some of the more radical entailments that are implicit in conventional liberalism. Some earlier liberals, notably J.S. Mill, based their liberalism on a robust standard of individual self-development. This meant that one could still apply critical theoretical standards to render judgment on whether the shared way of life in which individuals participate under a liberal or liberalizing regime is spiritually dead or spiritually alive. What distinguishes contemporary liberalism of the Rawls/Dworkin/Ackerman vintage is the injunction against applying any theoretical standards, let alone a robust one, for fear of derogating from the 'equal respect' that is owed to the moral choices of individuals, regardless of their content.[30] Despite the philosophical idiosyncrasies of his that I have surveyed in this essay, Rorty is a typical liberal in this respect, and the shallowness of the moral standard he applies to liberal society helps very well to illustrate the common failing of contemporary liberals.

The common thread joining the various versions of liberalism in our time is philosophical diffidence. This diffidence can take different forms, with different kinds of theoretical motivation: in utilitarian liberalism, it is sanctioned by the impulse not to impede the satisfaction of the wants and desires of all; for Kantian liberals, by the requirement to accord equal respect to all individuals (which rigorously debars one from raising questions about the equal legitimacy of the specific purposes elected by individuals); in the case of Rorty's pragmatist liberalism, by the urge for complete freedom in experimenting endlessly with a galaxy of social and cultural possibilities. To be sure, critical judgment is an impertinence, but the impertinence cannot be avoided since the alternative – taking the ends of our civilization to be beyond philosophical criticism – is an unacceptable price to pay for the wish not to appear illiberal. The real danger is that once the content of our social practices has been rendered immune to philosophical judgment, the moral autonomy affirmed by the second version of liberalism and the cultural freedom affirmed by the third version of liberalism will turn out in the end to be no more elevated than the wants and desires affirmed in the first version of liberalism.

What I like most about Rorty is that he punctures the presumption of theorists that they are, by their theorizing, helping to reorder the world.[31] At the same time, I can well understand what it is that many theorists find so irritating about Rorty: it is his frequent tone of smug self-satisfaction – his 'bourgeois aestheticism,'[32] to apply a label he himself seems to invite. (At least, that is the prevalent tone of *Contingency, Irony, and Solidarity*; the tone is quite different in some of the essays, especially the one on Unger and Castoriadis in *EOH*, 177–92.) To be sure, in calling the regime he celebrates that of the 'rich democracies,' there is a refreshing note of light self-mockery that is entirely absent from the more sober, less ironical theorizing of other liberals (such as Rawls and Dworkin). Still, the predominant rhetoric in Rorty's writing is a political-intellectual bourgeois smugness, as if to say, 'Aren't the rich democracies wonderful, and wouldn't the world be wonderful if it were composed exclusively of rich democracies?' In my own work,[33] I adopt exactly the opposite rhetoric: 'Aren't the rich democracies ghastly, and wouldn't the world be ghastly if it were composed exclusively of rich democracies?' The truth, of course (as Rorty no doubt realizes), lies somewhere between these two rhetorical extremities. But any kind of theorizing must make appeal to a certain rhetoric (here I agree *completely* with Rorty), and in order to have any force, such a rhetoric must move toward an extreme. Given the choice between these two opposing alternatives, I think the rhetoric I have chosen is closer to the historic vocation of Western theorists, from Socrates to Nietzsche. There is nothing more insufferable than a theorist who spends all his or her time saying how superior his or her own society is to every other society. (It is surprising that more theorists haven't found Rawlsian liberalism insufferable for this reason.) But again, Rorty, with his humour, his irony, his wit, is infinitely preferable to the more earnest self-congratulation of other liberals.

9

Foucault's Hyper-Liberalism

Michel Foucault clearly has enjoyed and continues to enjoy an eager reception as one of the major intellectuals of the left. However, as one reflects on the character of Foucault's political and existential commitments, it might be reasonable to ask whether his 'left libertarianism' shares more with the libertarianism of the right than his followers would care to acknowledge. One could at least take this up as a hypothesis for further analysis. In this light, it may not be so surprising that Foucault in his lectures of the late 1970s was, it appears, notably receptive to a range of market-based philosophies, encompassing forms of classical liberalism as well as various contemporary versions of neo-liberalism.[1] As I shall try to show, there is a consistent libertarian thread that eventuates in Foucault's *History of Sexuality* project, the second and third volumes of which are especially revealing in this regard. In the last years of his life, Foucault addressed 'ethical' questions having to do with the self's relation to itself by trying to locate in the Roman Stoics and other philosophies of antiquity what he called 'an aesthetics of existence'; by this Foucault meant 'the idea of a self which has to be created as a work of art.' My ultimate purpose in this essay is to pursue a critical dialogue with the texts and interviews that compose this last phase of Foucault's thought, probing the moral and political adequacy of Foucault's Nietzschean vision of the self's aesthetic self-creation.

Foucault's Libertarian Politics

It is from the perspective of political philosophy that I wish to approach

Originally published in *Critical Review* 9, no. 3 (Summer 1995). Reprinted with the permission of the Critical Review Foundation.

the thought of Michel Foucault. I want to explore what his thought contributes to normative understanding – that is, to our understanding of what constitutes a desirable human life, and of how society should ideally be constituted in order to facilitate the living of such a life. Several obstacles stand in the way of this undertaking. The first is that there is much in Foucault's body of work that simply escapes my understanding. Whether this attests to my limitations as a reader or whether it indicates shortcomings in Foucault's ability to communicate his ideas may be left to others to judge. A more serious obstacle is presented by Foucault's own strong reluctance to acknowledge that there *is* a normative vision to which he is committed. Thus, in much of his work he so to speak hides behind the façade of a normatively detached historiography (albeit a sensationally maverick historiography). Yet it is inconceivable that Foucault would have attracted the enormous following that he has by offering simply a putatively 'value-free' historiography.[2]

One can entertain the hope that some practitioner of the 'sociology of knowledge' will some day have an interesting story to tell about why the work of Michel Foucault generated such wide enthusiasm among certain intellectual élites for several decades in the latter half of the twentieth century. I will hazard one or two hypotheses of my own. What is interesting about Foucault's unique rhetoric is that he steadfastly resists pronouncing explicit moral-political judgments, yet of course he is judging *all the time*. Foucault refuses to come clean on his normative commitments, but rather 'insinuates' them throughout his work. This constitutes a kind of radical-left positivism that is somehow potently attractive to what I will call the hyper-liberal ethos of late modernity. The idea here is that one must avoid at all costs spelling out a normative vision, since it would ineluctably become the ground for a repressive regime of 'normalization.' This is clearly connected to the negativism that one associates with postmodern writers. The postmodernist claim is that we now inhabit an age in which all the grand metanarratives of the past have discredited themselves; hence, we are left with only 'deconstruction,' only 'genealogy.' But of course the notion that we live in an epoch devoid of metanarratives is itself a metanarrative, and implies, willy-nilly, a normative vision.

Given these difficulties, one should perhaps try teasing out Foucault's normative commitments by indirect means. Since Foucault is generally considered the leading Nietzschean of our time, and since he commonly presents himself as such, it might be helpful to define Foucault's normative vision against the background of Nietzsche's. In fact, however much it may serve rhetorical purposes for Foucault's followers to interpret him – or for Foucault to interpret himself – as the pre-eminent successor to the philosophical legacy of Nietzsche, it is easy enough to demonstrate that Nietzsche would have had absolutely zero sympathy for Foucault's political concerns. To this end, recall Nietzsche's unremitting hostility to anarchism as a political doctrine (as expressed, for instance, in *Gay Science*, § 370, *Genealogy of Morals*, 2nd Essay, section 11, *Twilight of the Idols*, 'Skirmishes,' § 34, and *The Antichrist*, § 58). Consider, by contrast, the end of the penultimate chapter of *Discipline and Punish*, where Foucault traces a Fourierist tradition of antipenal polemic. He concludes the chapter by noting that this Fourierist tradition was kept alive 'when, in the second half of the nineteenth century, taking the penal apparatus as their point of attack, the anarchists posed the political problem of delinquency; when they thought to recognize in it the most militant rejection of the law; when they tried not so much to heroize the revolt of the delinquents as to disentangle delinquency from the bourgeois legality and illegality that had colonized it.'[3] I don't think any reader of the book can fail to see this historical reference as a device by which Foucault declares his own political intentions; nor fail to see it as expressing Foucault's self-conception as the legatee of this political tradition. For Nietzsche, by contrast, anarchism in general is regarded as a form of Christian-inspired pathology.

One useful way of measuring the enormous distance between the respective political philosophies of Nietzsche and Foucault is to consider Foucault's indictment, in the 'Docile Bodies' chapter of *Discipline and Punish*, of the Napoleonic regime, which Foucault conceives as paradigmatic of disciplinary politics.[4] Here, Foucault criticizes Nietzsche's hero, Napoleon, for the very reason that Nietzsche adores him. In order to appreciate why Napoleon is consistently celebrated throughout Nietzsche's work, one should consult the end of *Beyond Good and Evil*, § 208, in which Nietzsche states with perfect clarity what he sees to be the fundamental political alternatives: *Kleinstaaterei* versus *große Politik* (that is, petty politics versus grand politics). What Nietzsche sees as *Kleinstaaterei* – as an intolerable splintering of political will – Foucault sees as a pervasive network of micronodes of power. Admittedly, this cannot be undone by some global act of macroliberation; rather, it must be met by a matching infinity of microresistance – by never-ending assertions of popular power directed against the normalizing power of the disciplinary society.[5] This should lead us to a more general grasp of the anti-Nietzschean thrust of Foucault's intention. Underlying all the analyses in Foucault's work is the thesis that post-Enlightenment humanism only *appears* to liberate, to liberalize, to loosen up laws and coercive constraints; while in fact, through greater scientific control and surveillance, it actually turns the screws all the more.[6] This is the precise reverse of Nietzsche's view, which is that the Enlightenment humanism of the nineteenth century *really is* softer, laxer, more tolerant, and so on, and *worthy of condemnation for this reason!* In all these respects, Foucault's power-philosophy directly inverts Nietzsche's theoretical ideal.

In trying to classify Foucault's normative vision, one is easily tempted to subsume it under the rubric of traditional anarchism.[7] But on reflection, this temptation must be resisted, for the classical anarchist conception is of the state as a concentration of political evil, such that abolition of the state suffices to secure a general liberation. Yet Foucault consistently rejects liberationist ideals. Presumably, he would view anarchist liberation from the state as just as much a naïve delusion as the Marxist ideal of liberation from the centralized power of capital. Because power is not housed in a singular control-centre, but is, rather, ubiquitously exercised across the whole social landscape, there is no prospect of a once-and-for-all liberation; instead, one must wage a ceaseless resistance against power wherever it asserts itself (which is everywhere).[8] This is, nonetheless, clearly a libertarian vision; and in common with any other normative vision, one must probe its claims to validity and the basis of its philosophical appeal (notwithstanding Foucault's own disinclination to submit his thought to this sort of testing).

Foucault could not possibly have exerted such a strong cultural impact if he had not expressed a certain truth that speaks to our situation. And indeed, such a truth can be located in his thought and in his work; it consists in a true insight into the massive normalizing pressures of modern life.[9] These are to be seen not only in the way that we are all regimented by the routines of a modern economy and of the bureaucratic organization of contemporary social life, but also, and above all, in the readiness with which people place the direction of their lives in the hands of technicians of everyday existence – psychotherapists, social workers, sexologists, and so on – who thereby function as all-powerful guardians of normality. But Foucault radicalizes this true insight to such an extreme that it becomes something utterly false – namely, the conception that *all* norms of social life are agencies of 'normalization.' To put this in a formula: Foucault is of the view that any normativity whatsoever is a mode of normalization, in his sense, and for this reason his genuine insights into contemporary life become sources of distortion and confusion.[10] One can see this especially in his libertarian stance toward questions of sexual morality.

Libertarian Sex

To sum up my (admittedly very sketchy) account of Foucault's political philosophy, I would suggest that there are basically two types of leftist intellectuals. The first type I will call social goods/social responsibility leftists; the second type I will call anarchist/libertarian leftists. Writing as someone who thinks of himself as belonging within leftism of the first kind, I would describe Michel Foucault as the most notable, most influential, and most extreme representative in our time of leftism of the second kind. The easiest way to illustrate this is by looking at some of Foucault's discussions of sexual morality. The texts I have in mind encourage one to think of Foucault as the sort of leftist intellectual whose idea of politics is to go on television with a few of his friends in order to defend pedophilia – and not just to defend pedophilia, but to express righteous indignation that there are some people around who think pedophilia needs to be regulated by the criminal justice system.[11] It seems staggering that a major intellectual like Foucault needs to agonize profoundly over the question of whether rape should be regulated by penal justice (even if, at the end of his agonizing deliberations, he comes to the uncomfortable conclusion that, well, yes, maybe one does after all need to regulate this in some fashion or other). The basic notion lying behind these ideas can be expressed in the following universal formula: law = repression; decriminalization = freedom.

This conception receives its clearest expression in an exchange between Foucault and his friends in the discussion entitled 'Confinement, Psychiatry, Prison.'[12] The exchange begins with Foucault prodding his interlocutors to accept (which they do eventually, albeit reluctantly) the proposition that rape, insofar as it is a matter for penal justice, has nothing whatever to do with sexuality. The crucial lines are actually spoken not by Foucault but by two of his interlocutors:

MARINE ZECCA: I can't place myself on the legislative level. Or on that of 'punishment' – that's what bothers me.
JEAN-PIERRE FAYE: From the point of view of women's liberation, one is on the 'anti-rape' side. And from the point of view of anti-repression, it's the opposite. Is that right?

Foucault does not challenge these statements, either immediately or later in the dialogue. He opts instead to challenge the intuitions felt by the women present that rape has to be put in some special category, distinct from other varieties of assault.[13] It seems obvious to me that Foucault lets pass without comment the statements I have quoted because they express perfectly his own views. But in fact these statements imply an outrageous way of thinking about rape: as if there were an obligation to protect the rapist against 'repression' that needs to be considered roughly on a par with, and weighed carefully against, society's obligation to protect women against rape! Moreover, I must say that I find it shocking that a legal reform commission in France would feel impelled to consult Foucault on these matters.[14] This is roughly equivalent to a tax reform commission in the United States consulting Robert Nozick on the question of how to establish a fairer tax system. Let me point out, finally, that when Foucault mentions the 'very radical' positions that were embraced by a magistrate with whom he had discussed these issues, the term 'radical' means minimal, or zero, regulation by the penal justice system.[15]

For Foucault, a social order as such is synonymous with sexual repression. This is why he is so critical of the idea that we might think of ourselves as sexually more liberated, relative to other, earlier epochs that we think of as more sexually repressed. It also explains why he is critical of Wilhelm Reich, who holds out the mere possibility of sexual emancipation.[16] From Foucault's point of view, a society that condemns pedophilia is still an essentially repressive society, no freer or more emancipated in essence than any other society. (It is interesting that in his judgments concerning Khomeini's Iran, these critical standards with respect to sexual repressiveness do not loom large in his assessment – presumably because he regards that society as a 'revolutionary' one, and therefore as deserving of greater interpretive charity.)[17]

Aesthetics of Existence

We turn now to the main purpose of this essay, which is to examine certain late texts and interviews by Foucault that, although they may appear to impart a new direction to his thought, in fact bring a, so to speak, new explicitness or new overtness to tendencies of thought that pervade his entire work. In the preceding section I emphasized issues of sexual morality, with the goal of placing in perspective Foucault's turn, in the last few years of his life, toward problems of the subject's self-relationship, which strikes many readers as out of character with – indeed, diametrically opposed to – the themes of his early and middle work. But if I have been right in attributing to Foucault a thoroughgoing libertarian impulse that is basic to his way of thinking, then this 'turn' is in no way anomalous; on the contrary, it is of a piece with, and represents a logical extension of, the general direction of his thought prior to the books on sexuality. Although, as we saw earlier, Foucault repudiates the anarchist faith that liberation awaits us beyond the state, he *is* an anarchist (indeed, a 'leftist anarchist,' assuming that this notion makes any sense) in the crucial sense that he shares the fundamental anarchist conviction that society constitutes a conspiracy to stifle each individual's longings for self-expression. This explains why Foucault is thoroughly sceptical of any global conception of social reform or social transformation: for him, it would necessarily signify merely another vehicle for society's conspiracy against his efforts at self-expression. So we see that Foucault's final books and interviews, far from being a radical break from his preceding work, are entirely consistent with the general thrust of his thinking *throughout* his work. Against the background of this larger interpretation of Foucault's career as a theorist, let us now look more carefully at some of these last interviews.

I want to begin with some of the interviews in the anthology edited by Lawrence Kritzman. In 'The Minimal Self,' Foucault's interviewer asks him what Jean Beaufret had asked Heidegger – namely, whether his philosophy yields an ethics. Foucault's answer merits close attention: 'If you mean by ethics a code which would tell us how to act, then of course *The History of Sexuality* is not an ethics. But if by ethics you mean the relationship you have to yourself when you act, then I would say that it intends to be an ethics, or at least to show what could be an ethics of sexual behaviour. It would be one which would not be dominated by the problem of the deep truth of the reality of our sex life. The relationship that I think we need to have with ourselves when we have sex is an ethics of pleasure, of intensification of pleasure.'[18]

Now, we cannot read this answer without asking ourselves what exactly Foucault means by 'ethics' in this context. One traditional alternative would be to say that ethics relates to how individuals conduct themselves in relation to *others*, and searches for normative standards that may be applied to questions regarding human conduct. Clearly, Foucault desires to subvert both aspects of this traditional definition: no normative standards, and no references to relations with others. What, then, qualifies this as 'ethics'? Foucault's answer: it relates to the self-relationship of the individual, and in particular, to the individual's concern with *intensifying* his or her own pleasures. To say that this way of delimiting the ethical is rather idiosyncratic would be an understatement of monumental proportions!

In turning to these 'ethical' concerns in his last two books, Foucault's purpose is not to provide a fuller, richer, deeper account of the moral self, but rather, just the opposite: to encourage people to invent new forms of self-relationship by showing that the possibilities of self-invention are unlimited. This comes out clearly in another statement in the same interview: 'people still consider, and are invited to consider, that sexual desire is able to reveal what is their deep identity.'[19] This is what Foucault rejects. His alternative is: living on the surface, and renouncing the idea of any 'deep identity.' In this light, sexuality is to be thought of as a play of possibilities lying on this surface; it doesn't give access to a deep identity. Hence the fundamental intention governing the Foucaultian ethics is not the idea of making ourselves more sensitive to the demands of social life by displaying the depth of sexual experience, but rather, that of liberating us to explore a wider range of possible ways of intensifying pleasure by exhibiting the superficiality of sex.[20]

Further light is shed on this whole problem of the definition of ethics in another of the interviews. In 'The Return of Morality,' Foucault states that what one has in Plato, Aristotle, and the early Stoics is a *unity* of 'conceptions of truth, politics, and private life': metaphysics, political theory, and moral reflection are inseparable.[21] What happened with mature Stoicism and with what one might call pre-Christian moral consciousness (Seneca, Marcus Aurelius) was that political theory dropped away, because its cultural context, the polis, ceased to exist; metaphysics also became less salient.[22] People were left with 'moral' life as a quasi-autonomous realm of private conduct (which is what the Stoics associated with the realm of philosophy). Although he never comes out and says so in *The History of Sexuality*, it is this aspect of Stoic thought that accounts for Foucault's greater sympathy for the Roman Stoics relative to the Greeks (which I think is perceptible when Volume 3 is compared with Volume 2, though one wishes Foucault were much more 'up front' about all this). Hence this statement: 'I would not entirely agree ... that the morality of antiquity was, throughout its history, a morality of the attention to the self; rather, it became a morality of the self at a certain moment.'[23] That is to say, Plato and Aristotle could not conceive morality as oriented strictly to the self, because for them moral life and political life were inseparable. It was only with the Stoics that moral reflection became thoroughly depoliticized, and it was for this reason that precisely the Stoics came so much closer to what *Foucault* understands by 'morality.'

The liberation of the self from the polis constitutes one side of the potential liberation that concerns Foucault; the other side has to do with a liberation from metaphysics – for instance, liberation from what Kant conceived as 'the metaphysics of morals.' Traditional moral philosophy had grounded its moral vision on a definite conception of the moral subject; it is the contemporary 'explosion' of traditional conceptions of the moral subject that clears the way to the open vistas to which Foucault beckons us: 'a moral experience essentially centred on the subject no longer seems satisfactory to me today. Because of this, certain questions pose themselves to us in the same terms as they were posed in antiquity' (that is, not in Plato and Aristotle but in the Stoics as Foucault presents them).[24] The 'moral subject,' as, say, Kant conceived it, no longer exists. In its place, we have a 'self' that isn't given, but that must be sought after, invented, experimented with, and 'constituted' by various contingent, revisable, malleable practices of 'self-crafting.' The self is the canvas upon which we explore various possibilities of artistic self-invention. At any point we can wipe the canvas clean and start again. This yields the outcome that the whole of morality is reduced to a single moral injunction, namely: Let a thousand flowers bloom! 'The search for styles of existence as different from each other as possible seems to me to be one of the points on which particular groups in the past may have inaugurated searches we are engaged in today. The search for a form of morality acceptable to everybody in the sense that everyone should submit to it, strikes me as catastrophic.'[25]

Foucault says explicitly that his interest in tracing back the history of sexuality is directly tied to a moral and cultural crisis that we are experiencing in the present (this link between past and present comes out in the passage just quoted). This crisis offers a unique opportunity: rightly grasped, it can be resolved in the direction of greater self-determination, new possibilities of personal liberation: 'If I was interested in Antiquity it was because, for a whole series of reasons, the idea of a morality as obedience to a code of rules is now disappearing, has already disappeared. And to this absence of morality corresponds, must correspond, the search for an aesthetics of existence.'[26] Already, Foucault points out, there are signs that things are moving in the welcome direction he favours. According to Foucault, there has been in recent years a profound change for the better insofar as people have been 'left to make up their own minds, to choose ... their own existence.'[27] Foucault's interviewer immediately recalls Foucault's seminars on Hayek and Von Mises, reflecting that 'liberalism ... seemed to be a detour in order to rediscover the individual beyond the mechanisms of power.'[28] We seem to be left with two extreme alternatives – either: subjectless power, or: pure, unconstrained self-direction. These are both unrealistic alternatives, but because Foucault conjures up in such a stark way the first extreme, he also offers the danger of lurching into its equally far-fetched opposite.

Even if one entirely accepts Foucault's thesis that the Stoics discussed in *The Care of the Self* introduced a conception of moral existence as a praxis of 'intensified' quasi-aesthetic self-crafting, and here I must point out that one has reason to be sceptical when one considers that it was precisely the Stoics, and not Plato and Aristotle, who were the originators of the natural law idea within the Western moral tradition – that is, the notion of the natural cosmos as a whole as the source not only of rational *norms*, but of *commands* of reason, comparable to the Judeo-Christian idea of the juridical commands of a Divine Legislator – again, putting these caveats aside, even if one accepts in its entirety the Foucaultian thesis concerning Stoic morality, one nonetheless cannot fail to observe that Foucault absolutely rejects the *content* of the Stoic teaching (one might say, rather, that he turns this teaching on its head). For after all, what defines the core of the Stoic teaching is the idea of a resolute mastery of the passions in order to liberate oneself from subservience to the contingencies of life, and from dependence on what exceeds one's powers of control. *Self*-control means restricting one's concerns to those which one *can* control, whereas desire renders one dependent on that which one cannot control. This doctrine not only extends the Socratic-Platonic moral tradition, but *radicalizes* it. Needless to say, there is nothing of this in Foucault; on the contrary, his primary 'moral' preoccupation is not mastery of the passions but the very opposite of the classical doctrine of *sophrosyne* – namely, *the intensification of pleasures*.[29] Of course, Foucault is perfectly aware that Stoicism represents a radicalization of Platonic morality; he wants to appropriate the Stoic absorption in the self while jettisoning the content of Stoic morality. To fathom the profound paradoxicality of Foucault's 'appeal' to the Stoic invention of a *techne* of the self, I think that one needs to read the passage quoted above in which Foucault states: 'The relationship that I think we need to have with ourselves when we have sex is an ethics of pleasure, of intensification of pleasure,' and then read the two long passages from Plato – one from the *Gorgias* and the other from the *Republic* – that Foucault uses to offer his initial explication of the idea of an art of the self; both of these celebrate the ideal of temperance and demand triumph over sexual frenzy.[30] It is a mark of the ingenious audacity of Foucault that just when he should be writing a book about the Marquis de Sade, he instead writes a book about the Stoics![31]

Here, a clarification is in order. I don't want to suggest that Foucault restricts his idea of an 'aesthetics of existence' to the Stoics. Rather, I think he intends it to be a general category embracing *all* pagan, pre-Christian moral experience. Thus, as I have just noted, in the section of *The Use of Pleasure* that introduces the term, Foucault cites Plato's *Gorgias*, Plato's *Republic*, and Xenophon's *Cyropaedia* (and in a corresponding passage in *The Care of the Self*, he cites Plato's *Alcibiades* and Plato's *Apology*).[32] So the *techne* of the self is certainly not an exclusively Stoic innovation; rather, as Foucault puts it in a crucial discussion in *The Care of the Self*, what the Stoics achieved in relation to earlier classical morality was 'an intensification of the relation to oneself'; 'the relations of oneself to oneself were intensified.'[33] Sexual austerity as demanded by the Stoics was, Foucault points out, not necessarily more *rigorous* than earlier Greek moralities; what distinguished the Stoics was their greater '*intensity*' (that is, intensity of concern with the self as an object of self-fashioning).[34] Nor did the Stoics represent the last instance of this cultural conception. In his first reference to an 'aesthetics of existence,' Foucault explicitly refers to the Renaissance as conceived by Burckhardt, and to Baudelaire.[35] I think one could generalize the thesis by saying that it is in epochs of ground-shaking moral-political *crisis* (Hellenism, the triumph of the Roman Empire over the Roman republic, Italy during the Renaissance, nineteenth-century Europe) that the individual assumes with much greater 'intensity' the burden of self-constitution. As Foucault puts it in *The Care of the Self*: 'The importance given to the problem of "oneself," the development of the cultivation of the self in the course of the Hellenistic period, and the apogee it experienced at the beginning of the Empire' cannot be construed merely as a function of 'individualistic withdrawal.' Rather, 'we need instead to think in terms of a crisis of the subject, or rather a crisis of subjectivation – that is, in terms of a difficulty in the manner in which the individual could form himself as the ethical subject of his actions, and efforts to find in devotion to self that which could enable him to submit to rules and give a purpose to his existence.'[36]

Without a doubt, Foucault conceives the present as a time of moral crisis in just this sense, and it is this commonality between the crisis of the present and the crises of past epochs that gives to these great precedents – Roman Stoicism, the Burckhardtian Renaissance, Baudelairean dandyism – their real salience for the present.

Let us now turn to Foucault's fullest statement of the view of 'ethics' that he formulated shortly before his death – namely, his interview with Rabinow and Dreyfus (April 1983) titled 'On the Genealogy of Ethics: An

Overview of Work in Progress.'[37] At the beginning of the interview, Foucault states very clearly why he finds ethical Stoicism of such appeal: the reason is that it is not a matter of 'ethics' at all; or rather, with the Stoics, ethics comes to be 'aestheticized': 'The principal aim, the principal target of this kind of ethics was an aesthetic one ... this kind of ethics was only a problem of personal choice ... it was not a question of giving a pattern of behavior for everybody. It was a personal choice for a small elite. The reason for making this choice was the will to live a beautiful life, and to leave to others memories of a beautiful existence.'[38]

Foucault characterizes two aspects of this aestheticized ethics that appeal to him: (1) there was no 'normalization' involved (that is, no demand that people conform to a preconceived norm); and (2) it did not impose a universalizing morality, but simply addressed itself to a small group of individuals seeking to perfect themselves. As I have already suggested, I find this a strange characterization of what we associate historically with Stoicism as a philosophical movement; but let us leave all of that to one side, and concentrate on what this aestheticized Stoicism means for Foucault. The brilliance of the Stoics, as Foucault understands them, is that they adhered to an extremely restrictive and austere sexual morality *without* imposing it as a universal normative framework in the way that Western moralities are typically cast: as an effort to 'normalize' people, and as the imposition of a universal moral code. Rather (as he presents it), it was offered as the means for exploring styles of life for a particular class of individuals.

Once again, Foucault draws a connection between our present post-Christian situation and the ancient pre-Christian situation. We have worked our way back to the aestheticized ethics discovered by the ancients 'since most of us no longer believe that ethics is founded in religion, nor do we want a legal system to intervene in our moral, personal, private life.'[39] Foucault points out that contemporary liberation movements feel themselves to be in need of an ethics, and that we are therefore obliged to go in search of new models of ethical reflection.

Again, Foucault emphasizes that ethics in late antiquity becomes more attractive, relative to what it was in Plato and Aristotle, owing to the depoliticization implicit in Hellenistic ethical life: 'A Greek citizen of the fifth or fourth century would have felt that this *techne* for life was to take care of the city, of his companions. But for Seneca, for instance, the problem is to take care of himself. With Plato's *Alcibiades*, it's very clear: you have to rule the city. But taking care of yourself for its own sake starts with the Epicureans ...'[40]

So: 'One of the main evolutions in ancient culture has been that this *techne tou biou* [art of knowing how to live] became more and more a *techne* of the self.'[41] Why does the latter represent an improvement? Foucault explains very clearly that the advantages of the Hellenistic and post-Hellenistic conception consist in its having insulated individuals against the normalizing structures of social life: 'Everybody has to take care of himself. Greek ethics is centred on a problem of personal choice, of aesthetics of existence. The idea of the *bios* as a material for an aesthetic piece of art is something which fascinates me. The idea also that ethics can be a very strong structure of existence, without any relation with the juridical per se, with an authoritarian system, with a disciplinary structure. All that is very interesting.'[42]

What matters to Foucault is not whether we opt for a morality of sexual austerity or a morality with an exactly opposite content; what matters is, one might say, the cultural motivation that impels one toward one morality or the other. Thus, the Greeks embraced the ideal of sexual austerity 'in order to give to their life much more intensity, much more beauty. In a way it's the same in the twentieth century when people, in order to get a more beautiful life, tried to get rid of all the sexual repression of their society, of their childhood. Gide in Greece would have been an austere philosopher.'[43] If we follow the Greek example, we are driven toward this challenge: 'Couldn't everyone's life become a work of art?'[44]

Here, Foucault's interviewers raise some very pertinent questions, and Foucault's answers to their challenge are highly illuminating. Rabinow and Dreyfus point out that the notion of submitting all the details of life (how one eats breakfast, how one has sex, and so on) to an art of self-perfection is actually a Californian project. Foucault replies that the problem is that people in California think that there is a truth about these things that they are capable of apprehending. Rabinow and Dreyfus respond that if one is obliged to create oneself 'without recourse to knowledge or universal rules,' how is this different from Sartrean existentialism?[45] Foucault's answer is very interesting: He notes that of course Sartre *wants* to break with the idea of the self as something given; but that in the end Sartre cannot help coming back to the idea of a true self – of a relation to the self that is judged to be authentic or inauthentic. The problem with Sartre is not his existentialism, but his failure to uphold it with utter consistency. The superiority of Foucault's conception of 'creating ourselves as a work of art' is that, unlike Sartre's, it avoids lapsing back into an ideal of the true self; that is, it perseveres in the idea of creating oneself *all the way down* (or to use Rorty's notion: the idea of *pure* contingency).[46] Sartre's problem is that he is an inconsistent existentialist. Rabinow and Dreyfus mention Nietzsche, and Foucault enthusiastically agrees that his view 'is much closer to Nietzsche's than to Sartre's.'[47] In short, Foucault's ideal is Sartrean existentialism *minus the appeal to authenticity* – that is, creativity *all the way down*. Only Nietzsche had the courage to descend into the abyss of the self without hoping to land eventually on some kind of bedrock – and if Foucault had read certain passages in Nietzsche (for instance, *Beyond Good and Evil*, § 230), he might well have concluded that even Nietzsche occasionally loses his nerve.

The same issue comes up again later in the interview, and again Rabinow and Dreyfus pose the right questions. Foucault repeats his analysis that Christian morality and the morality of antiquity actually share a commitment to asceticism, or sexual austerity. Therefore, what distinguishes the two moral visions is not their *content* but, one might say, the existential context into which this shared content is inserted. In antiquity, in sharp contrast to subsequent Christian practice, the austerity applied to the self 'is not imposed on the individual by means of civil law or religious obligation, but is a choice about existence made by the individual. People decide for themselves ...'[48] It is – like an individual freely choosing to enter the monastic life as an act of opting for a certain style of living, a (to use the ugly word we use today) 'lifestyle' – a self-chosen discipline. Foucault then begins the crucial exchange with the (quite implausible!) claim that 'we have hardly any remnant of the idea in our society, that the principal work of art which one must take care of, the main area to which one must apply aesthetic values, is oneself, one's life, one's existence. We find this in the Renaissance, but in a slightly academic form, and yet again in nineteenth-century dandyism, but those were the only episodes.'[49] Dreyfus and Rabinow rightly object: 'But isn't the Greek concern with the self just an early version of our self-absorption, which many consider a central problem in our society?'[50]

This restates the earlier challenge, and Foucault responds by restating his earlier answer: The problem with the contemporary 'cult of the self' is that it is not radical enough. It still presupposes a residual 'true self,' like Sartre's ideal of authenticity, to which one is obliged to seek to approximate. But a 'true self' is incompatible with the ideal of a self waiting to be fashioned as a work of art. Foucault concludes that therefore, his model, the 'ancient culture of the self,' is not identical to 'the Californian cult of the self' (as Rabinow and Dreyfus imply) but indeed, diametrically opposed to it.[51] What this means, surely, is not that the Foucaultian conception is less subjectivist than the Californian ideal; what it means, rather, is that the latter is *less radically* subjectivist than the former. Rabinow and Dreyfus express concern about the echoes of narcissism that they detect in Foucault's vision of the self as a work of art. In reply, Foucault complains that Californian narcissism goes wrong precisely in its appeal to authenticity. I don't see how one could draw any other conclusion from this exchange than that Foucault's ultimate view is that 'care of the self' = narcissism minus truth.

Let me now pose a couple of questions of my own. It seems to me that the intellectual adequacy of this Foucaultian view of aesthetic self-creation depends a great deal on whether it permits standards of judgment by which to appraise individuals' efforts to craft themselves as works of art – as either impressive or banal, as stunningly vivid or merely boring, as more meaningful/less meaningful, as more compelling/less compelling, and so on. Otherwise, it is hard to see how these merely aesthetic performances could retain their hold on our moral interest – that is, our interest in wanting to decide how (according to what content) we should live. Indeed, it is mysterious how they could even retain the interest of those who enact them. But I don't see how Foucault, or any other postmodernist, can allow us to ask just those questions that we need to ask if moral life (that is, the life of ordinary praxis and of choosing how to live) is not to become a gigantic bore. If the question of content is irrelevant, and if it counts equally as a existential work of art if we opt for a monkish life rather than the life of a sexual libertine, or vice versa, why doesn't this depiction of moral existence as the unconstrained choice of a style of living reduce moral life to the indifferent toss of a coin? If the existential artist maintains his or her artistic freedom by exercising the prerogative to splash a dollop of paint on the canvas without reference to independent standards of truth, beauty, or perfection, why isn't art reduced to a meaningless play of whim? These questions are implicit in Rabinow and Dreyfus's challenge, but Foucault fails to see that there is any problem here, and remains determined to carry his Nietzschean voluntarism to the furthest extremity without flinching. What a paradoxical outcome for a mode of thought whose original motivation was to debunk the idea of the autonomous subject!

Postmodern Platonism

Volume 1 of Foucault's *History of Sexuality* bears a Nietzschean title (*La volonté de savoir*); more surprisingly, the third volume of *The History of Sexuality* bears a *Platonic* title (*Le souci de soi*). It seems very striking indeed (to say the least) that the very last book published by Foucault should carry a title drawn from Plato.[52] I want to devote the last section of this essay to a closer examination of this curious fact. The Platonic text to which the title of Foucault's book directs us is a dialogue entitled *Alcibiades I* (127d–e), and in the Rabinow and Dreyfus interview, Foucault makes the strange claim that *The History of Sexuality* offers a reading of the dialogue: '*Le souci de soi* ... is composed of different papers about the self – for instance, a commentary on Plato's *Alcibiades*.'[53] But when one actually turns to the relevant text (namely, the published version of Volume 3 of *The History of Sexuality*), one sees in fact that there is no substantive account by Foucault (not even the trace of one) of what distinguishes his approach to the dialogue. There is precisely one direct citation of the *Alcibiades* in the book, where Foucault reports the Socratic view that one should put one's own soul in order before presuming to rule the city and manage its affairs; and he makes the observation – a fairly obvious one – that Socrates has in mind a practice of caring for oneself that goes well beyond what the Spartans took this to mean: physical and military training.[54] As well, there is a citation on the next page from a later Platonist to the effect that the way to be initiated into the philosophic life is by reading the *Alcibiades*.[55] *C'est tout.* The reader who doesn't yield to Foucault's authority will want to ask: Why is it, not only that Foucault *doesn't* provide the reading he says he offers, but that he *cannot* provide one, given the constraints of his basic intellectual commitments? For of course the dialogue itself embodies a Platonic commitment to giving a particular *content* to the 'care of the self,' which is what Foucault absolutely repudiates.[56] For Plato, the priority of the life of philosophy over the Alcibiadean lust for rule presumes that 'caring for the self' in *his* sense possesses an independent dignity and status that cannot be assured by the postmodern artist's impulse to splash any paint on the canvas that he or she chooses. (The great mystery that I have in reading postmodern authors is why they all seem to think that the greatest threat in the modern world is having to adapt to pregiven norms. It seems to me that a much greater threat is the prospect that what it means to opt for one way of life rather than another will be so trivialized that it will become impossible to see why one should exert the effort to make these choices at all.)

To close, I want, finally, to recall Jürgen Habermas's neat encapsulation of the impression that Foucault made on him, as a theorist and as a human being. Habermas writes that what characterizes Foucault is 'the tension, which resists easy categorization, between the almost serene scientific reserve of the scholar striving for objectivity on the one hand, and, on the other, the political vitality of the vulnerable, subjectively excitable, morally sensitive intellectual.'[57] Although one can hear a detectable tone of sympathy in this statement, what immediately came to my mind when I read it was Max Weber's famous phrase at the end of *The Protestant Ethic*: 'specialists without spirit, sensualists without heart.' Whether Habermas himself *intended* to bring to mind this Weberian image, I cannot say. But in any case, I think it captures beautifully what seems to me amiss in Foucault's theoretical universe. What Weber, of course, had in mind was that the pressures of late modernity would cause human beings to be bifurcated into two distinct types: spiritless specialists and heartless sensualists. What he could not have anticipated is that a paradoxical soul like Michel Foucault could combine within itself *both* of these types, and moreover, that such a figure could turn out to be one of the most influential intellectuals of the late twentieth century.[58]

II INTERROGATING MODERNITY

10

Do We Need a Philosophical Ethics? Theory, Prudence, and the Primacy of *Ethos*

One of the more interesting developments in moral theory in recent decades has been a very notable resurgence of modes of thought inspired by Aristotle's *Nicomachean Ethics*. Needless to say, this turn back to Aristotle within contemporary moral and political theory did not please everyone. In particular, Habermas and his followers charged that neo-Aristotelianism, with its appeal to notions like *ethos* and *phronesis*, rendered morality entirely dependent on the contingencies of given constellations of social life, and therefore abdicated the proper task of a moral theory, which is to supply universalist moral principles, as Kant, for instance, aspires to do in his practical philosophy. This essay tries to offer a response to the Habermasian challenge to neo-Aristotelian ethics. The object of my argument will be a heightened awareness of the gap between a *theory* of practical reason and the concrete demands of practical reason itself; this will, I think, allow me to defend Gadamer and other neo-Aristotelians against Habermas's charge that they hark back to an outdated philosophy that rests solely upon, as he disparagingly terms it, substantive 'worldviews.'[1] If Gadamer is correct in arguing for the centrality of notions like prudence and *ethos* to the constitutive reality of moral life, then Habermas's demand that ethics be grounded in 'theoretical knowledge' can be seen as basically hollow. Gadamer's emphasis on the ineradicable concreteness of practical knowledge suggests that even the full realization of Habermas's program (or any comparable one) leaves the tasks of practical reason in their actual content essentially untouched. Gadamer states in one place that it was 'on the basis of reasons and not

Originally published in *Philosophical Forum* 20, no. 3 (Spring 1989). Reprinted with the permission of *Philosophical Forum*.

out of neglect' that Heidegger in the *Letter on Humanism* balked at Jean Beaufret's plea for a new Heideggerian ethics. What were those reasons? An elucidation of these grounds will, I hope, help to clarify the limits of what one can accomplish with a new philosophical ethics.

Let us, then, start with an account of Habermas's challenge to the neo-Aristotelians. Habermas writes:

Classical natural right is a theory dependent on world views. It was still quite clear to Christian Wolff at the end of the eighteenth century that practical philosophy 'presupposes in all its doctrines ontology, natural psychology, cosmology, theology, and thus the whole of metaphysics.' The ethics and politics of Aristotle are unthinkable without the connection to physics and metaphysics, in which the basic concepts of form, substance, act, potency, final cause, and so forth are developed ... Today it is no longer easy to render the approach of this metaphysical mode of thought plausible.[2]

The nub of the argument so far is, clearly, that classical ethics is inseparable from classical metaphysics, and that the awareness of this inseparability has prompted contemporary advocates of Aristotelianism to shy away from a forthright systematic account of their principles (for obviously they lack the means to resuscitate an obsolete metaphysics[3]). This critique is, in my opinion, quite effectively negated by Alasdair MacIntyre. In the following passage, MacIntyre addresses the widespread assumption that 'ancient and medieval beliefs, including Aristotelian beliefs, in the objectivity of the moral order required as a foundation ... or were "based upon" theories about human nature and the nature of the universe':

This is an important, although a common misreading of the structures of ancient and medieval thought which projects back on to that thought an essentially modern view of the ordering of philosophical and scientific enquiries. On this modern view, ethics and politics are peripheral modes of enquiry, dependent in key part on what is independently established by epistemology and by the natural sciences (semantics has now to some degree usurped the place of epistemology). But in ancient and medieval thought, ethics and politics afford light to the other disciplines as much as *vice versa*. Hence from that standpoint, which I share, it is not the case that *first* I must decide whether some theory of human nature or cosmology is true and only *secondly* pass a verdict upon an account of the virtues which is 'based' upon it. Rather, if we find compelling reasons for accepting a particular view of the virtues and the human telos, that in itself will place constraints on what kind of theory of human nature and what kind of cosmology are rationally acceptable.[4]

Precisely the same point is made by Gadamer in the context of a challenge to recent efforts to derive a new ethics from the thought of Heidegger: 'The Aristotelian-Kantian inheritance still carries weight precisely because it is not grounded upon a metaphysics. Here I fail to see in what way Heidegger's [challenge to traditional metaphysics] lends itself to a direct application for the problem of a philosophical ethics. I think that Heidegger has warded off the question of an ethics on the basis of reasons and not out of neglect.'[5] In other words, it is not incumbent on Heidegger to produce a 'new' ethics, for the older ethical traditions have retained their abiding validity (or such validity as is proper to them). The debunking of traditional *metaphysics* does not at the same time suffice for the debunking of corresponding ethical traditions; so, at least in principle, traditional ethics can survive the demise of traditional metaphysical world-views. What is decisive, of course, is whether these ethical traditions continue to be reflected in the actual life and practices of historical societies; and this is something that is entirely independent of the efforts of philosophers and theorists. It is, as Gadamer – following Heidegger as much as Aristotle – terms it, a matter of *ethos*.

As the next stage of Habermas's polemic makes clear, however, Habermas is fully aware that certain qualified 'Aristotelians' like Gadamer 'withdraw' the *theoretical* claim of practical philosophy. As Habermas puts it, 'they *reduce* it to a hermeneutics of everyday conceptions of the good, the virtuous, and the just'[6] (hence his reference to this as 'reductive,' that is, reduced or contracted, Aristotelianism). However, in Habermas's view this tactical retreat does not rescue Aristotelianism from its contemporary predicament, but merely proves that such an emasculated Aristotelianism is incapable of meeting the demand that it *validate* itself at the level of theoretical knowledge:

If philosophical ethics and political theory can know nothing more than what is anyhow contained in the everyday norm consciousness of different populations, and it cannot even know this in a different way, it cannot then rationally distinguish legitimate from illegitimate domination ... If, on the other hand, philosophical ethics and political theory are supposed to disclose the moral core of the general consciousness and to *reconstruct* it as a normative concept of the moral, then they must specify criteria and provide reasons; they must, that is, produce theoretical knowledge.[7]

Implicit in this critique is a concern about the inherent *particularism* of any appeal to the prereflective *ethos* of given communities (hence the demand that these moralities be theoretically 'reconstructed'). The answer to such a challenge can be located, I think, in Gadamer's reference to 'the Aristotelian-*Kantian* inheritance'; for I think there can be little doubt that Gadamer, no less than Habermas, wishes to draw upon the Kantian universalism that is (today) also a part of the given ethical consciousness. Gadamer is *not* an Aristotelian in the sense that he wishes to revert ultimately to the self-assured political convictions of a particular privileged community (say, the Athenian polis). The ethical insight underlying Habermas's appeal to universal postulates of linguistic reason – an appeal that he sees as necessary to guard against the invidious implications of any such particularism – has already been 'fused' into the more comprehensive ethical tradition that Gadamer invokes. Consider the following sentence from *Truth and Method*, referring to *sensus communis* as 'the sense that founds community': 'What gives the human will its direction is not the abstract generality of reason, but the concrete generality that represents the community of a group, a people, a nation, *or the whole human race*.'[8] This is not, I think, a sentence that could have been written by Aristotle. In short, Habermas's fears that the renunciation of a steadfast 'theoretical' grounding for ethics will endanger the best universalistic impulses of modernity overlooks the fact that Gadamer's 'Aristotelianism' (denoting a participation in communally accepted basic norms) presupposes a prior fusion of Aristotelian *and* Kantian horizons.[9]

At this point, it starts to become rather unclear whether an Aristotelian like Gadamer has any more trouble distinguishing between legitimate and illegitimate consent than does Habermas; and if so, unclear also what exactly is gained by the heroic theoretical labours that Habermas's project of a philosophical ethics requires. Gadamer, as we have seen, holds that Heidegger had good reasons for turning aside the demand for a philosophical ethics. To the question that stands at the head of our essay, then, Gadamer answers: No, we do not need a 'new' philosophical ethics, for the ethics already to hand within the tradition are perfectly sufficient, and in any case, no 'new' ethics can serve to restore the *ethos* that animates ethical practice if indeed that *ethos* has dissipated within the life-practices of our society. This explains, more lucidly than Heidegger's account in the *Letter on Humanism*, why Heidegger was compelled to refuse Jean Beaufret's famous demand for a Heideggerian ethics.

When Heidegger asserts, in the *Letter on Humanism*, that the tragedies of Sophocles 'preserve the *ethos* in their sagas more primordially than Aristotle's lectures on "ethics," '[10] what is perhaps most interesting about this claim is the possibility that Aristotle himself might not have dissented from it in any decisive respect. That is, the conceptual articulation of the Greek *ethos* offered in the *Ethics* may have been composed from within an awareness that the essential force of this *ethos* had already exhausted itself. If so, Heidegger's seeming critique of Aristotle would actually agree with Aristotle's own awareness that he was describing an ethical culture that had been, since the emergence of the Sophists, in the process of losing its sway. In the same vein, Gadamer remarks that even so gifted a theorist as Aristotle could do nothing to restore *ethos* to the polis.[11]

Habermas, it seems, tends to trace Gadamer's aversion to a systematic ethics to the latter's reverence for cultural tradition, which involves a kind of idealistic historicism, which in turn leads easily into cultural relativism.[12] In my judgment, this is not at all the source of their theoretical disagreement. Rather, Gadamer's position derives from his emphatic understanding of the tense relationship between theory and prudence. As early as *Truth and Method*, Gadamer refers to how the Roman concept of the *sensus communis* contains 'a critical note, directed against the theoretical speculations of the philosophers; and that note Vico sounds again from his different position of opposition to modern science.'[13] More significantly, Gadamer's constant emphasis on Aristotelian *phronesis* is meant to bring to mind a polemical opposition between abstract theory and concrete prudence. According to Gadamer, Aristotle's distinction between the ideas of *sophia* and *phronesis* was 'developed by the peripatetics as a critique of the theoretical ideal of life.'[14] *Phronesis* is practical knowledge 'directed towards the concrete situation'; 'it must grasp the "circumstances" in their infinite variety.'[15] It is just this infinity of circumstance that theory as such is incapable of anticipating; and if ethical theory is in principle unequipped to deal with the concrete situation, this means that it stops short of precisely that concreteness that is at the heart of all moral knowledge.

The fact that Aristotle's ethics offers the merest sketch of what it is to achieve the mean in one's ethical conduct is an acknowledgment of this necessary limitation of theory.[16] What Gadamer ultimately draws from Aristotle's practical philosophy is the notion that one is always already participating in shared norms by which one is antecedently shaped, and that 'the ideal of the nonparticipating observer' who stands above it all is therefore a bogus one. While the given normative consciousness should never be conceived as immutably fixed and beyond criticism, 'it would surely be an illusion to want to deduce normative notions *in abstracto* and to posit them as valid with the claim of scientific rectitude,' for this would be to pre-empt the rightful task of *phronesis*.[17]

Here we confront what Gadamer, in his 1961 lecture 'On the Possibility of a Philosophical Ethics,' refers to as the vexing 'dilemma' of all philosophical reflection on ethics[18]: namely, that in order to philosophize about ethical norms, one must distanciate oneself from them, whereas in order to have experience of these norms at all, so as to be acquainted with that about which one philosophizes, one must first of all participate in them – and this participation never completely ceases, even in the furthest flights of theoretical distanciation. (This dilemma is not so pressing in the case of, say, a philosophy of natural science, where the content of the norms one seeks to validate does not enter into the very being of the philosophical observer who reflects on them, as *is* true – and necessarily true – for the moral philosopher.) This unavoidable tension between distance and involvement is at the heart of Gadamer's hermeneutics. The intractability of this dilemma carries important implications for any attempt to define a philosophical ethics. For Gadamer, it implies an essential finitude that characterizes any endeavour to bring philosophical reflection to bear upon ethical life. This finitude or conditionality of moral reflection is visible not only in the ethics of Aristotle, but even, as Gadamer shows, in the seemingly more ambitious attempt by Kant to ground moral principles. Kant, like Aristotle, insists that his moral philosophy makes available no new moral content, but merely clarifies and articulates the moral experience already shared in by ordinary people throughout the ages. Kant notes that a fault-finding reviewer of the *Foundations of the Metaphysics of Morals* 'really did better than he intended when he said that there was no new principle of morality in it but only a new formula. Who would want to introduce a new principle of morality and, as it were, be its inventor, as if the world had hitherto been ignorant of what duty is or had been thoroughly wrong about it.'[19]

The import of Kantian formalism, as understood by Gadamer, is less to inform us of the content of our duty than to confirm what duty *is*, in its very nature (to remind us of its unconditionality, when reason itself tempts us to treat duty as something that can be finessed). The purpose of Kant's ethics, on this reading, consists not in telling us what we ought to do, but rather, in telling us what it *means* to be subject to an 'ought,' what it *is* to be morally bound. According to Gadamer, Kant's attempts to derive content from the formula of the categorical imperative are entirely unpersuasive and contrived, and so what remains is the mere *form* of moral experience as the steadfast search for what is unconditionally valid and binding. Therefore *phronesis*, far from being displaced, retains its indispensable function within the drama of trying to *apply* the demand for moral unconditionality. Once again, the heart of moral experience lies in finding oneself cast into the concreteness of an ethical situation where no predetermined rule dictates an answer.[20]

As Gadamer puts it, practical philosophy, with its insistence on *phronesis*, 'does not propose any new ethics, but rather clarifies and concretizes *given* normative contents,'[21] and this, as we have seen, applies as much to Kant as to Aristotle. These given normative contents can only be supplied by *ethos*, which in turn is a function not of reflective consciousness but of our very being as shaped by life in society. So we see that what is most relevant to the understanding of contemporary practical reason is not the theoretical or metatheoretical grounding of principles, but the historical question of why the *ethos* of a coherent ethical life has decomposed. And for this purpose a historical reckoning such as that offered by Alasdair MacIntyre in *After Virtue* is a great deal more helpful than Habermas's attempt to supply grounding principles.[22]

Part of the explanation for the primacy of *ethos* is that in order for moral convictions to have force within the life of concrete societies, ethical intuitions must possess a great deal more self-certainty than they could possibly gather from merely theoretical demonstrations. (An insight of this kind is present in Hegel's and Nietzsche's analyses of Socrates, whose very appearance is seen as a symptom of moral decline within the polis.) As even Habermas concedes, 'the difference between what we always claim for our rationality and what we are actually able to explicate as rational can in principle never be eliminated.'[23] But for the demands of situated praxis, this is simply not enough: one must act *as if* unreflectively, embodying a sure sense of what is good and right; one must command a kind of practical assurance that even the strictest, most rigorous set of arguments fails to supply.[24] This is something made possible only by character and habituation, never by rational argument as such. As an Aristotelian would say, in order to live virtuously and to make the right choices, one's soul must be shaped by certain habits of virtuous conduct, in a way that renders superfluous, recourse to strict arguments. Judged by these purposes, the achievements of theory always fall short. This does not mean, of course, that the adequacy of one's judgments is measured by pure inner conviction; it means only that one's capacity to discriminate between good and bad judgments cannot be reduced to an abstract science.

Here we perceive the grounds of the tremendous modesty that characterizes Aristotelian ethics. Gadamer writes entirely in the spirit of Aristotle when he speaks of his 'profound scepticism regarding the role of "intellectuals" and especially of philosophy in humanity's household of life': 'The great equilibrium of what is living, which sustains and permeates the individual in his privacy as well as in his social constitution and in his view of life, also encompasses those who think ... [Even the Greeks, with their exaltation of *theoria*,] knew that such theory is embedded within the practice of conditioned and lived life and is borne along by it.'[25]

Habermas also, to be sure, often gives expression (especially in some of his more recent statements) to a similar sense of modesty in relation to the self-defined understandings of given societies.[26] The fundamental difference between them can, I think, be put as follows: For Habermas, any practical judgment insofar as it has not been theoretically validated is to that extent somehow suspect, or clouded by suspicion, as to its possible groundlessness. For Gadamer, on the other hand, any theoretical judgment as such carries a certain measure of stigma insofar as it stands unmediated by the concreteness of a particular social experience. It seems to me possible and desirable to embrace both of these points of view in a way that does justice to the imperishable tension between theory and practice.

The issue is not one of truth versus relativity, as Habermas tends to present it, nor of validated knowledge versus unvalidated opinion; the issue, rather, is one of the truth of generality versus the truth of specificity – that is, truth at the level of abstract principles versus truth embedded in immediate circumstances. Aristotle certainly does not repudiate the idea of moral truth when he insists that *phronesis* can only embody itself in the local encounter with 'ultimate particulars.' Nor does Gadamer. So it is not any kind of moral scepticism that prompts doubts about the project of a philosophical ethics, but instead the worry that it will have very little to teach us at the real locus of our ethical experience. What is intended is not an attenuation of moral reason, but its confrontation with an alternative account of moral reason – its 'localization,' one might say.[27] To use Gadamer's terms, the choice is between judging 'from a distance' and judging from within 'the demands of the situation'; so it is not a question of whether moral truths exist but of whether one gains access to these truths 'from the inside,' or whether they are imposed from 'outside' shared moral experience.

Gadamer's Aristotelian insight into the primacy of *ethos* may be expressed as follows: Good theory is no substitute for good socialization, and even the best theory is utterly helpless in the face of bad socialization.[28] Habermas, it would appear, agrees entirely with this formulation:

Moral theory proceeds reconstructively, in other words after the event. Aristotle was right in his opinion that the moral intuitions which theory clarifies must have been acquired elsewhere, in more or less successful socialization processes.[29]

How could anyone focus on moral intuitions and reconstruct them, before having them – and how do we get them? Not from philosophy, and not by reading books. We acquire them just by growing up in a family. This is the experience of everyone ... There can't be anyone who ever grew up in any kind of family who did not acquire certain moral intuitions.[30]

These statements certainly appear to draw Habermas as close to Gadamer's Aristotelianism as it is possible to get. And yet there remains a crucial gulf between them that may be discerned from the wide divergence in their respective stances toward modernity. For Habermas, modernity in itself is a gain, for it opens more and more aspects of human life to free, uncoerced examination and discursive argument, which renders these practices more 'rational,' and therefore more free. For Gadamer, in contrast, the effect of such 'rationalization' may be to loosen the hold of these practices (whether they are legitimate or illegitimate) insofar as they depend on *ethos*. Thus Habermas, while he seems to concede a great deal on the question of habituation, still does not follow through the full implications of his own admission of the primary role of moral socialization, as can be seen, above all, in his equation of modernity as such and emancipation. (How can the content of ethical life rest upon both habit *and* rational consensus? Surely this is an either/or.) For Gadamer, on the other hand, the legacy of modernity is far more ambiguous, for the rational and discursive examination of ethical practices may, in itself, contribute to the dissolution of those practices, to the extent that these practices express not our 'consciousness' but our 'being' as shaped by prereflective habituation.[31] (Consider the decline of the work ethic, the atrophying of shared culture, the decomposition of the family itself, and so on.) What may be inferred from this observation is not necessarily that these practices were in essence illegitimate, but rather, that there is a tension between *ethos* and 'rationalization' (that is, reason in the *Enlightenment* sense of bringing-into-explicit-consciousness) – a tension that Habermas persistently fails to acknowledge.

In a curious way, the contrast between these two positions vis-à-vis modernity shows Gadamer to be *less* of a relativist, more of a universalist, than Habermas; for whereas Habermas seeks to vindicate the universalistic truth contained within *our own* modern, Western rationality, Gadamer seeks to recover the truths of other times and other cultures that have been eclipsed by Western modernity. The irony is that Habermas, for all of his anti-historicism, embraces the supposedly higher claims of our own epoch, while Gadamer, criticized for his 'historicism,' is much more sceptical of the putative gains of modernity, and therefore further removed from the presumptions of the present.[32]

To reinforce our case, let us consider another Habermasian critique of Gadamer. Albrecht Wellmer, writing in defence of Habermas's project, offers the following characterization – mistaken in my view – of what he calls the 'left-Aristotelian' position.[33] The heart of this position, as he describes it, is the idea that while rational argument and agreement is certainly possible with respect to specific issues and problems, there are nonetheless basic norms, constitutive of political legitimacy, that are not in principle subject to rational dialogue. The crucial question here, as Wellmer construes it, is whether limits can be drawn, beyond which *in principle* rational argument and rational agreement are out of reach. If, in engaging in any rational discussion, we pursue a discursive continuum that leads to progressively more and more basic assumptions, then it is hard to see how any such 'boundary line' can ever be justifiably drawn. And if this boundary line can never be located in a fixed or determinate way, it follows, for Wellmer, that 'no norms, institutions or interpretations are in principle exempt from the possibility of critical examination.'[34] If this is intended as a refutation of Gadamer (Hannah Arendt is the only thinker explicitly mentioned by Wellmer), I think it fails to hit the mark. The basic premise of Wellmer's argument (the interminable continuity of rational discourse) is, in my opinion, sound, but it does not yield the conclusion that he seeks to draw from it (that is, the refutation of 'left Aristotelianism'). What the argument obscures is a fundamental ambiguity surrounding the term 'in principle.' I think that Gadamer (and Arendt, for that matter) would happily admit that there are no principled limits to rational discussion of social norms. (This is, after all, what defines the tradition of political philosophy.) What *is* at issue, though, is whether it is realistic to demand or expect that such rationally-arrived-at consensus could actually uphold the life of an entire society (or whether it is even coherent to posit such a consensus as an ideal norm at which to aim). Here indeed Gadamer would fault Habermas's theory for rationalistic utopianism. If, as any 'left Aristotelian' must believe, *ethos*, not rational agreement, is the condition of virtue, it would be completely implausible to posit the possibility of a good or reasonable society, any more than any other society, founded upon rational consensus. To say this, however, is not to banish notions of reason and unreason in the evaluation of different societies. The idea that social norms should not be submitted to critical reason is hardly a view one would expect from a devoted student of Plato and Aristotle like Gadamer. (To put the point rather provocatively, one might say that where Gadamer opposes critical theory is not in its commitment to reason but in its sociological naïvety – a naïvety that is, of course, as critics from Rousseau and Hegel onwards have insisted, a crucial aspect of the legacy of Enlightenment rationalism.)

Habermas himself, of course, denies that the idea of rational consensus is any kind of utopian ideal; rather, he insists that it furnishes merely a critical standard for distinguishing the legitimacy or illegitimacy of given forms of social organization. But even as a standard for judging actual societies, such a regulative idea presupposes that it is meaningful to conceive of societies whose members are not just socialized *to* reason but socialized *by* reason,[35] and it is the coherence of precisely this conception that is here in question. Furthermore, if Habermas agrees with Gadamer that philosophical ethics is necessarily situated posterior to ordinary moral consciousness, and that to this extent no such ethics, however well-grounded, can actually 'pre-empt' practical judgment, and if he agrees that even the most impeccably grounded theory leaves open the task of application with respect to particulars,[36] what in substance remains of Habermas's demand that everyday communication receive a 'justification or grounding' whose validity is elevated above 'the mere de facto acceptance of habitual practices?'[37] Is it not the case that the challenge to supply reasons or grounds for a particular judgment will arise *within* the immediate situation of praxis, as Gadamer thinks, and that a formal inquiry into conditions of validity such as Habermas pursues will have little or nothing to contribute toward satisfying the internal demands of practical reason in all its immediacy and concreteness? We are left, it seems, more unsure than ever about what one may hope to accomplish with a systematic '*Diskursethik*' – apart from seeking merely to repel the most virulent forms of relativism. But even supposing that this last intention defines the sole object of the enterprise,[38] one might still ask: Does one need a systematic ethics in order to fend off relativism, as Habermas implies in relation to Gadamer?[39]

The disputation between Gadamer and Habermas ultimately comes down to a question of the relative priority of theory and prudence. Habermas's position, as we saw in the passage I quoted from 'Legitimation Problems in the Modern State,' is that a reliance upon prudence alone, without resort to theoretical criteria, risks sliding into a denial of universal principles of justice and equality. Therefore *phronesis* is not enough: one requires theoretical knowledge of correct norms. Gadamer's clearest and most forceful answer to this challenge is contained in his letter to Richard Bernstein, appended to *Beyond Objectivism and Relativism*:

Aristotle's *Politics* ... comes into its own and makes the transition from ethics to politics only because it presupposes the results of the *Ethics*: first and foremost, a common, shared normative consciousness. The *Politics* proposes, so to speak, the doctrine of a political constitution for a society that still knows what *ethos* and *phronesis* are. Both your own [Bernstein's] and Habermas' argument assert that this is precisely the knowledge we no longer possess today. This fact fundamentally alters the task of the transition from ethics to politics; if I understand correctly, it now becomes the transition from practical philosophy to social science. But practical philosophy insists on the guiding function of *phronesis*, which does not propose any new ethics, but rather clarifies and concretizes given normative contents. To this extent, I share Rorty's criticism of Habermas' claim to scientific status. As I have put it elsewhere, I cannot really make sense of a *phronesis* that is supposed to be scientifically disciplined, although I can imagine a scientific approach that is disciplined by *phronesis*.[40]

The priority of *phronesis* over science that Gadamer here asserts follows from the dependence of any ethical understanding upon *ethos* or habituation (as Gadamer puts it: one cannot be convinced by argument to be virtuous). If in fact the technicization of modern life, or the 'disenchantment of the world,' or whatever, has caused us to lose this *ethos*, then no theoretical grounding of a philosophical ethics could possibly allow us to recover it. In that case, our situation would be truly desperate; it would be as forlorn as Heidegger describes it when he says that 'only a god can save us' – namely, the descent of a new *ethos* as a dispensation of being. But here Gadamer is just as critical of Heidegger as he is of Habermas: just as no philosopher can legislate a new *ethos*,[41] so no philosopher can rule out new constellations of ethical life arising out of existing communal solidarities. (It is in reference to *Heidegger* that Gadamer speaks of the 'terrible intellectual hubris' involved in dismissing 'life as it is actually lived with its own forms of solidarity.'[42]) The *ethos* may indeed be tenuous in the technological age we now inhabit, but if it were genuinely as bleak as Heidegger expresses in his cry for new gods, then certainly no provision of a philosophical ethics would yield consolation enough.

11

Rescuing the Rationalist Heritage

Imagine a social theory that seeks to combine the boldest truths of German speculative philosophy with the analytical precision of contemporary Anglo-American philosophy. Such a theory, let us suppose, is equally at home in the traditions of American pragmatism, post-Wittgensteinian speech act theory, and German hermeneutics. Let us assume, moreover, that this theory incorporates the best critical insights of Marx, Nietzsche, and Freud, while eliminating the elements of folly and extravagance in these teachings. It takes the best from both Marxist and Weberian social theory. Imagine, too, that the theory offers a comprehensive radical epistemology as a foundation for its theory of society, as well as a firm grounding in the latest research in philosophy of language, linguistics, cognitive developmental psychology, and other social sciences. Finally, let us presume that the enterprise is rounded off with an encyclopedic survey of alternative contemporary theories, showing how each contributed to, or stood in the light of, the theory advanced to encompass them all. Such a theory, we might think, would go as far as humanly possible toward establishing a basis for social knowledge in our present circumstances (that is, telling us the truth about ourselves). This, without much exaggeration, is precisely the aspiration of the work of Jürgen Habermas as it has unfolded during the last two decades.

The magisterial scale on which Habermas presents his developed reflections in *The Theory of Communicative Action* matches this heroic con-

Review of Jürgen Habermas, *The Theory of Communicative Action*, vol. 1, *Reason and the Rationalization of Society*, trans. Thomas McCarthy (London: Heinemann Educational Books, 1984), and *Philosophical-Political Profiles*, trans. Fredrick G. Lawrence (London: Heinemann Educational Books, 1983); originally published in *The Times Higher Education Supplement*, 22 May 1984. Reprinted with the permission of The Times Supplements Ltd.

ception of the task. Habermas seeks to define his position through dialogue with the 'classics' of sociological thought – namely, the work of Durkheim, Weber, G.H. Mead, and Talcott Parsons. In this first volume, his main interlocutors are Max Weber – who characterized modernity as an 'iron cage' – and those who carried forward Weber's legacy within Western Marxism. For Weber, Western rationalism is both a supreme achievement unique to Occidental culture, *and* an 'iron cage' that encloses us more and more tightly in its grip. Marxists from Lukács onwards have been forced to acknowledge the compelling force of Weber's analysis, transposed into the neo-Marxist category of reification. Adorno and Horkheimer bring this theoretical development to its conclusion of ultimate despair, leaving critical theory at an uncomfortable impasse. This is the situation to which Habermas responds.

The book has both a substantive thesis and a methodological thrust. As regards the substantive thesis, the basic underlying intuition, I think, is that people are locked into systems of administrative rationality without any effective say over the kinds of shared existence that ought properly to be matters of collective determination. The iron cage thus has a real political dimension: depoliticization of the public sphere, and an eclipse of any meaningful experience of citizenship.

As for the methodological message of the book, it can be summed up in a sentence or two: One cannot practise sociology without being implicated in the substantive contests over social truth. One participates in the truth claims of social actors; one is never suspended neutrally above the fray. This argument is undoubtedly correct. The two strands of the work, substantive and methodological, link up in the following way: Social life is about the shared pursuit of truth. This orientation to practical truth guides our judgments about how society should be organized (to facilitate the collective detection of truth); it also guides our understanding of the relationship of the social-scientific investigator to the social actors, whose perspectives he or she both shares and critically evaluates.

The contemporary context is relevant. Our situation, as Habermas understands it, is one in which antirationalism and relativism are rampant, as displayed both in the vestiges of liberal positivism and in the new appeal of Nietzschean poststructuralism. In an interview published in 1981, Habermas says that his theory of rationality is addressed to those 'who cannot swallow such a prudish word as rationality without turning red.' As he remarks, 'the tragedy Lukács described as *The Destruction of Reason* now reappears as farce in our liberal cultural weeklies.' The basic problem, as Habermas sees it, is that in the political conflicts that characterize contemporary society – say between those who exalt economic growth and those who abhor it – 'both sides turn against the heritage of Western rationalism.' His purpose, therefore, is to draw upon all available philosophical resources in order to rescue this rationalist heritage.

In his preface, Habermas describes how he struggled between seeking to pursue the analytical aims of the philosopher and remaining true to the interests of the sociologist, who must ask what purpose such conceptual analysis should serve. The implication is that the sociologist in Habermas kept him from becoming lost in the details of conceptual inquiry pursued for its own sake ('as *l'art pour l'art*'). Indeed, my own opinion is that the importance of the work owes more to its sociological motivation than to its conceptual achievement. (For all my sympathy for Habermas's project, I find it difficult to see how the classification of speech acts, for instance, can make any substantial contribution to the grounding of social theory.)

One of the problems is that Habermas despairs of philosophical inquiry as traditionally conceived. Philosophy, he says, can no longer furnish 'totalizing knowledge.' Instead, it should direct itself toward 'formal conditions of rationality' in knowing, in linguistic understanding, and in acting. Current philosophy is postmetaphysical, limited to a theory of rationality. Habermas rejects both 'substantive theories of nature, history, society' *and* transcendental philosophy in the Kantian tradition: 'All attempts at discovering ultimate foundations ... have broken down.' What is left is the project of a formal (but not transcendental) analysis of conditions of rationality.

Perhaps the most promising dimension of Habermas's enterprise is the theory of modernity reserved for Volume Two, and sketched by Thomas McCarthy in his introduction. Despite a penetrating analysis of the destructive implications of instrumental rationality, Habermas nonetheless remains sanguine toward the Enlightenment attitude of increasing rationalization, refusing to rule out the prospect that communicative rationality could yet succeed in breaking out of the bind in which it presently finds itself. Modern forms of life, however irrational they may be, nevertheless circumscribe 'a potential for reason.'

Habermas still adheres to an Enlightenment concept of reason: the greater the degree to which ways of life are based on explicit, conscious, argued-out adducement of reasons, the more rational these ways of life become. This, basically, is why he feels constrained to affirm Weber's rationalization process and the modern forms of life that go with it. There are, of course, serious objections to this concept of reason, some of which have been very thoughtfully and penetratingly articulated by Hans-Georg Gadamer (based on reflections inspired by Heidegger).

Habermas takes care to qualify this concept of rationality by insisting that it cannot be used 'to judge the totality of a form of life.' The idea of the good life, as a concrete possibility, cannot, he says, be derived from the formal concept of reason (although, he concedes, the modern age permits no other concept of reason). The problem remains, however: if Habermas can succeed only in delineating a formal or procedural conception of reason, and if modernity itself rules out 'substantive' standards of rationality, such as were available with premodern conceptions of rationality, from where are we to derive the guidance necessary for reconstructing our actual forms of life – a guidance the furnishing of which is, surely, the whole rationale of Habermas's theory? This, I believe, is where the notion of a concretely embodied wisdom that transcends formal criteria of rationality is unavoidable. Practical wisdom is something we are inducted into *from within* (by *ethos* and education) rather than something to which we gain entry under the direction of *external* rules and methods.

Relevant here is Habermas's well-known controversy with Gadamer. Although Habermas tends on occasion to portray Gadamer as a cultural relativist, Gadamer does not hold that there is no truth to practical questions; rather, he holds that practical reason achieves truth only in its *concretization*. Formal conditions of rationality do not suffice, apart from the concrete ethos and the fostering of intellectual virtues by which we are initiated into the truth of practical reason from within.

At one point, Habermas suggests that the notion of communicative rationality goes back to the classical idea of *logos*. In Plato's dialogues, opinions are examined by a process of dialectic in which each party is challenged to 'give an account' that provides reasons or grounds for whatever claim has been put forward. For Habermas, all discourse, whether theoretical or practical, should ideally meet this original standard of ancient dialectic. However, in Plato's dialogues the arguments are not addressed to a 'universal audience,' as implied by Habermas's model; rather, they take into account the concreteness of a *particular* audience.

Habermas assumes that what is decisive for rationality is the liberation from all contexts of power, coercion, and domination. But it should be obvious from ordinary experience that this is, at best, merely a necessary, not a sufficient, condition. Generally, our arguments only have force for those who already share certain prior understandings with us, and those who fail to gain access to this circle of understanding miss the point, not because of constraints on the formal conditions of discourse, but rather because they lack the concrete level of insight required for the relevant understandings. It should be evident that someone may well continue to lack the capacity for such insights even if *all* formal constraints were removed.

Habermas is determined at all costs to uphold for his work the status of a strict scientific discipline, as opposed to 'mere' hermeneutics. On the other hand, he has himself admitted that the truly formative insights are not won by science, but come through experience and habituation: 'In my convictions there is also a dogmatic centre. I would rather abandon scholarship than allow this centre to soften, for those are intuitions which I did not gain through science, that no person ever gains that way, but rather through the environment of people with whom one matures, with whom one discusses and in whom one recognizes oneself.' It should not be necessary to add that to admit this is *not* to relinquish claims to truth.

To begin to appreciate the distance that separates Habermas's concept of rationality from that which still prevails in much of Anglo-American analytical thought, we may compare his concept of rationality with the one taken for granted by John Rawls: 'Rationality is taking effective means to achieve one's ends.' It should be clear that Habermas removes any presumption that individuals are the sole rational arbiters of their own ends. The question becomes this: What is justifiable in the arena of collective discussion and decision? In other words, rationality is measured by the standard of *intersubjective* validity.

The strengths of Habermas's position are visible in his divergence from Rawls; conversely, the weaknesses of his position can be seen in what he shares with Rawls. Habermas's grounding of morality, though it claims to be purely formal, to a certain extent already presumes to know the outcome of the (anticipated) ideal discourse. For instance, how are we supposed to know, in advance of actually conducting such a distortion-free discourse, that the emancipatory argument will prove to be the well-grounded one? Perhaps it is actually the emancipatory ideology *itself* that is a source of distortions. At least if Habermas embraced a substantial concept of moral rationality, he could have some warrant for claiming to foretell the anticipated outcome, in advance of actually conducting the requisite discourse in a domination-free society. This is the very same theoretical problem that plagues Rawls's contractualist construction.

I should add a note of caution concerning the difficulties of accessibility posed by the style of the text. Habermas is notorious for the density of his writing, yet I hope that this will not overly discourage readers. At times, making one's way through the prose is like struggling through a thicket sharp with thorns and bristles. When Habermas says that 'communicative actors take up yes/no positions on criticizable validity claims,' he simply means that, as modernity takes hold, we increasingly make conscious, reflective judgments, as opposed to adhering unreflectively to traditional norms and customs. When Habermas refers to a 'colonization of the lifeworld,' he means merely that imperatives of administrative efficiency have displaced issues of moral and cultural identity. And so on. This problem of textual opacity is not helped by the host of Germanicisms such as 'action-theoretic,' 'thematizing,' and 'rationality problematic.' For this reason, readers seeking a more gentle initiation into his thought might be well advised to turn to the lighter and more discursive essays collected in *Philosophical-Political Profiles*. These essays are highly recommended, especially the wonderful essay 'The German Idealism of the Jewish Philosophers.'

However, in *The Theory of Communicative Action* there are also moments of surprising lucidity. For instance, Habermas's survey of his predecessors, from Weber through Lukács to Horkheimer and Adorno, in the final chapter of Volume One, is clear, concise, and often brilliant. In fact, one should look to this chapter for the guiding centre of Habermas's work. In his survey we come to see that his authors apply different labels for what is really the same basic phenomenon: Weber calls it the 'iron cage,' Lukács calls it 'reification,' Adorno calls it the 'administered world.' Habermas himself refers to it as the process whereby subsystems of purposive-rational action encroach upon structures of intersubjectivity of the lifeworld. The volatility of contemporary public opinion (as can be observed, at the moment, in the course taken by the American primaries process) testifies to the acuteness of Habermas's diagnosis that political decisions are 'decoupled' from concrete, identity-forming contexts of life within a political life choked by bureaucratic administrative systems.

I have little doubt that Habermas, in *The Theory of Communicative Action*, has written a major work, possibly one of the decisive works for the very urgent issues that beset our own times. Certainly, there was a critical need for someone to address anew, in a systematic way, the dilemmas that Weber had placed irrevocably on the agenda of modern theory, and it is most unlikely that anyone could be better qualified for this task than Habermas. Whether Habermas has finally achieved his purpose, I cannot venture to say. Clearly, the conception of communicative rationality is marked by important strengths, as well as by important weaknesses. One eager reviewer has gone so far as to declare that *The Theory of Communica-*

tive Action 'will play a role in the 1980's similar to the one that John Rawls' *Theory of Justice* played in the 1970's.' Whether there are valid grounds for this expectation, again, I cannot pretend to judge; in any case, it is much too early to predict exactly how the work will be received in the Anglo-American world. But it will surely be fascinating to see what kind of reception *is* accorded to *The Theory of Communicative Action*. Among other things, it will give us important clues as to whether we are at last beginning to get beyond the individualism and moral scepticism that run so deep in our intellectual life and in our public culture generally.

12

Accepting Finitude

One of the most encouraging intellectual events of the 1970s was the emergence of Hans-Georg Gadamer as a real presence on the English-speaking philosophical scene. Not only has Gadamer attained prominence as a star pupil and exponent of Heidegger, but more and more he has gained attention as a major thinker in his own right. English-speaking students and admirers of Gadamer's work are fortunate indeed that his memoirs are now available in Thomas McCarthy's excellent series, 'Studies in Contemporary German Social Thought.' The book offers a set of charming and richly detailed sketches of Gadamer's experiences as student and teacher in the course of his very ample and illustrious career. Gadamer, now 85 years old, still teaches with an astoundingly youthful vigour, and can scarcely be said to have retired in any sense.

Although the term 'hermeneutics' gets used today with more frequency than understanding, the basic experiences on which Gadamer builds his theory are quite simple and familiar ones: that the experience of responding to and being captivated by a work of culture is not a solely 'aesthetic' phenomenon, but rather, changes the very being who experiences it; that in confronting such a transformative object of understanding, one does not suspend who one is or where one comes from but attempts – in opening oneself to the truth of what is alien – to join what one already is with what addresses one; that the 'event' by which this truth discloses itself is not under the sovereign control of a 'subject,' but is rather

Review of Hans-Georg Gadamer, *Philosophical Apprenticeships* (Cambridge: MIT Press, 1985), and Joel C. Weinsheimer, *Gadamer's Hermeneutics: A Reading of Truth and Method* (New Haven: Yale University Press, 1985); originally published in *The Times Higher Education Supplement*, 15 November 1985. Reprinted with the permission of The Times Supplements Ltd.

the refutation of all subjectivism. These experiences, self-evident as they are, were never theoretically articulated as such until Gadamer did so.

Gadamer's hermeneutics offers a kind of philosophy of limitations, or what Gadamer once called 'a metaphysics of finitude.' It provides no transcendental grounding for human experience, as sought by Gadamer's neo-Kantian and phenomenological teachers. Rather, it accepts the finitude that is implicit in the actual historical dialogue in which we find ourselves immersed, prior to any theoretical reflection. However, this attention to the historical dimension of our experience does not entail any relativization of the idea of truth, as many have claimed in response to hermeneutics. On the contrary, Gadamer attempts to situate such claims to truth – whether of art, culture, or history – in the concretely actualized setting within which we first experience them. The 'truth' of a compelling and revelatory poem is something we encounter in a pretheoretical experience, as participants who are moved by a work of art, not as detached spectators who seek epistemological grounding in a cognitive method before venturing a judgment. This aspect of Gadamer's philosophy – its embrace of finitude without forgoing the claims of truth – is expressed in Gadamer's preoccupation with the relationship between philosophy and poetry, and in the fact that he develops his hermeneutics under the banner of the philosophic poetry or poetic philosophy of Plato.

While Gadamer rarely departs from the concerns of the 'pure' philosopher, wholly absorbed in the movement of ideas, one may detect a kind of social-political dimension to his work. As expressed in *Philosophical Apprenticeships*, it can be formulated as follows: to wrest the objects of humanistic or cultural understanding out of the clutches of the middle classes, and to restore the seriousness of the humanities against the bourgeois monopoly of cultural pretensions. One finds a key to this intention in the following passage: 'My hermeneutical attempt ... sought to go beyond the bourgeoisie's blind faith in education [bourgeois *Bildungsreligion*], and to bring it back to its original powers.' In another place he remarks: 'The calm distance from which a middle-class educational consciousness takes satisfaction in its educational achievements misunderstands how much we ourselves are immersed in the game and are the stake in this game.' In a more cutting passage, Gadamer relates how he had tried to suggest to Ortéga y Gasset that he should 'follow up the *Revolt of the Masses* with a book on the revolt of the middle class, but he of course did not do this. Instead world history has taken up precisely this choral refrain and shouted its theme in unison into our ears.' In this antibourgeois animus, we perceive the continuing impact of Heidegger's radicalism.

It is said by many critics, in a sense intended to impugn his work, that Gadamer is a historicist. But does it sound like the utterances of a historicist when Gadamer exclaims: 'Is that not what thinking means – to be between the times and to question beyond all time?'; or when he offers the motto borrowed from Goethe: 'He who philosophizes is not at one with the premises of his times'; or when he says that the true philosophical function of scepticism is 'to harden what no scepticism can kill because it stands fast as superior truth'? As Gadamer has stated his position: 'The hermeneutical experience is the experience of the difficulty that we encounter when we try to follow a book, a play, or a work of art, in such a way as to allow it to obsess us and lead us beyond our own horizon. It is by no means certain that we can ever recapture and integrate the original experiences encapsulated in those works. Still, taking them seriously involves a challenge to our thinking and preserves us from the danger of agnosticism or relativism.'

The fundamental lesson of Gadamer's hermeneutics is that the really decisive insights in the humanistic pursuits like art, history, and philosophy exceed what we are able to establish by methodical reasoning and demonstrable proof. As Gadamer quotes Hegel: 'Arguments are a dime a dozen.' To say this, however, is not to renounce truth, but to acknowledge the very condition of its possibility in the human sciences. Joel Weinsheimer, in his splendid commentary on *Truth and Method*, succeeds in capturing this insight in a way that is admirably faithful to Gadamer. Perhaps the fact that this very fine study is the work of a professor of English is an indication that literary critics and students of literature, who have been infatuated with the deconstructionist creed of Derrida in recent years, are now at last beginning to turn to the less dazzling but more salutary guidance of Gadamer.

13

Hannah Arendt and Leo Strauss:
The Uncommenced Dialogue

Nowhere in Hannah Arendt's published work does she mention Leo Strauss. This seems rather curious. Both arose from the same intellectual milieu. They knew each other personally, starting in the early 1930s.[1] Both felt the strong impact of the encounter with Heidegger, which remained a continuing influence upon each of them. Both were preoccupied throughout their careers with ancient political philosophy and its relevance for contemporary politics. Being German Jews, they were both driven from Germany in the early 1930s, and both settled permanently in the United States. At various times, they were affiliated with the same institutions – the New School for Social Research and the University of Chicago – and in the 1960s they actually taught at the same university. Yet they made no explicit mention of each other's work, even when both were beginning to have a major impact on the discipline they shared.

I find it hard to conceive that there is not some manner of tacit or latent dialogue with Strauss to be found in Arendt's work. For instance, when she argues in *The Human Condition* that it was an error of the Platonic tradition of political philosophy to place the *vita contemplativa* and the *vita activa* in a hierarchical relation, it is hard to imagine that she did not reflect on Strauss's reassertion of that hierarchical relation. Or again, in her Kant lectures, when she celebrates Kant because he was one of the few philosophers who sought to liberate philosophy from 'sectarianism,' from its confinement within a 'school,'[2] it is nearly impossible not to suspect that Arendt had in mind, among other things, Strauss's founding of a 'school.' If I am right in this conjecture, there is perhaps merit in the

Originally published in *Political Theory* 18, no. 2 (May 1990). Reprinted with the permission of Sage Publications, Inc.

attempt to draw out this unspoken dialogue into an open dialogue, and to imagine the lines of debate in an intellectual confrontation that never really materialized.

The most obvious difference between Arendt and Strauss is, of course, that Strauss's main concern was with ancient *philosophy*, whereas Arendt was highly critical of ancient philosophy, while she idealized – if not, as her critics charged, romanticized – ancient politics. Arendt was by no means the first modern thinker to oppose ancient praxis to ancient theory. In fact, within the history of modern political philosophy we encounter a deep and essential tradition that celebrates ancient practice at the same time that it denigrates ancient theory. Machiavelli, in the Introduction to Book I of *The Discourses*, writes that imitation of the ancients is the highest need of modern politics, yet in Chapter XV of *The Prince* we get what seems to be a wholesale rejection of the philosophy of the ancients. Rousseau, in the *First Discourse*, extols Sparta as the paragon of ancient praxis while condemning Athens for being overwhelmed by the vanities of philosophy (although, strangely, Socrates is nonetheless one of the heroes of the essay). Nietzsche, from *The Birth of Tragedy* onward, mounts a bitter polemic against Socratic philosophy, yet he writes glowingly of Greek politics as the indispensable spur to 'the unique sun-height of their art.'[3] This preference for ancient politics over ancient theory culminates in Nietzsche's comparison of Plato and Thucydides in *Twilight of the Idols*. Finally, Heidegger, in his *Letter on Humanism*, depicts Greek theory as having embodied an utter falsification of ethical existence as soon as 'ethics' is isolated as a distinct science (hence Aristotle is ranked unfavourably next to Sophocles)[4]; but in *An Introduction to Metaphysics* he exalts the founding deeds of great statesmen within the polis as an aspect of the highest experience of being.[5] Hannah Arendt represents but the latest expression of this notable modern tradition running from Machiavelli to Heidegger.

What does Arendt reject in classical political philosophy? Primarily, she rejects the view that the contemplative life is categorically superior to the life of political involvement, and that the latter has to be judged ultimately by the standards of the former. In fact, it might be said that her book *The Human Condition* is in its entirety an attempt to challenge the latter assumption by offering a ranking of human activities according to standards that are immanent within the *vita activa* itself. Plato made clear enough what he thought of the dignity of political life when he described Pericles, in the *Gorgias* and elsewhere, as nothing but a show-off pandering to the Many. Aristotle indicated that his view on this question was considerably more charitable than Plato's when he remarked in Book 6 of the *Nicomachean Ethics* that 'we think that Pericles and men like him have practical wisdom' (as opposed to 'men like Anaxagoras and Thales [who] have theoretical but not practical wisdom').[6] But by Book 10 of the *Ethics*, it is certainly clear that Aristotle's ultimate standard of judgment is very nearly identical to Plato's. In Arendt's view, Kant was the first of the great philosophers to question radically this traditional view. We all know the famous quotation in which Kant declares that he too shared this ancient assumption until he was liberated from it by his reading of Rousseau.[7] But if the contemplative life is no longer presumed to constitute the final standard for measuring the rest of human existence, which had entailed that politics could appear as, at best, 'a second-rate form of human activity,'[8] then the possibility is opened up of a revindication of the dignity of political life. As Arendt puts it: 'The abandonment of this hierarchy [of the philosophical way of life versus the political way of life] ... is the abandonment of all hierarchical structures.'[9] By challenging the former supremacy of the *bios theoretikos*, Kant facilitates the ordinary citizen's recovery of his or her lost dignity.

The central argument of *The Human Condition* is not so much a positive argument for the virtues of politics, as a negative argument about the vices of subjectivization – the dissolution of a common world owing to the hegemonic activities of labour and consumption. Those who are sympathetic to Strauss are hardly likely to fault Arendt for being moved by concerns of this kind; Allan Bloom, the most influential of Strauss's followers, speaks in a very similar vein of the attenuation by modernity of the 'inherent political impulse in man,' the replacement of politics by the administrative state, 'the disappearance of citizens and statesmen,' and, above all, the privatization inherent in modern life that leaves individuals bereft of any 'common object' or 'common good.'[10] Arendt's political philosophy is fundamentally a root-and-branch critique of modern subjectivism. She turns to politics because it alone can save us from the crippling process of subjectivization through which our experience is turned more and more private, from experience of a common world to that of our own inner world. Art, religion, morality – increasingly, each of these is privatized by the subjectivizing tendency of modernity. Politics alone offers a chance of arresting this fearful process because politics by its very nature is public or it is nothing. But to serve this purpose, political life must be defended against both modern and ancient detractors: from the moderns who see politics as the product of instrumental motives and instrumental to economic goals;[11] and from the ancients who see politics as a dark cave surveyed from the light and height of the contemplative life.

To begin assessing the differences in philosophical perspective between Arendt and Leo Strauss, it is probably best to try to define those differences in relation to the two poles of Strauss's lifelong reflection: nature and history. Certainly, Arendt did not look to the polis for a standard of 'natural' politics, as Strauss appeared to do.[12] Arendt would unquestionably have rejected the idea of the polis as a timeless norm; she would in all probability not even have been able to make sense of the idea. Like Rousseau, she saw the highest achievement of politics to be a transcendence of nature. Let me add, however, that in my opinion Arendt misjudged the extent to which political philosophy can free itself from, or hold itself aloof from, reflection on human nature. (This obviously parallels Kant's strenuous attempt – also in vain – to avoid basing his practical philosophy on an appeal to a conception of human nature.) Arendt thought it was wrong to base political philosophy on philosophical anthropology, and thought that she could somehow avoid doing so. But, of course, *The Human Condition* can itself be read as the great statement of a philosophical anthropology, or can easily be restated as such. I must say that I myself have no deep antipathy to the appeal to nature; but at the same time, it is not entirely clear what the predicates 'natural' and 'contrary to nature' add to the more modest-sounding affirmation that one alternative is superior to another alternative, that better reasons can be adduced on behalf of one than on behalf of the other, and that these things are not matters reducible to sheer preference. If that is all that one intends, then the language of 'natural right' seems to me unobjectionable. If something more is intended, then one may fall into a dogmatic naturalism that Strauss always claimed he wanted to avoid.[13]

As far as the issue of historicism is concerned, we may identify two different renderings of the meaning of historicism. According to the strong version, what is good or bad, desirable or undesirable, true or false, is essentially governed by the needs and aspirations of distinct cultures, so what is morally true for the citizens of the ancient polis may be untrue for the denizens of the modern state, and vice versa. The weak version is that we can only come to an understanding of, or obtain access to, what is good, desirable, true, on the basis of a wealth of historical experience (as Hegel, for instance, affirmed); so that while the moral truth is a matter of discovery rather than invention, the content of this truth is historically disclosed, perhaps in a fashion that is never-ending, never definitively in our possession. (Strauss tends to conflate these two meanings of historicism.) In respect to the former (strong) rendering, Arendt is every bit as anti-historicist as Strauss.[14] Indeed, to be a thoroughgoing critic of modernity, as both Strauss and Arendt are, one *must* be a vigorous anti-historicist! But in relation to the latter (weak) rendering, Arendt and Strauss seem to be deeply at odds. Arendt states: 'What is the subject of our thought? Experience! Nothing else! And if we lose the ground of experience then we get into all kinds of [abstract] theories.'[15] It would be quite peculiar, from this point of view, if thousands of years of political experience had taught us nothing that had not already been evident in the time of Plato and Aristotle. For Strauss, by contrast, the most that historical experience can teach us is to appreciate more profoundly the truth of ancient wisdom (although it may leave us entirely in the dark as to how to apply this wisdom in our own circumstances – as Strauss himself acknowledges quite openly[16]).

The political content of this timeless wisdom is made evident to us in a remarkable published exchange of correspondence between Strauss and Karl Löwith. Strauss writes:

I *really* believe ... that the perfect political order, as Plato and Aristotle have sketched it, *is* the perfect political order ... One can show from political considerations that the small city-state is in principle superior to the large state or to the territorial-feudal state. I know very well that *today* it cannot be restored [though maybe tomorrow it can? – R.B.]; but ... the contemporary solution, that is, the completely modern solution, is *contra naturam* ... Details can be disputed, although I myself might actually agree with everything that Plato and Aristotle demand (but that I tell only you).[17]

In a subsequent letter, Strauss clarifies what he has in mind: 'I assert that the polis – as it has been *interpreted* by Plato and Aristotle, a *surveyable, urban,* morally serious (*spoudaia*) society, based on an agricultural economy, in which the *gentry* rule – is *morally-politically* [i.e., but not according to the needs or interests of philosophers – R.B.] the most reasonable and most pleasing.'[18] For all her supposed infatuation with the Greek polis, this is certainly not the sort of affirmation that one is likely to encounter anywhere in the writings of Hannah Arendt. Once again, Arendt is too deeply wedded to modern Kantian egalitarianism to be much attracted to the prospect of permanent rule by a gentry within a highly exclusive and homogeneous community. But, to come back to the question of historicism, the fact that Arendt opts for Kant over Plato does not mean that she embraces a historicist position in the culpable sense we defined earlier. What is actually involved in the political-philosophical contention between Plato and Kant is not the commitment to a transhistorical truth versus a relativistic affirmation of the prejudices of modernity, but rather, these questions: Where does the truth lie? And who has got it right? The choice is not between modern historicism and the transhistorical standards of the ancients, but between two competing accounts – egalitarian and anti-egalitarian – of what is transhistorically true. After all, the affirmation of human equality is equally a truth-claim that is intended to have a validity that cannot be relativized.

I think it follows from my discussion that the differences between Strauss and Arendt on the questions of nature and history are perhaps somewhat less radical than they appear at first glance. Where, then, do we look in order to locate their real differences? To answer this question, I want to consider two large issues: first, the source of the 'crisis of modernity,' and then, once again, the problem of equality. As we shall see, the two issues are closely interconnected; in both cases we shall find ourselves returning to the question we started with – namely, the relationship between philosophy and politics.

Strauss and Arendt have both been branded 'nostalgics' because both are committed to the view that there is a crisis of modernity. But they offer radically different accounts of what defines and what precipitated this crisis. What explains the crisis for Strauss is an intellectual transformation. In this respect, Strauss's account bears close affinity to the accounts offered by Nietzsche and Heidegger. For the latter, the decisive moment of the Western destiny occurred when the 'tragic philosophy' of the pre-Socratic Greeks was supplanted by (what Nietzsche refers to as) the 'cowardly' philosophy of Socratic rationalism.[19] After Heraclitus and Parmenides, it was all downhill for Western civilization. Strauss's account differs only in respect of a shift in the perceived moment of catastrophe. By his account, the fateful undoer of the West was not Plato but Machiavelli. After Machiavelli, the *vita contemplativa* was no longer the centre of gravity of human existence, and the philosophers ceased courting the gentlemen and instead began courting the plebs. For Arendt, in stark contrast, what shapes our world is not intangible ideas, but tangible 'events': the invention of the telescope, the expropriation of monastic property in the wake of the Reformation, the election of Hitler as German Chancellor, the launching of Sputnik. This yields an entirely different account of the crisis of modernity that does not consist simply in fixing upon two or three heroic thinkers as the ultimate source of the rot.

Arendt would certainly agree with Richard Rorty in taking issue with Strauss's view that 'reference to what had been happening in European intellectual life helped explain the coming of fascism.'[20] Contrary to the intellectual's typical overestimation of the political influence of intellectual battles:

The fact that, as Bloom says, 'German thought had taken an anti-rational and anti-liberal turn with Nietzsche, and even more so with Heidegger,' does not do much to tip the balance in favour of the bad guys, any more than the popularity of Deweyan pragmatism among American intellectuals of the 30's does much to explain why fascism did not happen here. Disagreements among intellectuals as to whether truth is timeless, whether 'reason' names an ahistorical tribunal or a Habermasian free consensus, or whether the 'inalienable rights' of the Declaration are 'grounded' in something non-historical, or are instead recent inventions (like education for women, and the transistor), are just not that important in deciding how elections go, or how much resistance fascist takeovers encounter.[21]

A similar issue is engaged in Arendt's (public and private) dialogue with Eric Voegelin. As Arendt writes in reply to Voegelin: 'what separates my approach ... is that I proceed from facts and events instead of intellectual affinities and influences.'[22]

Strauss's fundamental view is that the 'crisis of the West,' a practical crisis, is the outcome of an intellectual crisis – in particular, the crisis (or series of crises) in the historical development of political philosophy.[23] To borrow a formulation employed by Thomas Pangle, the idea here is that what is decisive in the moral life of any society is 'an explicit public theology or philosophy' that ultimately shapes the opinions, habits, and dispositions of a people. Without the support of such a public philosophy, any existing *ethos* – including one that incorporates the moral residues of older public philosophies – will by necessity eventually decay.[24] (This, by the way, is the same analysis as offered by Plato in Book X of *The Republic*, of the deficient *paideia* of the poets.)[25] Therefore, the ultimate source of the moral and political deficiencies of the American republic, for instance, are attributable not to the contingent failings of its statesmen or its citizens, or to the nature of its social and economic institutions, but, more profoundly, to the character of the philosophy relied upon by its original founders. I must confess that I am rather sceptical (as Arendt would be) of the implicit claim that the American polity would be in a less sorry state than it is today if its founders had read more Cicero and less Locke. I do not deny the intellectual power of Locke and the other modern political philosophers; nevertheless, it may well be that the relationship between public *ethos* and public philosophy is the converse of the one that Pangle asserts: namely, that Locke influenced (or found a spontaneous resonance within) a particular political culture because his thought naturally suited the lived experiences and evolving aspirations of the historically embodied individuals who composed that culture.

We have now begun to approach more closely the decisive question, which is the relationship between philosophers and nonphilosophers in society and at the site of historical change. To carry the Arendt–Strauss debate to its next stage, I will need to offer a more extended presentation of some of Strauss's (typically guarded) formulations. In 'On the Intention of Rousseau,' Strauss states very clearly what he takes to be the essence of the ancient wisdom he commends: 'The basic premise of classical political philosophy may be said to be the view that the natural inequality of intellectual powers is, or ought to be, of decisive political importance. Hence the unlimited rule of the wise, in no way answerable to the subjects, appears to be the absolutely best solution to the political problem.'[26] However, society being what it is, the rule of the wise is to say the least a highly remote prospect; therefore one should settle for the next best possibility, namely, 'the rule, under law, of the gentlemen over those who are not gentlemen.' In other words, for Strauss the decisive political consideration relates to one particular fact of nature that overshadows all other potentially relevant natural facts: namely, the natural superiority of intellect of philosophers over nonphilosophers. In an ideal world, this natural fact would be directly translated into political practice; but because the permanent antagonism between 'science and society,' or between those who love wisdom and those who inhabit the cave, is *also* a natural fact, the occurrence of this ideal is not to be expected.

To be sure, what mainly concerns Strauss is the timeless validity of the natural hierarchy governing the relationship of philosophy and politics (as well as the natural inequality implicit in this hierarchy, between those fitted for the life of philosophy and those fitted merely to be citizens). But as we saw earlier in the correspondence with Löwith, Strauss at the same time is committed to the timeless validity of a particular standard of political life. Let us be perfectly clear about what this doctrine asserts. It says not just that men of leisure ('idling in Epicurean gardens'[27]) are politically superior to men and women who must work to feed themselves and their families, but that philosophers, by their very nature as philosophers, possess an intrinsic claim to political knowledge that surpasses that of artists, novelists, lawyers, diplomats, journalists, and even professional politicians. Now it is, to say the least, not entirely obvious why 'the natural inequality in the possession of intellectual gifts' should have the crucial *political* importance that Strauss attributes to the classical political philosophers.[28] As we all know, one may possess the most stupendous intellectual gifts, or even be the greatest thinker of one's epoch, and yet for all that be utterly stupid politically. This is certainly one of the lessons that Arendt drew from the experience of 1933. The fact that Heidegger was (as Richard Rorty describes him) 'your average Schwarzwald redneck'[29] does nothing to detract from his intellectual gifts or his superiority as a philosopher; what it *does* do is rule out any direct political translation, even in a ideal world, between inequality in the realm of the intellect and inequality in the realm of politics. (And it is not only Heidegger's infamous *Der Spiegel* interview that drives this point home; one can gather it as well from a reading of Plato's *Seventh Letter.*)

To assume that there should be an automatic correlation between intellectual gifts and natural entitlement to rule strikes me as thoroughly dubious, both theoretically and practically. It seems more reasonable to say that intellectual gifts and political gifts simply represent two quite distinct human capacities. To paraphrase Arendt: one commonly encounters people of very high intelligence who are deficient in judgment, just as there are people of rather ordinary intelligence who nonetheless *do* possess good judgment[30]; to this we might add that the possession of exceptional intelligence *and* excellent judgment is almost a kind of freak of nature, rarely to be expected. Perhaps not surprisingly, one finds a similar thought in Kant: in the *Critique of Pure Reason* (B172–173) he notes that all the learning in the world cannot make up for lack of judgment. A related point, stated more bluntly, is put by Rorty: 'You can be a great, original, and profound artist or thinker, and also a complete bastard.'[31] Or again, Conor Cruise O'Brien, in a counter to the Platonism of Simone Weil: 'Does the love of good depend on the light of intelligence? It hardly seems so; we can all think of rather stupid people who are kind and honest, and of quite intelligent people who are mean and treacherous.'[32] These are, we might say, *Kantian* (or Rousseauian) insights.

We now turn more directly to the problem of equality. As Strauss presents the political doctrine of the classics, there are fundamentally three classes in any society: the philosophers, the gentlemen, and the non-gentlemen (the vulgar).[33] Politics involves the rule of the society by one of these three groups. The ideal would be rule by the philosophers, but this is impracticable. Next best, and a little less impracticable, would be rule by the gentlemen, to some extent on behalf of the philosophers ('the gentlemen's virtue is a reflection of the philosopher's virtue; one may say it is its political reflection ... The rule of the gentlemen is only a reflection of the rule of philosophers'[34]). The norm is rule by the non-gentlemen: at best, democratic rule mitigated by aristocratic aspects of the constitution (what the ancients called the mixed regime); at worst, unmitigated rule by the vulgar. For the most part, this last possibility is what we have now – that is to say, mass democracy. Central to this teaching is the idea of intellectual, moral, *and political* inequality. The fact of intellectual inequality is self-evident. However, the correlation between intellectual inequality and moral and political inequality needs to be established by argument. As we all know, of course, philosophers since Rousseau and Kant have presented important arguments to deny this correlation. As far as *political* inequality is concerned, Strauss asserts that the fact of intellectual and moral inequality is so decisive that the very possibility of political converse among the three classes is more or less ruled out: 'The gentlemen and the others disagree ... as regards the end of man or the highest good; they disagree regarding the first principles. Hence they cannot have genuinely common deliberations ... What [is] observed regarding the gentleman in his relation to the vulgar applies even more to the philosopher in his relation to the gentlemen and a fortiori to all other nonphilosophers: the philosopher and the nonphilosophers cannot have genuinely common deliberations.'[35]

In the reflection on Kant presented in her lectures published in 1982, Arendt adopts a position on the relationship between politics and philosophy that is as radically antithetical to Strauss's as any can be; and if Strauss's characterization of the core political doctrine of classical philosophy is an accurate one, then Arendt is as deeply opposed to classical political philosophy as Strauss is committed to it. Although it has become conventional to describe Arendt (in my view quite wrongly) as a kind of 'Aristotelian,' she misses no opportunity to criticize both Plato and Aristotle – precisely for holding the views that Strauss attributes to them. Rather, her philosophical hero, she tells us, is Kant[36] – and again, precisely because he repudiates the Platonic–Aristotelian doctrine of the rule of the 'wise' over the 'vulgar'[37]: '[For] Kant, the philosopher clarifies the experiences we all have ... [For instance,] the task of evaluating life with respect to pleasure and displeasure – which Plato and the others claimed for the philosopher alone, holding that the many are quite satisfied with life as it is – Kant claims can be expected from every ordinary man of good sense who ever reflected on life at all.'[38] That is, one does not have to be a Plato to reflect on the discrepancy between the happiness one seeks and the happiness life confers. Common deliberation is possible.

The basic problem here is nicely captured in a passage from Pascal that, significantly, is cited by both Arendt and Strauss.[39] Pascal writes that

Plato and Aristotle amused themselves with the subject of politics 'as if laying down rules for a lunatic asylum'; these writings on political philosophy – their least philosophic and least serious – were addressed to madmen, strictly for the purpose of rendering 'their madness as little harmful as possible.' One way of restating the difference between Strauss and Arendt is that for Strauss this text describes an ever-present, immutable predicament of the philosopher, who must live in a community that ultimately is not his own (which, to be his own, would have to be a community of philosophers); for Arendt, on the other hand, the passage defines a relationship between philosophy and politics that can and ought to be transformed. Strauss is in agreement with the philosophical tradition from Plato to Pascal according to which what makes the philosopher a *political* philosopher, a philosopher of politics, is first and foremost the concern for his own survival. The philosopher's primary social and moral commitment in the polis is to keep philosophy alive in the polis. But this self-preservation of the philosopher cannot be taken for granted. In the wake of Socrates, the philosophers are understood to constitute an endangered species. As Strauss puts it: 'There is a fundamental disproportion between philosophy and the city.'[40] But suppose one were able to redefine one's understanding of philosophy so that the community of philosophers and the community of ordinary citizens were no longer fundamentally at odds with each other. Then, presumably, one would have a reason for concerning oneself as a philosopher with politics that was not chiefly dictated by the preoccupation with brute self-preservation. This, according to Arendt, was the fundamental achievement of Kant.[41] (Admittedly, the philosopher's relation to the polis is a two-way street: it depends not just on the philosopher's attitude toward his or her society, but on the actual organization of the society itself. A society constituted in such a way that its leaders are capable of dispatching hit squads to assassinate a disfavoured novelist is hardly likely to encourage a relationship between philosophy and politics other than the one postulated by Strauss.)

In our earlier discussion of Strauss, we noted that he regards the differences in perspective among the philosophers, the gentlemen, and the sub-gentlemen as unbridgeable and politically irredeemable. There is a further, more radical, implication to Strauss's argument. Crucial to his assertion of a natural order of distinct classes of human beings is a corresponding denial of a single, universal morality. In agreement with Nietzsche, and in opposition to Kant, Strauss holds that there is not one morality but different moralities, each binding for a different class of souls, governed by the 'pathos of distance.' Strauss states this view most explicitly in a conversation with Jacob Klein that is transcribed in 'A Giving of Accounts.' Citing section III.8 of Nietzsche's *Genealogy of Morals*, Strauss states that the philosopher's practice of the moral virtues 'is not different from the asceticism of a jockey, who in order to win a race must live very restrainedly, but that is wholly unimportant to the jockey, what is important is to win the race ... [O]ne may say similarly of the philosopher, what counts is thinking and investigating and not morality.'[42] It follows from this that Kant is *wrong* to uphold the unconditional universality of the moral law. At best, the philosopher abides by morality for instrumental reasons, not because it is universally binding.[43] In other words (although Strauss does not fully spell this out), the vulgarian's morality is *virtue is what pays*; the gentleman's morality is *virtue for its own sake*; the philosopher's morality is *virtue is what's good for philosophy*. In contrast to all this, what Arendt draws from both ancient practice and modern philosophy is a certain conception of equality as central to human dignity. (For Strauss, on the other hand, human dignity is grounded upon 'the dignity of the mind,'[44] which means that it is inseparable from the *in*equality of intellectual endowments.)

One of the leading concepts that Arendt attempts to extrapolate from ancient political experience is the notion of isonomy, or political equality, which she interprets in contradistinction to the *natural* equality asserted by the tradition of modern political philosophy (Hobbes, Locke, Rousseau). Although it presupposes to some extent an equality of condition, isonomy does not depend on any claims about the natural equality of individuals; it is, rather, a conventional or constructed equality contrived specifically so that one can enjoy political freedom *in the company of one's peers* – which for Arendt is the only political freedom with any authentic meaning. ('The Greeks held that no one can be free except among his peers.'[45]) The possibility of a 'body of peers,' joined in the experience of shared citizenship, is a deliverance of *nomos*, not *physis*. Precisely because men are not by nature equal, they 'needed an artificial institution, the polis, which by virtue of its *nomos* would make them equal. Equality existed only in this specifically political realm, where men met one another as citizens and not as private persons ... The equality of the Greek polis, its isonomy, was an attribute of the polis and not of men, who received their equality by virtue of citizenship, not by virtue of birth.'[46] According to this understanding, to enter upon political activity in concert with others is as such to constitute a realm of equality that is not grounded in the nature of the individuals concerned, but is, quite deliberately, a work of human artifice, motivated by the love of political freedom. In the light of this ideal of isonomy, it is not surprising that Arendt in one place refers to jury service as the political experience *par excellence* in our contemporary world: people from different walks of life, with different types of competence, join in a commonality of judgment simply by virtue of sitting together around the same table.[47] In Book III, Chapter 11 of *The Politics*, Aristotle gives expression to a similar argument on behalf of the nonexpert judgment of the many.

I conclude with some brief remarks in regard to Arendt's 'classicism.' Arendt has very little confidence that reflection on ancient practice will, by itself, dissolve the perplexities of the present. Certainly her theoretical writings, as much as they are inspired by certain ancient conceptions of political life, do not presume to furnish an exit from these perplexities. Of *The Human Condition*, she writes that 'this book does not offer an answer. Such answers are given every day, and they are matters of practical politics, subject to the agreement of many; they can never lie in theoretical considerations or the opinion of one person.'[48] At all times she emphasizes what is novel and unprecedented, unforeseen and unforeseeable – the element of surprise in human affairs. Far from hoping for reliable guidance from ancient experience, she insists that the radical novelty of the modern situation demands a 'new science of politics' (here she cites de Tocqueville).[49] Arendt, unlike Strauss,[50] is a 'Burkean' when it comes to the relationship between theory and practice; that is to say, she is deeply sceptical about the extent to which the uniqueness of circumstance and the contingency of the particular can be anticipated or commanded by theory. Like Burke, she constantly inveighs against the pretensions of theory. Indeed, she faults most of the tradition of Western political philosophy for privileging theory over practice, as if the content of political life were merely a kind of imperfect embodiment of intellectual archetypes. If this means that Arendt is infected with 'historicism,' it is, I would say, a very salutary historicism (like Burke's), intended to avert the follies that result from the typical hubris of the theorists.

The impetus behind Arendt's affirmation of politics and active citizenship was neither romanticism nor utopianism, but *fear* and *dread*. She began her career as a political philosopher with a deep and serious reflection on totalitarianism, and everything she wrote afterwards was a consequence of what she saw there. Modern men have an unprecedented capacity to be sheep, easily herded by ruthless shepherds, or to become mindless bureaucrats like Eichmann. The quintessentially modern possibility is the life of the herd – to be a functionary or to be the slave of functionaries. Modern life itself is an assault upon human dignity: atomized, 'massified,' and deracinated. Her whole subsequent reflection on possibilities of collective agency is a response to this grim prospect, and has the aim of identifying ways that human beings in the modern age might recover a sense of efficacy and self-respect.

Straussians accuse Arendt of being nostalgic about the Greek polis, and about Athenian democracy in particular.[51] But as we all know, Strauss himself has been accused by countless critics of a similar nostalgia. It would be more profitable, I think, to put aside such mutual recriminations, to give both thinkers the benefit of the doubt, and to assume that neither was particularly nostalgic about ancient politics (such nostalgia would be in any case quite pointless). We may assume, rather, that both looked to ancient experience and ancient ways of thought for help in articulating their deep disquiet about the horrendous potentialities of modern political societies. And it seems hardly necessary to add that one does not require nostalgia about earlier societies in order to have rational grounds for such disquiet concerning modernity.

APPENDIX

Response from a Colleague, with a Rejoinder*

Critical Response from Thomas L. Pangle

June 11, 1988

Dear Ronnie,

[1]   I read your paper on Arendt and Strauss with great interest and profit. You state forcefully key issues dividing Strauss and Arendt, and I think this is certainly the clearest juxtaposition of the two I know of. I wish I could have read this before I wrote the short section criticizing Arendt in my forthcoming book on Locke and the Founders. My considered reaction may have to wait a longer time for rumination over your many points, but I thought I would clarify things a bit for myself, and anticipate the conference, by trying to put down my initial questions and observations. I'm not sure if the conference will allow time or opportunity for even the beginning of a worthy response to your carefully thought out invitation to a dia-

* This exchange of letters, previously unpublished, has been slightly edited for publication.

logue, and besides I think I will get things clearer if I try to set them down on paper.

[2] I begin with my puzzlement as to the character of Arendt's recourse to classical political practice, a puzzlement which broadens into a continuing puzzlement as to what she means by 'politics' altogether. You start by saying that 'Arendt represents but the latest expression of' a 'tradition running from Machiavelli to Heidegger, a tradition which includes Nietzsche as well as Rousseau (p. 106). But with the apparent exception of Rousseau (about whom more later), every adherent of this tradition manifestly endorses a hierarchial conception of politics, and very plausibly claims to find such a hierarchical conception in classical practice. And opposition to hierarchy seems to be at the very core of Arendt's conception of politics, as you later stress. How can Arendt be an 'expression' of a tradition with which she disagrees at the very core? And secondly, how can she interpret Greek political experience as non-hierarchical?

[3] Your presentation of Arendt's notion of 'isonomy' did not remove my perplexity. I do not see any instance of Greek history which reflects such a notion of isonomy. The one text to which you refer, in Aristotle's *Politics*, seems to me to be so far from asserting the political equality of all citizens (that is, their equality in terms of judgment or practical wisdom) that it in fact presents an argument for democracy on the explicit grounds that democracy will allow for the manifestation and constructive employment of the inequality among citizens. Only when the majority pools its talents might it equal or surpass the talents of the few (Aristotle does not for one minute say that every member of even the best majority is equal or even close to being equal in practical wisdom, and he explicitly asserts the continuing superiority of the 'excellent' or 'virtuous' to each member of the many taken individually).

[4] But let us move beyond Arendt's questionable appeal to or evocation of a certain notion of the Greek political experience and ask about her conception of politics as such. How can politics be conceived apart from hierarchy? Is not ruling the very essence of the political – ruling, and being ruled, the regime, expressed in law, entailing coercion? Is politics separable from foreign policy, hence the preparation for war, the struggle for freedom and empire? And even if or when ruling rotates, or is rule under law, ruling remains ruling (law-making, at the peak), and being ruled remains being

ruled – and the specific virtues of politics are the virtues or excellences of rulers and ruled (see especially *Politics*, Bk. 3, chap. 4 end). The contest among the regimes is a contest over who should rule and ultimately over what kind of person or over what qualities, what virtues, are the truly or legitimately ruling. I would argue that in denying hierarchy, Arendt is denying and denigrating, rather than affirming and elevating politics. I think that Aristotle is correct in making rule the essence of politics, and I think this is surely not a matter of mere theorizing. Where in human history has there ever been found a political life that is not centered on ruling, and which does not include coercion? Arendt's claim to appeal to 'experience' seems to be contradicted by her central concept, her concept of the political, which has no historical or experiential correlate. Arendt's 'abandonment of all hierarchical structures' (p. 107) is the abandonment of all human political experience as it has been known in fact or in history. It is Strauss, against Arendt, who appeals, in the name of Aristotle and against contemporary attempts to deny the political, i.e., the omnipresence of rule or hierarchy, from 'our notions' (about citizenship, the regime) to 'our experience' (*City and Man* [Chicago: University of Chicago Press, 1977], p. 46).

[5]   These reflections lead me to my puzzlement as regards the relation between Arendt and Kant. I am handicapped by the fact that I have not read your edition of Arendt's lectures on Kant. But I find it difficult to associate Arendt's concept of politics, her contention that dignity is found principally in the public realm of political action, with Kant – the great apostle of liberalism, who insists so strongly on the distinction between the public and private realms, or on the distinction between the demands of virtue and the very limited legitimate demands of justice or public law and governmental activity. If anything, Arendt seems closer to Rousseau, but without admitting Rousseau's compelling proof that a just society is necessarily a closed society.

[6]   But I have a broader and deeper doubt about the evocation of Kant. For Kant, there is a single, supreme, synthetic a priori principle of morality, the categorical imperative, which is the sole, absolute, trans-historical ground of all morality for God as well as mankind. You never so much as allude to this ground.

[7]   I think your attempt to avoid the question of nature or natural right on pp. 108 points to the grave difficulty, for of course Kant's own

political philosophy is emphatically a philosophy of natural right. The idea that we can only get as far as 'the more modest-sounding affirmation that one alternative is superior to another alternative, that better reasons can be adduced on behalf of one than on behalf of others' sounds to me like (from Kant's point of view) a lapse into that sort of mixture of pragmatic and moral that Kant excoriated in the eclectic Aristotelian Christian Wolff (see Kant's *Groundwork*, Preface near the end). You seem to describe or speak of a Kantianism divorced from the *metaphysics* of morals: how can there be such a thing?

[8]   My question is simply this: does or does not Arendt (do or do not you) accept the doctrine of the categorical imperative? If so, how do you deal with the enormous difficulties? I have in mind the following questions. How can a clear and specific articulation of the virtues, of friendship, of love, of beauty, be deduced from such a barren formalism? How can one make sense of the Kantian discussion of happiness and its relation to virtue (I have in mind especially the central role played by the afterlife and God in Kant's moral philosophy)?

[9]   If you abandon the doctrine of the categorical imperative, then what foundation do you have in Kant (or outside Kant) for your moral egalitarianism? The question of the foundation is absolutely central to Kant: how can Arendt ally herself to Kant and abandon this question? In other words, I do not see how the issue of nature can be avoided. Either we possess or we do not possess knowledge of human nature, of the soul, of God, of the good, sufficient to allow us to say with confidence we know what is good for man as man, at least in principle. If we do not have such knowledge, then we are on the first step of the Socratic dialectical ladder, and are compelled to recognize the superiority of the philosophic life as the life which is lived in clear-sighted awareness of our ignorance. Do you (or Arendt) do justice to the irresistible dialectic that leads to the superiority of the philosophic life as the life of Socratic scepticism – the meaning of the contemplative life for Strauss? This scepticism issues in definite (if not 'a priori' or 'metaphysical') principles of moral and political action. Above all, this scepticism reveals the unjustified dogmatism, the blindness or the boastfulness or the unawareness, that underlies and pervades the life of all of us who are not philosophic – including 'artists, novelists, lawyers, diplomats, journalists, and even professional politicians' (p. 112). Unless of course, the art-

ist is himself philosophic (e.g., Horace, Lessing, Goethe) in the sense indicated here.

[10] Your characterization of Strauss's position as one that equates 'intellectual superiority' with the right to political superiority misses or blurs Strauss's point, I think. It is not a question of 'intellectual gifts' or of what you speak of as 'men of leisure' (p. 112), or of 'learning' or 'originality' (p. 113 – you are quoting Rorty) or 'very high intelligence' or 'exceptional intelligence' (p. 113). All this I think is misleading. The question is one of being a philosopher, and not just any kind of philosopher but a philosopher in the Socratic sense. Heidegger from the classical point of view must be considered as a very high form of distorted philosophy; Strauss does not agree with you and Rorty that Heidegger's political stand does 'nothing to detract from his superiority as a philosopher' (p. 113; see Strauss's characterization of Machiavelli in *Thoughts on Machiavelli* [Glencoe, Illinois: The Free Press, 1958], p. 13. ['a perverted nobility of a very high order'] and also pp. 294–8 and see his characterization of Heidegger in *Studies in Platonic Political Philosophy* [Chicago: University of Chicago Press, 1983], p. 34 top and also p. 30). The possible perversion of philosophy is a theme of Socrates (*Republic* Bk. 6 and Aristophanes' *Clouds*), although it is perhaps true that classical political philosophy was not fully aware of the ways or the extent to which philosophy or philosophic talent could be distorted (see Strauss's confession of wonderment on p. 298 of the Machiavelli book): I wonder whether this is not perhaps for Strauss the deepest lesson to be learned from modernity that could not have been learned without modernity. If so, it is a lesson that only strengthens the need to insist on and protect the purity of political philosophy as Socratic political philosophy.

[11] It seems to me that in your characterization of the classical notion of the best regime you do not appreciate enough the purity of the notion of Socratic political philosophy. For Strauss at least, it is not quite correct or sufficient to say that the wise cannot rule because 'society is what it is' (p. 112), or that 'the ideal would be rule by the philosophers, but this is impracticable' (p. 113). This makes it sound as if the wise or the philosophers want to rule, or would be better off if they did rule, and the opposite is emphatically the case (*City and Man*, pp. 124–8; cf. *Republic* 346e–7e).

[12] I return stubbornly to what I regard as the fundamental question, the question of nature or of the ground for Arendt's position, and to a contrast with Rousseau. You associate Arendt's position with Rousseau's on two fundamental counts: both see politics as a 'transcendence of nature' (p. 108) and the denial of the political relevance of intellectual inequality is a 'Rousseauian insight' (p. 113). The second point seems to me very dubious once one takes into account Rousseau's teaching on the Legislator, which cannot be separated from the *Social Contract* or the General Will or Rousseau's political teaching as a whole. The teaching on the lawgiver explicitly states the necessity for deception and manipulation of the entire citizen body of a healthy republic; in other words, it contradicts in the strongest way Arendt's claim as to the autonomy of citizenship. This leads to my grave doubts about the first point, or about the conclusion Arendt or you draw from it. For Rousseau, the fact that politics transcends nature is at the least a profoundly ambiguous fact. In the final analysis, it is a fact that signals the inferiority of the political to the philosophic life – the latter life being foreshadowed in some measure by the life of the lawgiver, but only foreshadowed. For Rousseau, the human being of the highest sort is not a citizen and is superior to the citizen; Rousseau recovers in some measure the classical standpoint, though with a different conception of the philosophic life, admittedly (*The Dreams of a Solitary Walker*).

[13] I think that the neglect of the theme of nature leads, finally, to a fundamental contradiction in Arendt or in your presentation of her central conception of isonomy. You say that 'isonomy does not depend on *any* claims about the natural equality of individuals' (my italics); but on the next page you say that 'precisely because men are *not* equal, they "need an artificial institution, the polis, which by virtue of its *nomos* would make them equal"' (quoting Arendt, your italics). So then the ground *is* an assertion about nature – the assertion that men are not equal (otherwise they would not need the artificial institution, the polis)! Arendt's thought does rest, as all coherent thought must, on a claim about human nature. You foreshadow this contradiction on p. 108, but you do not deal with or resolve it.

[14] I think this weak point can and must be pressed. What is the ground or argument for this claim about human nature? And what is the

ground for opposing or attempting to conquer nature by artifice? What gives the artificial a higher status than the natural, and perhaps more grave, what in the world allows us to suppose that nature can be overcome? What distinguishes Arendt's position from the impossible, or the merely visionary?

[15] Connected with this is the amazing silence in Arendt about the challenge posed by the claims of religion or revelation – a silence you reproduce in your paper, and which again, it seems to me, leads to a certain distortion of the position of Strauss. Just as Arendt fails to come to grips with the issue of nature or our ignorance of nature and the consequences the Socratic dialectic draws, so she seems to me to fail to come to terms with the comprehensive alternative posed by the religious traditions – and the Socratic response again. Aristotle can lead his gentleman addressee to avoid the religious issue only because he can implicitly assure him that contemplative men like Aristotle himself have or are dealing with these very high questions (for Aristotle, the contemplative life is closely associated with God, and one of the key functions of the discussion of the contemplative life in the *Ethics* and *Politics* is to introduce and acknowledge the religious question); Kant cannot guarantee the integrity of the moral life without a critique of both reason and theology that culminates in a '*Religion within the Limits of Reason Alone.*' Strauss made the theological-political question '*the* theme.' How does Arendt come to grips with God?

[16] Finally, it seems to me that the most disputable part of your paper is your claim that Strauss or the classics deprive political life of its dignity or treat it as 'a second-rate form of human activity' (p. 107). To rank politics above all other ways of life except philosophy is surely not to treat it as second-rate. As I have already indicated, it seems to me that true politics, as it is and has been known in human historical experience, is denied by Arendt in the name of an evocation of a kind of community that does not and never has existed. Moreover, her evocation of Periclean Athens (without mentioning its imperialism), her praise of the love of glory, her endorsement of Machiavellian republicanism, her silence on the positive as well as the negative role religion may play in limiting political ambition – her tendency to unleash activism or ambition or the longing for shattering and resounding revolutionary action – all seem to me to share something with Heidegger that is politically frightening or irrespon-

sible. Strauss, in contrast, insists that politics, political ambition, the love of glory, the hope for change or for satisfaction from public life, must all be moderated, severely moderated, in the light of all that we know from historical experience about the severe limits of human knowledge, in the light of our strong sense of the unchangeableness of nature mingled with our imperfect knowledge of that nature, and in the light of the superiority of the way of life that lives preoccupied with thinking about our problematic situation. It is true that Plato in the *Gorgias* deflates the grandeur of that popular imperialist Pericles (p. 106); but I think you are a little unfair to Plato in your failure to mention the fact that the *Gorgias* concludes with the elevation of the unpopular, anti-imperialist Aristides – Aristides the wet-blanket; 'Aristides the Just' (526b). Aristides vs. Pericles, I would say, is Platonic politics in a nutshell.

Well, I look forward to more discussion and express again my appreciation for your provocative and penetrating discussion.

Tom P.

Reply to Pangle

June 21, 1988

Dear Tom,

Again, many thanks for your extremely generous and challenging response to my essay. Your letter has, much to my advantage, forced me to formulate some of my ideas a bit more clearly. No doubt, they still fall well short of the standard of clarity that I would wish for, and therefore I offer the following thoughts in a spirit of continuing dialogue.

ad para. 2 = My statement that Arendt stands within a 'tradition running from Machiavelli to Heidegger' meant to say no more than that she shares a certain rhetoric with a line of earlier thinkers. That no reference to theoretical content was intended should be evident from the fact that both Rousseau and Nietzsche were included in this 'tradition.'

ad paras. 3–4 = It may well be the case that isonomy is a theoretical fiction as far as the life of the Greek city-states was concerned. But Arendt would certainly not agree that she imagines 'a kind of community that does not and never has existed' (para. 16). She does openly acknowledge, however, that such episodes of isonomic freedom are extremely rare and fleeting (perhaps they are actually less exceptional than she makes out). A recent example of the experience of isonomy might be the attempt by shipyard workers in Poland in 1980–81 to seize some control over their own destiny. This is a rather dramatic example, but much more modest examples can easily be found.

= This leads to the complicated question of the function of utopian reflection, which, you will agree, has illustrious roots in classical political philosophy. The utopian possibility as a critical standard for reflection is not refuted by historically infrequent occurrence. This is surely the case with Plato's idea of an ideal regime where reason is master over desire, despite the fact that in just about all known regimes, desire is everything. Why should it be any the less valid for Arendt's ideal conception of deliberation among peers? It seems strange for a resolute anti-historicist to decide between a utopia founded on hierarchy and a utopia founded on equality on the basis of what normally prevails. And to assert that the former accords with 'nature' hardly suffices as a conclusive argument.

= To this, I would add: What remains of Strauss' anti-historicism if the standard of judgment is no longer *what is best* but *what is typical*? I had always assumed that according to the way of thinking of classical teleology, what is *natural* is defined by what is best, not by what is typical. (Cf. Aristotle, *Politics*, Bk. 1, chap. 2: 'nature is an end: what each thing is ... when its coming into being is complete is, we assert, the nature of that thing.') How can one accuse Arendt *both* of excessive historicism *and* of insufficient attention to historical actuality? Surely, what is finally at issue between Arendt and Strauss is not whether hierarchy or equality is the norm, historically speaking, but whether hierarchy or equality is the highest possibility in human life, the most appropriate realization of man's nature, etc.

= To summarize: I have no doubt that the notion of isonomy as it relates to the reality of ancient Greek politics is an idealization, to say the very least. But as a good anti-historicist, I don't see that this suffices to dispose theoretically of the idea of isonomy.

ad para. 5: 'Arendt seems closer to Rousseau [than to Kant]' = Arendt is closer to Kant at least insofar as she affirms his conception of political cosmopolitanism, and rejects Rousseau's assumption that 'a just society is necessarily a closed society.' But you are right that she typically understates Kant's commitment to liberal politics, and perhaps, therefore, also understates the relationship between cosmopolitanism and liberal politics.

ad paras. 6–9 = Arendt states very explicitly that she rejects the doctrine of the categorical imperative. Her Kantianism, as I described it, is encapsulated in the passage from *Critique of Pure Reason* (B859) that I cited in n. 38: 'Do you really require that a mode of knowledge which concerns all men should transcend the common understanding, and should only be revealed to you by philosophers? ... we have thereby revealed to us ... that in matters which concern all men without distinction nature is not guilty of any partial distribution of her gifts, and that in regard to the essential ends of human nature the highest philosophy cannot advance further than is possible under the guidance which nature has bestowed even upon the most ordinary understanding.' I don't see why one can't embrace this teaching (contra Plato) while acknowledging theoretical difficulties in the doctrine of categorical imperative.

= I'm not sure that the description 'barren formalism' does justice to Kant's moral thinking, but I would agree with you that Kant fails to offer a sufficient account of the full range of moral experience. But where does this leave us? Everything of course would be fine if Kant's philosophy were beset with theoretical difficulties while Plato and Aristotle's philosophy were beset with none, but this is surely to oversimplify our theoretical situation. *All* positions in the history of philosophy are beset with difficulties; but rather than making us succumb to despair, this should keep alive in us a sense of the challenge of the original Socratic enterprise. (Corresponding to your objection, one might have put a like challenge to Strauss, that he ought not have appealed to classical philosophy until he had satisfactorily resolved the problem of natural science posed on pp. 7–8 of *Natural Right and History* [Chicago: University of Chicago Press, 1974] – which of course he never did.)

ad para. 9: You very rightly celebrate Socratic scepticism. But wouldn't it be proper for the philosopher to direct his scepticism also at this self-serving notion of his own superiority? The philosopher has the upper hand over the artist, the poet, the musical composer by virtue of his superior capacity to articulate questions about the relationship of truth and beauty, *logos* and music. But the artist, poet, composer are superior to the philosopher in their power to create the works of beauty that elicit theoretical reflection in the first place. Similarly, the philosopher surpasses the statesman in his capacity to articulate questions about the possibilities and limits of political life; but the statesman is superior in enacting the deeds that, again, elicit theoretical reflection in the first place. It strikes me as a case of illegitimately 'judging in one's own case' when the philosopher presumes to decide which of these diverse and cross-cutting inequalities is the ultimate, humanly definitive inequality.

= Your contrast between the openness of Socratic philosophers and the closed horizons or 'blindness' of all non-philosophers as such strikes me as itself somewhat dogmatic. Is it not true that even those philosophers who most pride themselves on their 'Socratic scepticism' can turn out to be, in the realm of praxis, more dogmatic than the least reflective ordinary citizens?

= To restate the gist of my argument: It is most unseemly for philosophers or aspiring philosophers to congratulate themselves on their own superiority. This presumed superiority is all the more suspect when we reflect on the abysmal practical judgments (moral and political) sometimes made by the greatest philosophers, while ordinary citizens of quite modest intellectual capacities often make relatively sound judgments. To echo the challenge of I.F. Stone's recent book: Why should we judge Socrates intrinsically superior to his fellow-citizens in the polis when we know that he had the poor sense to hang out with the likes of Critias, Charmides and Alcibiades?

ad para. 10: On the question of whether Heidegger's politics detracts from his greatness as a philosopher = Would you go so far as to say that Frege was less of a philosopher because his politics were akin to Heidegger's?

= You object to the misleading generality of my account of the relation between intellect and entitlement to rule. Strauss' own phrase is 'natural inequality of intellectual powers' (Rousseau essay ['On the Intention of Rousseau,' in *Hobbes and Rousseau*, ed. M. Cranston and R.S. Peters (Garden City, NY: Anchor Books, 1972)], p. 288), or 'natural inequality of men with regard to intellectual gifts' (ibid., p. 289), which – even if one excludes the philosophers of which one does not approve – still is of quite a general scope. Let us put aside Heidegger. Would one want to be ruled by, say, *Strauss*, subject to the prudence he may or may not have possessed (notwithstanding his undoubted intellectual powers or intellectual gifts)?

= To judge by the 7th Letter, Plato's effort to intervene in Syracusean affairs was not a great deal more well-considered than Heidegger's misguided attempt to constitute himself the spiritual leader of the 'Nazi Revolution.' If so, that would indicate that Heideggerian politics were a disaster not because Heidegger's philosophy was flawed (though that may be true as well), but simply because sometimes (more often than not, in fact) even good or great philosophers make bad (or atrocious) judgments. (But perhaps you have a different reading of the 7th Letter that puts all of this in a different light.)

ad para. 12: 'For Rousseau, the human being of the highest sort is not a citizen and is superior to the citizen.' This is certainly not what Kant read in Rousseau; and it is not what I read in him either.

= I am inclined to read Rousseau's doctrine of the lawgiver in a quite different light than you do. Indeed, what it is meant to emphasize, in my view, is that will, and will alone, confers political legitimacy; even a general will that bases itself on false premises (supplied by the lawgiver) forfeits none of its ultimate authority. This is certainly quite a striking and even shocking doctrine relative to the rationalism of ancient political philosophy. (Therefore the doctrine of the lawgiver, far from betokening an accommodation with ancient rationalism, stands in the greatest contradiction to ancient rationalism. Will, not wisdom, is the source of all authority.) I cannot agree that the *Reveries of a Solitary Walker* finally discloses, contrary to the impression given by all of his earlier works, that Rousseau reasserts the old hierarchy of philosopher and citizen. Nor can I accept Strauss' argument, in 'On the Intention of Rousseau,' that Rousseau's aim was as much to safeguard philosophy from being compromised by society as to defend society against philosophy. (Where, for instance, is the textual support for Strauss' claim that 'since he considers science superior in dignity to society, one must say that he attacks the Enlightenment chiefly in the interest of philosophy' [p. 268], or for the claim that central to Rousseau's thought is 'the admission, and even the emphatic assertion, of the natural inequality of men in the most important respect' [p. 289]?) But obviously, to pursue these issues in detail would carry us too far afield.

ad para. 13 = I certainly agree with you that 'all coherent thought must rest on a claim about human nature.' Insofar as Arendt thought otherwise, she was mistaken (as I point out in my essay). But while the *question* of human nature is unavoidable, the grasping for answers can never be too humble (this goes as well for the question of nature as such). This point is brilliantly stated in a favourite quotation of mine: 'It is much easier to identify the undesirable than the desirable, the *malum* than the *bonum*. That diabetes, epilepsy, schizophrenia, hemophilia are undesirable, to afflicted and fellow men alike, is noncontroversial. But what is "better" – a cool head or a warm heart, high sensitivity or robustness, a placid or a rebellious temperament, and in what proportion of distribution rather than another: who is to determine that, and based on what knowledge? The pretense to such knowledge alone should be sufficient ground to disqualify the pretender' (Hans Jonas, *Philosophical Essays* [Chicago: University of Chicago Press, 1974], p. 152).

ad paras. 13–14 = Here you pose some really searching questions, and they have forced me to recognize some unfortunate muddles in my earlier formulations. Kant's view is that all rational beings (of which human beings are the most familiar subset) have in principle equal access to apprehension of the moral law, and since all other facets of human experience are infinitely paltry in relation to the grandeur of the moral law, human beings *really are* equal in the most fundamental respect. This is not what Arendt says. What she says, roughly, is that the experience of isonomy contributes so powerfully to the prospect of human dignity that human beings ought to cancel out their various inborn inequalities through the artificial equality offered by political citizenship. My essay left rather unclear the substantial discrepancy between Arendt's argument and Kant's argument. How can one characterize as essentially egalitarian a theory that recommends artificial civic equality as a means of overcoming natural human inequality, and how can one describe this theory as of Kantian inspiration when it makes no reference to the only kind of equality that really mattered to Kant: moral equality as rooted in common subservience to a categorically binding moral law? However, the two positions are not as straightforwardly contradictory as they may appear (i.e., human beings either are or are not by nature equal). While Arendt certainly does not place the kind of overarching emphasis on the moral law that Kant clearly does, her notion that all human beings have an equal claim to human dignity which is perfected in isonomic citizenship amounts to a reaffirmation of Kant's moral egalitarianism. This can be seen most clearly in contrast to Strauss' view that human dignity is compatible with, indeed demands, the affirmation of basic inequality.

= As I indicated in my essay, I believe that any theoretical claim can without too much difficulty be restated in the language of nature and natural right. For instance, in regard to isonomy: although Arendt means by it the *artificial* creation of *political* equality among *naturally unequal* individuals, the doctrine can be restated in terms of the necessity of such equality among unequals for the realization of the highest human possibilities, or for the flourishing and fulfilment of human nature. So on the basis of this teleological restatement of the doctrine, one could say that while Arendt argues that equality is a product of artifice, in a deeper sense there *is* in effect a natural equality of men.

= To be sure, there is nothing illegitimate in the appeal to nature as such. The point is, though, that it is hard to say what extra force is carried by the invocation of nature, beyond the simple claim that a theoretical proposition is valid, or otherwise, why this extra force is warranted. (What is the difference between the proposition 'X is true' and the proposition 'X is true by nature'?)

= Again: *Any* theoretical claim may invoke nature. Arendt's egalitarian claims, no less than Strauss' hierarchical claims, can be couched in the language of nature. But the problem remains, how do we theoretically vindicate such claims? As finite beings, of course, we do the best that we can. Still, it seems improper that one set of theoretical claims should be given greater weight than another set of claims simply because it *claims* for itself the authority of nature.

= The question of the relationship between nature and artifice seems to be a very complicated one. Relative to what was the norm a couple of generations ago (to say nothing of what was the norm in antiquity), the practices of contemporary medicine appear infinitely 'artificial' (= the product of artifice). But does this by itself prove that it is not better to intervene artificially in order to save lives that would previously have been left in the hands of God or nature? This seems to suggest that the boundary between nature and artifice is not fixed once and for all, but must to some extent be judged relative to context. Moreover, it seems that Aristotle himself, in *Nic. Ethics* V.7, acknowledged (quite sensibly and with good reason) this very complexity.

= You criticize Arendt because it is not clear that her theorizing possesses an ultimate ground. (This objection recurs throughout your comments.) But where is the ground in Strauss? In the 1971 preface to *Natural Right and History*, he speaks of his 'inclination to prefer' classical natural right. That is hardly the language of someone fully confident of his grasp of an ultimate ground. And indeed he very openly acknowledges the deep problematicality of appeals to nature in the context of modern experience (*Natural Right and History*, pp. 7–8; *Thoughts on Machiavelli*, p. 299) – which is not to say that a return to Aristotelian teleology is necessarily impossible. Hans Jonas' philosophy of nature in *The Phenomenon of Life*

[Chicago: University of Chicago Press, 1982] is an attempt to supply the sort of ultimate ground that Strauss implies is required, but that Strauss himself never attempts to offer.

ad para. 15 = Arendt's position on 'the theologico-political question' was that religion in the politically relevant sense had to such an extent lost its hold on the public life of modern Western societies that there would be little point in devoting much energy to questions of political theology. Of course, not all societies have been secularized, nor is it in principle impossible that modern societies could be 'unsecularized,' but I don't think the latter prospect would have been much welcomed by Arendt. I tend to share this view.

ad para. 16 = I agree with you that Arendt did not pay sufficient attention to the imperialism of Periclean politics. And it is also true that in her theoretical writings she sometimes went over the top in her celebration of 'glory,' etc. (although even in *The Human Condition* [Chicago: University of Chicago Press, 1973] she wrote: 'the old virtue of moderation, of keeping within bounds, is indeed one of the political virtues par excellence' [p. 191]). But if one looks at her more concrete, practical writings, and compares them with the more directly practical texts of Strauss (e.g., the Introduction to *The City and Man*), it becomes much more debatable which of the two, Arendt or Strauss, was more committed to a politics of moderation, and which of them gave greater encouragement to a politics of imperial ambition.

= As you may know, while the Right tended to see Arendt as a flaming radical, the Left always considered her far too conservative for their liking. While, obviously, merely 'splitting the difference' between Left and Right is no test of prudence, this is nonetheless not a bad indicator of having successfully avoided political extremes. Her writings on questions of concrete political practice were always distinguished by a careful attention to contingencies of historical situation, feasibility, realism, and so on. This is what I referred to as her 'Burkeanism.' The opposite attitude I find in the following passage from Strauss' attack on Burke at the end of *Natural Right and History*: '[Burke] rejects the view that constitutions can be "made" in favor of the view that they must "grow"; he therefore rejects in particular the view that the best social order can be or ought to be the work of an individual, of a wise "legislator" or founder ... According to the classics, the best constitution is a contrivance of reason, i.e., of conscious activity or of planning on the part of an individual or of a few individuals' (pp. 313–14). I take chap. 31 of *The Human Condition* to be a deliberate reply to this ancient conception.

= As one might expect, on questions of concrete prudence, Arendt's views were occasionally rather eccentric, but more often they were hard-headedly realistic and sober. Overall, I don't think it would be fair to characterize her politics as wildly utopian or 'visionary' (para. 14).

= Obviously, I would like to believe that the concern for more expansive possibilities of citizenship is not simply the product of softheadedness or sentimentalism. Arendt's idea (intended to be sober and hardheaded) is that without such more expansive possibilities, modern societies would continue to succumb to the overwhelming power of destructive ideologies.

= Finally, a word concerning Platonic politics (para. 16). It is true that Plato, in the *Gorgias*, applauds Aristides. But in the *Meno* (94a), Plato seems to say quite clearly that Aristides too, no less than Pericles, fails the ultimate political test, which is to provide a sound and secure pedagogy of virtue. Therefore the suggestion offered in the *Meno*, more radical and perhaps more authentic than what is suggested in the *Gorgias*, is that *all* statesmen fall short of the decisive political standard, a standard that Socrates alone satisfies.

I must apologize for the fact that this rejoinder contains so many rhetorical questions. It is the expression not of any confidence I feel that I have the answers, but of the fact that I am myself still struggling with all these questions. Again, I am very much in your debt for your wonderful generosity in offering such a thorough and probing response to my paper. Have a good summer!

Yours,

Ronnie

14

Eros and the Bourgeoisie

We are fortunate to have one last book by Allan Bloom, in which he gathers together the fruits of a lifetime of acute reading, and of forceful teaching based on the books that were most important to him. In *Love and Friendship*, Bloom returns to the three lodestars of his previous scholarly work: Plato, Shakespeare, Rousseau.

Although he undoubtedly relished the fame and fortune, Bloom was not altogether well-served by his rise to bestsellerdom. The popularity of *The Closing of the American Mind* entrenched the image of him as a guru of neoconservative culture criticism, to be ideologically reviled in the pages of the *New York Times* and elsewhere. Bloom himself, as we know from the introductory chapter of *Giants and Dwarfs*, was not terribly comfortable with his reputation as an official spokesperson for cranky conservatism.[1] There will no doubt be readers who, upon perusing the introduction of *Love and Friendship*, will quickly conclude that they are in for another dose of priggish neoconservative moralizing. But this would be unfair to Bloom.

Other readers will voice a quite different complaint: that Bloom, by handing over the stage to his favourite authors, relieves himself of the exigency of giving a positive account of his own of the grand themes that concern him. But this objection, too, is rather unfair, for there is a coherent narrative underlying the commentaries presented in the various chapters. Bloom is drawn to Rousseau's project to re-eroticize human existence because he shares Rousseau's sense of the flatness of a bour-

Review of Allan Bloom, *Love and Friendship* (New York: Simon and Schuster, 1993); originally published in *Review of Politics* 56, no. 4 (Fall 1994). Reprinted with the permission of *Review of Politics*.

geois world that has been drained of eros. It is the great deficiency of liberalism, from Hobbes and Locke onwards, that it fails to take sex seriously enough, just as it is the great virtue of Plato and Rousseau that they never fail to give sex its due within the economy of human experience (p. 104). (See pp. 46–7: Rousseauian education locates its essence in the question of erotic intensification, whereas Lockean education devotes comparable attention to the problem of bowel regularity.) Bloom rightly draws to our notice the striking passage in *Emile* in which Rousseau avers that even religious fanaticism, insofar as it is a source of 'grand and strong passion which elevates the heart of man,' is to be preferred to the deadening effect of bourgeois rationality, which pacifies the human spirit as it domesticates the passions (p. 85, citing pp. 312–14 of his own edition of *Emile*).

Each of the novels that concern Bloom in Part One revolves around the antinomy between romance and the bourgeoisie. As presented by Bloom, Jane Austen, Stendhal, Tolstoy, and Flaubert offer four different responses to this contradiction between antibourgeois eroticism and the unerotic conventionalism of *les bourgeois*; three of these teachings somehow hopeful, the fourth deeply pessimistic. The teaching of *Pride and Prejudice* is that the antinomy can be ameliorated by an attitude of reserve, noble simplicity, and above all, irony. The teaching of *The Red and the Black* is that even a moment of true passion can suffice to redeem the frustrations of life in a world of social vanity. The teaching of *Anna Karenina* is that even when romantic love leads to tragedy, it confirms rather than annuls the seriousness of the ethical bonds governing human life, and finds therein a dignity that redeems the tragedy. And finally, *Madame Bovary* offers the not at all redemptive teaching that, contrary to the promise of Romanticism, the antinomy is a hopeless one, because the emptiness of bourgeois life is too abysmal to be cured by romantic love. The farcical aspects of bourgeois existence that are satirized by Flaubert are fully perceived by the other writers as well; what sets Flaubert apart is that he no longer offers the Romantic consolation that one can transcend the farce and be elevated to something higher. Bloom says enough to indicate that the verdict attributed to Flaubert is also his own, namely, that Romanticism was not vanquished but simply expired from the inner exhaustion of its own limited possibilities. (On the limits of Romanticism, see pp. 137, 151, 233, 242, 259–60, 262, 300.)

Rousseau, better than anyone, dramatizes the problem of 'the decay in human connectedness' (p. 100) that is a concomitant of life in bourgeois society, and offers romantic and matrimonial love as an antibourgeois tonic. Bloom is vastly more sympathetic to this Romantic project than the average contemporary reader of Rousseau, yet he nonetheless sees it as an ultimately defective solution to the eroslessness of modernity. As a corrective to Rousseau and his Romantic legacy, Bloom devotes the rest of the book to Shakespeare and then Plato. Bloom considers Shakespeare superior to the Romantic novelists because he is able to celebrate love at its most sublime without blowing it up out of all proportion or allowing it to crowd out other valuable dimensions of human experience, and because Shakespeare can accept human nature pretty much as it is, rather than feeling obliged to 'reconstruct the soul' (p. 269) in order to satisfy some artificial project of Romantic redemption. (On Shakespeare's superiority to Romanticism, see pp. 269, 307, 315, 345, 373, 396.) Plato, too, is accounted superior to the Romantics, again because, according to Bloom, Plato takes his bearings unstintingly from nature, rather than from an artificial reconstruction of the human situation in pursuit of a contrived and unsustainable idealism. Plato's great advantage, of course, relative to Rousseau and his followers, is that he never had to contend with the bourgeoisie!

Rousseau, for all of his profound debt to Plato, must be situated on the modern side of the 'quarrel between the ancients and the moderns' (p. 35); and given Bloom's own commitments in this quarrel (that is, as a partisan of the ancients), he is obliged to record the limits of Rousseau's understanding of the nature of eros. One of the gravest of these deficiencies is Rousseau's slighting of friendship and the primacy he accords to the relationship between lovers: 'There is no way that friendship could be considered, as it is by Aristotle, to be the highest relationship.' For a prototypical Romantic like Rousseau, friendship arises merely out of the need to have someone 'with whom to discuss one's mistress' (p. 147; cf. pp. 425–6). The moderns are concerned only with love, whereas the ancients can give both love and friendship their due (and in this respect, Shakespeare counts as a bona fide ancient). On a cursory reading of the book, it may appear as if Bloom actually follows the moderns in this respect; for despite the symmetry announced in the title, there is hardly any discussion of friendship in the first 400 pages of Bloom's book (nor, for that matter, is there much discussion of friendship in the last 120 pages of the book). Yet this deceptive imbalance directs us to a crucial section on Montaigne, where Bloom makes known his real sympathies. Once again, the symmetry of love and friendship is upset, but this time in a much more profound sense, and in the reverse direction. Through much of the book, Bloom appears to be defending the claims of love in a world where Romanticism has lost its hold, but really his book is intended as an argument on behalf of friendship. It is on this basis that Bloom seeks to persuade us of Plato's superiority to Rousseau: Rousseau, with his idealism, provides no viable human relationship capable of mediating the extreme demands of individuality and the extreme demands of political community – something Plato *does* provide with his ideal of philosophical friendship. Bloom agrees with Montaigne that love and friendship are not mutually harmonious neighbours, but rather competitors between which one is required to choose, which in turn entails the establishment of a rank order that assigns each its relative worth within the hierarchy of human relationships.[2] This hierarchy, for Bloom, is decisive, and it seals his verdict on Rousseau and his successors: Romantic love points down to sex (the union of bodies); friendship points up to philosophy (the union of souls).

Nonetheless, whatever Bloom's ultimate philosophical reservations about the Romantic movement, there is, relative to our de-eroticized times (in both the Romantic and classical meaning of eros), clearly much that Bloom sympathizes with in the Romantic impulse. Bloom's singular aim throughout his life as an educator was to restore the image of philosophy as something that could speak not just to reason or to the intellect but to the soul – as addressing those ultimate concerns with art, religion, and politics capable of moving all human beings to passion in facing their choices in life. This intention to re-eroticize philosophy was bound to make Bloom appear, as he surely realized, rather naïve and sentimental. Hence his affinity with the great Romantics. It is tempting to regard it as an act of self-description when Bloom says of Stendhal that the great paradox of his writing is its unvarnished realism about human deeds and motives, joined to idealism in its view of love (p. 162). Bloom's endeavour to draw philosophy back into the realm of eros also obliged him to seize every possible opportunity in piquing contemporary sensibilities. Naturally, this established Bloom in the eyes of his critics as an arch-conservative, whereas he clearly took himself to be the practitioner of a misunderstood kind of radicalism. Again, it is tempting to see Bloom as offering a self-description when he writes that Stendhal's disdain for bourgeois society – a society that finds its true home in democratic America, where everybody is the slave of shopkeepers' opinions, and where there is no opera – 'could be interpreted as the expression of an aristocratic preference ... But actually he is arguing for an Emilean self-legislation, accessible to even the poorest of men, rather than for the haughtiness of the old regime' (p. 160).

In order to be a philosopher in Bloom's sense, one has to be something of a Romantic, and how difficult it is to be a Romantic in the twentieth century! In a sense, the entire book is an argument intended to render plausible the provocative maxim with which Bloom concludes *Love and Friendship*: that Great Sex depends on Great Books. Bloom learns from Rousseau that 'Imagination ... constitutes the quasi-totality of the sexual life of human beings' (p. 121); and imagination, in turn, feeds on the either rich or feeble nourishment provided by the literature emotionally or intellectually available to a given culture. If literature loses its power for us, we therefore pay a higher price than we realize.

Is the problem the disappearance of a certain kind of literature, or is it the disappearance of the social reality that it presupposes? Bloom would say that this is a false dichotomy, for what makes the reality real is our capacity to be gripped imaginatively by the literary evocation of a world. Perhaps. One reason for scepticism is Bloom's persistent assumption that whatever shapes human beings, for good or ill, ultimately comes from philosophers:[3] in *The Closing of the American Mind* we learned that everything questionable in contemporary culture comes from Nietzsche; in *Love and Friendship* we learn that everything good in the culture of the Romantic novel comes from Rousseau. And it is not too much of an exaggeration to say that for Bloom, all the insights of Shakespeare are already available in either Plato or Machiavelli. In any case, if it is indeed true that the eclipse of the great tradition of the Romantic novel leaves us in a world from which eros has ebbed away, Allan Bloom, with his observant reading and elegant writing, can help us think about what this means.

15

Left-Wing Conservatism:
The Legacy of Christopher Lasch

In the debates that commanded the attention of political philosophers in the 1980s, critics of liberal individualism came to be called 'communitarians.' Like me, Christopher Lasch has serious reservations about this label, and offers a preferred alternative: 'populism.' In this essay, I want to propose another label that I think is more precise than either of these: namely, 'left-wing conservatism'; moreover, Lasch himself presents a superb illustration of the appropriateness of the label I am proposing.

Christopher Lasch wrapped up a very productive, indeed prolific, career as a historian, cultural commentator, and social critic with two interesting books, *The True and Only Heaven*[1] and *The Revolt of the Elites and the Betrayal of Democracy*.[2] Notwithstanding much unfair criticism of Lasch's contribution as a culture critic, his writings offer exemplary displays of critical intelligence (to say nothing of an enormous breadth of scholarship); and if one were looking for a model of intelligent social criticism, one could certainly do worse than to draw inspiration from Lasch's last two books.

The True and Only Heaven is a sprawling work. Its chapters alternate between theology, syndicalism, the intellectual history of pessimistic social thought, American cultural history, and the kind of sharp social criticism for which Lasch was famous through much of the 1970s and 1980s. On the whole, Lasch seems to put himself forward as a late-twentieth-century American Rousseau, and his discussions of the idea of progress tend to cast contemporary America in a distinctly unflattering light,[3] in much the same way as Rousseau's debunking of progress in his first and second *Discourses* served to puncture the conceit with which the Parisian Enlightenment taught eighteenth-century Europe to regard itself. At least one notable critic of the book puts the whole exercise down to Lasch's 'mood' – as if one had to be a chronic dyspeptic in order to fail to celebrate liberal modernity's contribution to the cause of human happiness.[4]

The Introduction to *The True and Only Heaven* is an immensely thoughtful and quite moving retrieval of the intellectual and political ground covered by Lasch in the course of his career as a cultural observer and social critic. In it, Lasch refers to how he drew insight from the English Marxism of Raymond Williams and E.P. Thompson into 'the way in which capitalism thwarted the need for joy in work, stable connections, family life, a sense of place, and a sense of historical continuity.'[5] Later in the book, Lasch quotes Williams's observation that 'he had "discovered themes profoundly related" to his "sense of the social crisis" of his time "not in the approved list of progressive thinkers" but in "paradoxical figures" like Burke, Carlyle, and Ruskin, who defied left-wing canonization but usually had more interesting things to say about modern life than those who marched under the banner of progress.'[6] This is as good a description as Lasch ever furnishes of his own intention in *The True and Only Heaven*, namely, 'to reconstruct a tradition of social criticism resistant to conventional political classifications,' and thereby to nourish 'insight into the "redefinition of what politics should be" – the lesson radicals most need to master.'[7]

Lasch's central theoretical purpose is to develop a systematic contrast between liberalism as an ideology of progress and what Lasch designates as a 'populist tradition' that, starting with Thomas Paine, William Cobbett, and Orestes Brownson, served to articulate civic and cultural anxieties (or at least scepticism) about the liberal ideals – namely, 'progress, large-scale production, and the proliferation of consumer goods.'[8] This tradition of populism – Paine's ideal of 'a democracy of small shopkeepers and artisans,'[9] Cobbett's assault upon 'the machinery of modern credit,'[10] and Brownson's polemics against wage labour – although it obviously had some relation to the liberal tradition, was closer in spirit to republican thought. The 'political economy of liberalism' entails 'a more and more specialized division of labor'[11]; the 'political economy of republicanism,' on the other hand, sought to 'restore the old system of real home industry.'[12] Populists, then and subsequently, adhere to a vision of an independent citizenry, self-employed and self-sufficient; whereas liberals promote dependency both by focusing employment on factory labour and by encouraging 'tutelary powers in the state.'[13] In Lasch's account, even John Locke counts as an honorary 'populist' because the type of property he vindicates is that of petty producers, not anything that might be associated with industrial capitalism.[14]

This 'tradition' continues with (as Lasch presents these thinkers) the attempts by Thomas Carlyle, Ralph Waldo Emerson, and William James to keep a Calvinist ethos alive in an age in which Calvinism was theologically discredited. Next, the story shifts to the syndicalism of Georges Sorel and the guild socialism of G.D.H. Cole; the argument here is that the failure of guild socialists to break with progressivist thinking caused them to sell out the radicalism of syndicalist ideals. This turn from theology to syndicalism may seem like a puzzling leap, but Lasch's attempt to draw the two together is both deliberate and central to his narrative. The discussion of Sorel in Chapter 7 is pivotal because it helps clarify Lasch's pervasive theme of the intersection between social philosophy and religion. In fact, it is impossible to overlook the centrality of religion to Lasch's concerns in this book (as is true, as well, of his final book, *The Revolt of the Elites*). His point is that social concerns and 'theological' concerns are inseparable. All the thinkers who fascinate Lasch – Carlyle, William James, Sorel – are preoccupied with the same set of concerns: What can motivate human beings to a feeling of real devotion or reverence in a progressivist epoch? What in the modern world can supply a counterpart to the experiences that elicited religious piety or military ardour, longing for the transcendent or willingness to sacrifice, in earlier ages? If one thinks of, for instance, syndicalist projects of social reorganization as mere social–economic alternatives, one will fail to comprehend the lofty cultural–metaphysical aspirations that gave meaning to the syndicalist project of a figure like Sorel.[15]

The heart of the book is Lasch's defence of nineteenth-century agrarian and artisanal populism.[16] Living in the twentieth century, we tend to see liberalism and socialism as exhausting the social–economic alternatives. But for Lasch, these two, far from exhausting the alternatives, are actually on the same (progressivist) side, the more radical alternative – craft-based resistance to the industrial and corporate organization of economic life, small-scale production, and property ownership based on co-operatives – having been crushed by the march of 'progress.' Hence, syndicalist ideals of co-operative ownership are absolutely central to the story Lasch wants to tell about how anti-industrial conservatives were the real radicals.[17]

So one clear entailment of Lasch's argument is that, in terms of the fundamental alternatives that his narrative aims to present, liberalism and Marxism are on the same side.[18] Both are ideologies of progress; both opt unreservedly for large-scale production and the depreciation of localism. The characteristically progressivist attitude toward the past is: 'Let the dead bury their dead' – a phrase that Marx quite aptly borrowed from Christ as quoted in *Matthew* and *Luke*.[19] Those living in the present have enough to occupy them without being distracted by a look back to the past. For the Christian, the imperatives of other-worldly salvation must unconditionally trump competing loyalties and obligations; for Marx and other progressivists, the demands of this-worldly salvation are similarly uncompromising. One could easily take Marx to be speaking not just for himself and for his comrades-at-arms, but for his capitalist adversaries as well, when he writes: 'The social revolution of the nineteenth century cannot draw its poetry from the past, but only from the future.'[20] The fate of the preindustrial crafts is a crucial case in point. Consider, for instance, the pathos of the following passage from Seamus Murphy's beautiful book, *Stone Mad*, describing the eclipse of the world of the stonemason: 'Didn't you hear the news? Turner's Cross church is to be built in concrete. Isn't that nice blackguarding? What the hell is the world coming to at all when they're going to build the House of God in mud?'[21] For a critic of progress, the death of craftsmanship is an utter catastrophe. Conversely, for a partisan of the progressivist vision, like Marx, the death of craftsmanship is a small price to pay for the onward march of history.

Lasch knows perfectly well what liberals and conventional leftists will say in response to his seemingly pastoralist vision: they will cry, 'Nostalgia!' – and assume that the mere utterance of this epithet suffices to dispatch the critic's challenge.[22] So, to try to pre-empt this dismissal, Lasch himself, very early on in the book, attempts to mount his own critique of the nostalgic impulse.[23] The argument is not fully clear, but the basic thrust of it is that nostalgia is an *ally* of progress because it sentimentalizes and infanticizes the past, rather than presenting memory of the past as a secure ground for mature experience of the present: 'Nostalgia evokes the past only to bury it alive.'[24]

These themes are so central to the book that Lasch could have given his tome this title: *Progress versus Memory, Memory versus Nostalgia*. He could also have titled it *In Defence of the Petty Bourgeoisie*. Lasch's purpose throughout the book is to reconstruct the sources of a literary–theological–philosophical tradition that rebels against modern hubris – a philosophy of limits that expresses 'a sensibility ... that runs against the dominant currents in modern life'[25]; and he doesn't hesitate to connect this philosophy with its class basis: it is 'the sensibility of the petty bourgeoisie.'[26] Lasch's heroes in the book – Emerson, Carlyle, William James,

Sorel, G.D.H. Cole, Josiah Royce, Reinhold Niebuhr, Martin Luther King – 'embodied the conscience of the lower middle class.'[27] What defines this sensibility? According to Lasch, what needs to be appreciated is 'the moral conservatism of the petty bourgeoisie, its egalitarianism, its respect for workmanship, its understanding of the value of loyalty, and its struggle against the moral temptation of resentment.'[28] The great failure of American liberalism, so Lasch argues, is its incapacity to appreciate 'what is valuable in lower-middle-class culture.' Liberals themselves, he continues, had to pay a high price for this failure of moral imagination: 'Their attack on "Middle America" ... eventually gave rise to a counterattack against liberalism – the main ingredient in the rise of the new right.'[29]

The last chapter of Lasch's intellectual history (though not the last chapter of the book) is an account of the pessimistic social theology of Reinhold Niebuhr, and of what it contributed to the hope-animated and hope-nourishing politics of Martin Luther King, Jr. The key idea here is Niebuhr's conception of the need for a 'spiritual discipline of resentment.'[30] Lasch uses King to illustrate how basing one's politics on a foundation of 'petty bourgeois' virtues like individual responsibility and self-discipline, upheld by the communal resources of church and locality, can bring about astonishing social change. These things – religiosity, rootedness in a particular culture, communal solidarity, and the upholding of the petty bourgeois virtues of individual responsibility, moral discipline, and neighbourhood-based self-help – constituted, in Lasch's view, the greatness of the original civil rights movement; but these sources of moral and spiritual strength were no longer present when Dr King took his movement north in the 1960s. Rather, Lasch argues, the movement lost its way when it could no longer mobilize popular energies on the basis of family, church, and neighbourhood, and when, instead of building on a shared culture, it had to resort to social-democratic notions of enforcing social justice through the power of the state. Populist virtues of individual and communal empowerment turned into liberal vices: deracination, and the evisceration of self-respect as people were encouraged to think of themselves as passive victims.

In a similar vein, Lasch, in the final two chapters of the book, takes on some of the most difficult political debates in America in recent decades: desegregation, abortion, affirmative action, school prayer, the 'permissive' culture, 'family values,' and so on. In each case, Lasch argues that liberals make things too easy for themselves when they portray opponents of liberal policies as simply backward-thinking reactionaries or ignorant masses, often in the grip of racism. If one reads Lasch's argument here –

as some critics do – as an effort to align himself with Archie Bunker, then it is arguable that many of his political judgments in this part of the book are questionable at best, militantly illiberal at worst. But it seems to me that one can interpret Lasch's endeavour in a more generous fashion. His project is to show how the attitudes of the white lower middle class concerning family, church, and patriotism came to be treated by suburban liberals as something to be sneered at and looked down upon. Hence it is no surprise that these former constituents of the Roosevelt coalition, realizing that they were no longer being taken seriously as partners in a cultural dialogue, succumbed to a right-wing backlash. The point is not to embrace blue-collar conservatism; the point is to come to a better understanding of how white-collar liberals caused Middle America to feel so resentful and alienated, so that the left can avoid such political mistakes in the future. Only in this way – by taking better account of populist sentiment in Middle America – will the left be able to marshal the political resources needed for the struggle that really needs to be fought: the challenge to atrocious conditions of social inequality in America and to the control of the country by corporate capitalism. Lasch concludes the book with a brilliant exposé of the sham 'conservatism' of Reaganite ideology, of its duplicity in manipulating lower-middle-class anxieties and resentment of the cultural arrogance of élites as a cover for its real agenda: a reckless unleashing of capitalism in its least conservative aspects.[31]

To be sure, Lasch's book is full of instructive discussions of intellectual history, syndicalist political economy, politics, and much else; but at the centre of everything is his insistent voice as a culture critic and moralist. Consider the following cultural indictment that he addresses to his fellow citizens:

The unwholesomeness, not to put it more strongly, of our way of life: our obsession with sex, violence, and the pornography of "making it"; our addictive dependence on drugs, "entertainment," and the evening news; our impatience with anything that limits our sovereign freedom of choice, especially with the constraints of marital and family ties; our preference for "nonbinding commitments"; our third-rate educational system; our third-rate morality; our refusal to draw a distinction between right and wrong, lest we "impose" our morality on others and thus invite others to "impose" their morality on us; our reluctance to judge or be judged ...[32]

What conservative could articulate better than this the sorts of (legitimate) cultural anxieties that provided the populist bases for the New Right? Passages like the one just quoted provoke Stephen Holmes to refer to Lasch as someone who is 'easily unmasked as a cultural conservative cloaked in a leftish fleece.'[33] This is pure slander (though Holmes is hardly alone in accusing Lasch of being a pseudo-leftist). Lasch's credentials as an egalitarian radical are irreproachable, and there is not the slightest reason why one cannot be both a stringent critic of capitalism's assaults upon justice and solidarity *and* a critic of the miserable standards of moral and cultural experience in contemporary liberal society.[34] It is true that Lasch, in common with anti-egalitarian conservatives, is very critical of the welfare state and of the paternalistic impulses of social democracy.[35] But, whether one agrees or disagrees with Lasch that one should always try to avoid reliance on the state as an agent of egalitarian reform, this is no reason to accuse him of dissembling a more-than-professed affinity with 'conservative lookalikes.'[36] Lasch believes that the left needs to adhere to a more ambitious social ideal than liberalism's idea of the welfare state as a dispenser to passive recipients of social-democratic entitlements. His inspiration is, as cited earlier, the civil rights movement's ideal of black self-help, and this is indeed an extremely powerful model of activist citizenship. Again, Lasch's celebration of petty-bourgeois notions of civic virtue is intended as a foundation for radical politics.

Clearly, Lasch is convinced that the progressivist narrative of ever-expanding contentment, moral improvement, and, eventually, universal affluence has been thoroughly discredited. But contrary to what Lasch's critics say, *The True and Only Heaven* is *not* a counternarrative of Spenglerian decline; on the contrary, it is a plea for agency (which presupposes hope): 'A sober assessment of our predicament, one that would lead to action instead of paralyzing despair, has to begin by calling into question the fatalism that informs this whole discourse of progress and disaster. It is the assumption that our future is predetermined by the continuing development of large-scale production, colossal technologies, and political centralization that inhibits creative thought and makes it so difficult to avoid the choice between fatuous optimism and debilitating nostalgia.'[37]

However, if human beings are to be able to mount resistance and mobilize forms of counter-agency against the modernist dynamo, what is required, once again, is a secure cultural infrastructure as a ground for agency.[38] This explains why Lasch's critique of the liberal critique of particularism is one of the persistent themes in the book. 'Man grasps the universal only through the particular'[39]: this is the truth that Lasch thinks is missed by those who celebrate the prospect of progress toward liberal cosmopolitanism and a transcendence of all forms of tribalism or parochialism. Both politically and theologically, the cosmopolitan ideal fails to grasp that, as Lasch puts it, 'ultimate loyalty to the creator of being has to be grounded in loyalty to families and friends, to a particular piece of earth, and to a particular craft or calling.'[40]

After reading this book, most people will find it hard, if not impossible, to avoid posing these questions: Is there anything that anyone can now do to reverse the hegemony of a wage-based economy and to reinstate a more craft-based regime? And if not, how can this kind of historiographical exploration help us address our current predicaments? This seems to me beside the point when it comes to measuring Lasch's contribution. The business of a social philosopher is above all to articulate the essence of presently lived social reality, and it seems to me undeniable that dimensions of contemporary existence that never get articulated in standard works of liberal political philosophy *do* get articulated in this book. For instance, Lasch offers the following penetrating observation concerning 'the narrowing of political debate in the twentieth century':

In the nineteenth century, people asked whether the work was good for the worker. Today we ask whether workers are satisfied with their jobs. A high level of "job satisfaction" then serves to refute those who deplore the division of labor, the decline of craftsmanship, and the difficulty of finding work that might leave workers with a sense of accomplishment. The liberal principle that everyone is the best judge of his own interests makes it impossible to ask what people need, as opposed to what they say they want.[41]

To ask for nostrums is always unreasonable.[42] If a work of social theory helps us to become more thoughtful and enlarges the boundaries of our social imagination, then that is reason enough to feel grateful toward its author.

The True and Only Heaven, with its many digressions and odd shifts of topic, is a strange and perhaps overambitious book. It is difficult to follow the thread of Lasch's story of modern hopes and disappointments since he refers to such a bewildering variety of texts and intellectual movements. It is a lot easier to get a handle on *The Revolt of the Elites*. Needless to say, the themes of his book on progress are very much in evidence in this final collection of essays. The basic overarching 'metanarrative' is the same: he assembles basically the same villains and the same heroes, although he also adds a few new wrinkles to his social theory. The fundamental moral armature of the whole analysis is the opposition between rootedness and mobility.[43] The heroes are farmers, shopkeepers, and blue-collar workers who know where they come from, and who feel little desire to rise up to somewhere else. The villains are white-collar careerists who have lost touch with the past, and who owe loyalty only to their own ambitions. In Lasch's theoretical universe, *mobility* is what defines the current social dispensation, and his overriding aim is to attack it as a social ideal, as well as to expose to searching cultural critique those who embody it in their lives.

The new professional-managerial élite is destroying people's sense of place, as well as the idea of continuity between the generations (with its attendant notions of social obligation) that *had* at least been a virtue of the previous bourgeois élites.[44] Multiculturalism appeals to the new élites, patriotism doesn't: 'Theirs is essentially a tourist's view of the world.'[45] Social mobility is not egalitarian but anti-egalitarian because it increases the arrogance of the winners and the despair of the losers.[46] A sounder understanding of equality would involve notions of a common culture and common experiences that would mitigate the polarization of classes.[47] The privileged class becomes ever more privileged, while the majority become ever more demoralized by job insecurity, unemployment, and collapse of the solidarities previously supplied by the labour movement. The mobility of capital becomes the all-encompassing principle of social existence.[48]

These problems generate a 'democratic malaise' because the conception of equality associated with the idea of social mobility is a betrayal of the notion of equality that originally defined American democracy: '[The American ideal] was nothing less than a classless society, understood to mean not only the absence of hereditary privilege and legally recognized distinctions of rank but a refusal to tolerate the separation of learning and labor. The concept of a laboring class was objectionable to Americans because it implied not only the institutionalization of wage labor but the abandonment of what many of them took to be the central promise of American life: the democratization of intelligence.'[49]

When equality, originally defined as a rough parity of condition and civic experience, comes to be redefined as the opportunity to break free of one's native class and ascend to the upper reaches of the social hierarchy, this implies a corruption of the democratic ideal itself. The most important choice a democratic society has to make, as Lasch rightly points out, is 'whether to raise the general level of competence, energy, and devotion – "virtue," as it was called in an older political tradition – or merely to promote a broader recruitment of elites. Our society has clearly chosen the second course.'[50] And his conclusion is that 'careerism tends to undermine democracy by divorcing knowledge from practical experience, devaluing the kind of knowledge that is gained from experience, and generating social conditions in which ordinary people are not expected to know anything at all. The reign of specialized expertise ... is the antithesis of democracy.'[51]

Lasch's basic political aim is to challenge the existing lines of political debate: those on the right celebrate the market and damn the state; those on the left damn the market and celebrate the state. Lasch wants to say 'a plague on both your houses,' and to argue for a realm of local self-help and voluntary civic spirit that needs defence against *both* the market *and* the state.[52] What he seeks is 'a third way' between the market and the welfare state.[53] Libertarians of the right believe in the untrammelled authority of the market. Social democrats believe in compassion enforced by colossal state bureaucracies. 'Populists,' as Lasch presents them, believe in both individual responsibility *and* communal norms, in both self-reliance *and* the notion of a common good – in a communitarian morality that is grounded locally, not at the remote level of the state.

Lasch is as sensitive as any conservative to the evils of bureaucracy and centralized social planning; and he is entirely faithful to the radical tradition in his awareness of the evils of class division. What he seeks to do, ultimately, is to combine the conservative's anxieties about the deterioration of the moral and cultural infrastructure of social life (family, religion, education, mores) with the old-fashioned radical's assault upon the unjust privileges of class. The political ambiguity of Lasch's preferred term 'populism' (for of course there are populisms both of the left and of the right) underscores the political paradox that is at the core of Lasch's left-wing conservatism. Politically speaking, *The Revolt of the Elites* is an argument for a radically egalitarian vision; this argument favours universal self-government, and therefore universal achievement of civic competence. Yet culturally speaking, it is an argument on behalf of Middle America – on behalf of religion, patriotism, self-reliance, and devotion to the claims of local community and neighbourly co-operation. It seeks to affirm the reasonableness of Middle American anxieties about the collapse of the family, the collapse of moral and cultural standards, and the threatening character of the centrifugal forces at work in the relations between the racial, ethnic, and sexual groups that define contemporary American society. In this way, Lasch's political vision situates itself at a point of intersection between American radicalism and American conservatism (although the conservatism is sometimes more conspicuous than the radicalism).[54]

Many liberals are bound to be quite uneasy about all the talk, in Lasch's writings, of 'spiritual malaise,'[55] 'spiritual disrepair,'[56] 'spiritual desiccation,'[57] 'spiritual torpor,'[58] 'moral and cultural disorder,'[59] 'moral collapse,'[60] and so on.[61] Richard Rorty, for instance, writes: 'People start writing books about spiritual plight only when they have pretty much given up on politics – when they can no longer figure out what concrete practical measures might help. Then they say that only moral regeneration, or a return to religion, or a revolution in philosophy can do any good.'[62]

This seems to me very unfair. The talk in Lasch of moral and spiritual breakdown is not an escape from politics but an attempt to come to terms with how political sentiment ebbs and flows in a real-life society: for instance, how contemporary America moves from left to right and (perhaps) back again from right to left. It is an attempt to take seriously the concern with moral order or moral disorder of legitimately anxious parents, neighbours, and citizens. As argued above, Lasch wants above all to make sense of why America in the 1980s was so responsive to the siren-song of the New Right.[63] How on earth did it come to pass that 'liberal' became a dirty word in American political discourse? And indeed, anyone who reads Chapter 11 of *The True and Only Heaven* will have a much better understanding of how the New Right turned the 'L-word' into such a damaging epithet.

This isn't to say, however, that there aren't problems in how Lasch conceives his role as a critical intellectual. In Lasch's view, what discredited liberalism more than anything, and rightly so, was 'liberal intellectuals' sense of alienation from America,'[64] and the cultural arrogance this implied; what social critics need, above all, is a 'philosophy of loyalty.'[65] This conception of the relationship between intellectuals and citizens is put forward most explicitly in an important section of *The True and Only Heaven* defending Michael Walzer's idea of connected social criticism.[66] Yet Lasch's social criticism is more disconnected than he intends it to be. He wants to connect with the populism of Middle America, but the dominant *ethos* of Middle America is progressivist and optimistic, hence very remote from the social and religious pessimism of the 'populist' intellectual tradition that Lasch is trying to construct. Much as it may be true that Lasch has considerable sympathies for the moral world of Middle Americans – for their religiosity, their anti-statism, their anti-elitism, and their anxieties about the unravelling of the moral fabric – the average American does *not* share either Lasch's moral reservations about capitalism or his qualms about material progress. Americans want their politicians to be broad-grinned optimists, not brooding pessimists. The last thing that Lasch wants to be is a socially alienated intellectual. But given the progressivism, optimism, and consumerism that are at the core of American life, as opposed to Lasch's own 'producerism,' pessimism, and anti-progressivism, it is hard to see how he could be anything other than a far-out-of-the-mainstream social critic.

I close with a reflection on the perils of theory and practice. Lasch was apparently the philosophical inspiration behind a major address to the American public by a president of the United States – an address so major that in the eyes of many, it actually came to define that presidency (namely the Carter presidency).[67] This is a practical effect of theory that vastly exceeds the sort of influence that the average theorist or intellectual can hope to exert. Yet its consequence was, arguably, the sinking of that presidency (or at least an important contribution thereto) and the election of a more upbeat alternative, Ronald Reagan. One cannot imagine this outcome being received by Christopher Lasch with anything less than horror and revulsion: Reagan as a president was determined at any price to see only sunshine and hope, never malaise or anxiety; and Reagan's sunniness helped obscure the fact that his policies contributed hugely to the exacerbation of the very class divisions and class polarization that were the source of Lasch's pessimism. Christopher Lasch was not the kind of praxis-minded theoretician who hopes to use theory as an instrument to change the world,[68] and his intention as a social theorist was surely to help citizens become more thoughtful and reflective about their situation in the contemporary world. Yet, strangely enough, he too, in this respect, could not prevent his well-intentioned theorizing from being drawn into the whirlwind of political practice. The ironies of theory and practice seem unavoidable; this should give us theorists some pause.[69]

16

Hermeneutical Generosity and Social Criticism

It is possible to read Charles Taylor's *Sources of the Self* as a magisterial attempt, not only to respond to the whole range of debunkers of modernity – from Adorno on the left to Allan Bloom on the right – but to respond as well to the postmodern conception that we now inhabit a universe of metaphysical groundlessness, decentred selves, and deconstructable traditions. Taylor wants to argue against the postmodernists that far from being centreless selves stitched together from bits and pieces of deconstructed traditions, we can as modern selves draw upon inner structures of moral aspiration as resources for a coherent experience of our own selfhood. If it succeeds, Taylor's narrative of the modern self can refute the postmodernist claim that we must forsake the very possibility of a unified self nourished by unified traditions. In fact, what the postmodernist claims is not only that this experience of fracture and groundlessness is the appropriate *description* of our current situation, but also that we should welcome the postmodern situation as a *liberation* from metaphysically grounded visions of unified selfhood and unified tradition. I think it is true that theory should avoid a reckless debunking of modernity as a whole; and Taylor seems to me completely right to challenge the postmodern vision as normatively attractive. But it may be suggested that in his effort to vindicate the dominant moral impulses of modern life, Taylor gives us a picture of our condition that is a little more reassuring than our contemporary situation actually warrants. Moreover, this resolve to survey the modern landscape with a bountiful interpretive generosity (sometimes to the extent of giving modern identity the benefit of the

This is an expanded version of an article originally published in *Critical Review* 9, no. 4 (Fall 1995). Reprinted with the permission of the Critical Review Foundation.

doubt) is dictated by Taylor's conception of what it is to do social theory; it is precisely this conception that I wish to explore in this essay.

Reflexivity is inherent in the very enterprise of theory. That is to say, it belongs to the nature of theory for the theorist to reflect on what he or she is doing as a theorist, and to give an account of the character of one's activity as a theorist. I want to begin with a distinction that Taylor himself offers, in one of his essays, between two perennial archetypes of the practice of social theory. This will provide a framework for thinking about Taylor's contribution as a theorist; it will also allow me to explore some of my own puzzles about what the activity of theory entails. In 'The Motivation behind a Procedural Ethics,' Taylor sketches ideal-types of two radically opposed conceptions of what it is to do theory.[1] The first, which he labels 'revisionist,' is illustrated by Plato's political philosophy in *The Republic.* Plato resolutely rejects the quest for citizen honour that drives life in the Greek polis, and confronts this lived experience of the polis with an utterly revolutionary vision of human life and the human good. Taylor describes this as 'the classic case of a revisionist doctrine': 'The internal goods, the citizen dignity and fame, are savagely reinterpreted as a grasping after mere appearances, simulacra.' The exemplar of the alternative conception of theory is Aristotle's critique of Plato, which is labelled 'comprehensive' in the dual sense that it *encompasses* the full range of existing goods, and seeks to *understand* why these goods are experienced as good: 'We cannot just legislate the goods people are actually seeking and finding as goods out of court. What could the highest good be if it did this? On what basis could we establish a highest good that had this property? A theory of justice must begin with the kinds of goods and the kinds of common practices organized around these goods that people actually have in a given society. Ethical theory has to comprehend given practice; it cannot just abstract from it.'[2]

Significantly, Taylor says that these archetypal images of theory present us with an impossible choice: 'I do not propose to decide this [issue] by fiat in favour of Aristotle; there is no one-sided resolution of this conflict. We all must recognize allegiance both to the Platonic and to the Aristotelian sides of this dispute, both to the revisionist and the comprehensive approach.'[3] However, notwithstanding this avowal of impartiality, I want to argue in what follows that Taylor, in his own practice of theory, is very much slanted to the Aristotelian model of comprehensive theory.

Here we need to engage the issue of Taylor's historicism, which is inscribed at the very core of his interpretive enterprise. The clearest and most forceful account of his basic enterprise is offered in section 19.2 of

Sources of the Self. According to Taylor's account of moral theory as presented there, moral truth consists in overcoming forms of blindness or distortion in our moral self-understanding.

> It is widely thought that no constitutive good could have such a fragile ontological foundation as this, a niche simply in our best self-interpretation. Unless it is grounded in the nature of the universe itself, beyond the human sphere, or in the commands of God, how can it bind us? But there is no a priori truth here. Our belief in it is fed by the notion that there is nothing between an extra-human ontic foundation for the good on one hand, and the pure subjectivism of arbitrarily conferred significance on the other. But there is a third possibility, the one I have just outlined, of a good which is inseparable from our best self-interpretation.[4]

This is undoubtedly a compelling picture of moral theory, but it contains a crucial ambiguity: What are the boundaries of the self that is submitted to this exercise in self-interpretation? Are we seeking to address the human condition globally, or are we more directly concerned with the conditions of modern selfhood as we now live it, on the basis of a specific history? Taylor's practice of interpretation in *Sources of the Self* suggests the latter. In order to clarify what is at stake here, I want to supplement Taylor's distinction between revisionist theory and comprehensive theory by borrowing William Galston's helpful distinction between 'deep description' and 'wide justification'; in fact, I want to endorse Galston's conclusion that 'the wide justifiers have the better case.'[5]

Galston defines deep description as 'the elucidation of basic structures of moral belief within our political culture,' whereas he associates wide justification with 'the traditional philosophical effort to scrutinize the premises of a political culture in light of (the possibility of) transcultural standards.' Beyond the various arguments that one might adduce on behalf of wide justification, I have a special reason for favouring it over deep description – namely, my commitment to a certain kind of radical social criticism that, as I conceive it, depends on assuming a Platonic distance from shared identity, whether it is the local identity shared with members of one's own polis, or a much more broadly defined shared identity, say, that of Occidental modernity. Here my concern is not with the whole range of forms of social criticism (encompassing not only the narrowly political arts of speech-making and pamphleteering but also novels, poetry, and all the visual arts); rather, I'm primarily concerned with one particular mode of social criticism, namely, philosophy. A case needs to be made on behalf of the *philosopher* as social critic because – at least according to Michael Walzer's specification of the meaning of social criticism – Plato, Spinoza, Friedrich Schiller, Marx and Nietzsche, Walter Benjamin and Roberto Unger are not to be considered social critics because they don't feel themselves obliged to address their projects of philosophical criticism exclusively to fellow citizens within the horizon of shared concerns of some specific national community.[6] Indeed, one might go so far as to say that as Walzer conceives social criticism, even Charles Taylor himself counts as a social critic only when he writes a book like *The Pattern of Politics*, not when he writes a book like *Sources of the Self*. If so, then it is no exaggeration to say that Walzer's account calls for a defence of philosophy itself as a practice of social criticism.[7]

Getting Out of the Cave

I share the Socratic conception of philosophy defended by Galston in Chapter 2 of *Liberal Purposes* – that is, the conception according to which one necessarily starts off in some particular cave, and then does one's damnedest to rise intellectually out of that cave. In fact, I would say that Galston himself is not 100 per cent faithful to the Socratic conception, for the Socratic ideal stipulates that one's first intellectual duty is to do battle against the underlying assumptions of one's *own* cave: those born in a *liberal* cave ought to devote their chief theoretical energies to challenging individualist assumptions, whereas those who find themselves initially in an illiberal cave are entitled to appreciate the virtues of liberal individualism. So while in his role as a theoretician for Clinton's Democratic Party it is perfectly reasonable for Galston to write books defending liberalism, his first duty *qua* Socratic theorist is to *challenge* the reigning assumptions of a liberal society, not to give liberal citizens a better understanding of their own aspirations. Now it may well be true that no theorist ever fully ascends out of the cave in which he or she starts – that is, *in some respects*, Socrates never did get out of that Athenian cave – but the intelligibility of the very *aspiration* to rise out of the cave depends on there being in principle an 'outside' to which one might aspire. For theorists like Michael Walzer and Richard Rorty, however, this 'outside' is in fact a phantom; there is nothing outside the cave to which one might intelligibly aspire, and philosophy in the Socratic mode is therefore based on a delusion.

Now when one considers *Sources of the Self* and *The Malaise of Modernity* relative to this Socratic ideal of philosophy, I think the striking modesty of Taylor's enterprise will be apparent. For Taylor's project in those works is addressed to the inhabitants of modernity, bringing to their attention aspects of their own deeper existential commitments, features of the modern cave that have escaped the notice of the cave-dwellers. Hence what one gets in these books is, from my point of view, a very forceful defence of modernity and a rather timid critique of modernity. I should hasten to add, however, that I have no doubt that Taylor, unlike Walzer and Rorty, believes there to be an 'outside the cave' that is an intelligible object of philosophical aspiration.[8] One might say that Taylor's undertaking in a work like *Sources of the Self* is to *mediate* between the Socratic perspective and the cave-dweller's perspective: his idea of 'sources' indeed suggests that there are certain experiences within the cave that, rightly interpreted, offer intimations of what's outside the cave. One can, as it were, summarize the intention of Taylor's interpretive project by saying that what is attractive about the project of a self-interpretation of modernity is that it allows us to apprehend what's outside the cave without ever having to leave the cave.

Returning to the alternatives of deep description and wide justification: Galston appears to have in mind primarily Walzer's practice of theorizing. Indeed, Walzer does seem more single-mindedly committed to deep description, whereas Taylor genuinely fluctuates between the two conceptions of theory. Still, I think it is fair to say that *Sources of the Self* is decidedly a deep description enterprise rather than a wide justification enterprise (although the community that is being favoured with a deep description in that work is a rather large one – namely, Occidental modernity as a whole, rather than some more specific national community, as in Walzer's work). It strikes me that what governs Taylor's work as a whole is the 'historicist' presumption that if we make a sufficiently generous effort to understand why modern selves have come to be what they are and why modern moral aspirations have evolved in the direction that they have, these moral aspirations, and the selves that they constitute, will show themselves as perfectly reasonable and worthy of aspiration.[9] (I qualify this as 'historicist' in the Hegelian sense that the modern identity has unfolded as an intelligible story, and that it is the chief task of the philosopher to reconstruct this intelligible story in its rational intelligibility.) This, at least, is the intention that defines the theoretical–interpretive enterprise laid out so grandly in *Sources of the Self*: what we require is a suitably ambitious narrative of the self-unfolding of modern identity so that the moral *telos* of modernity can be apprehended as quite reasonable and indeed compelling. But, clearly, this Taylorian practice of comprehensive theory presupposes the historicist confidence that there really is an immanent narrative structure here rather than just a tissue of contingencies, and it may be hard to sustain this Hegelian or quasi-Hegelian confidence in the absence of Hegel's metaphysical assumptions.

John Dunn, with his usual incisiveness, explains the perils of this theoretical strategy of *tout compris*:

Since [Taylor] is a Catholic he could scarcely fail to see some force to 'demands that come from beyond our own desires or aspirations, be they from history, tradition, society, nature, or God.' But, as well as being a Catholic, he is also very much a Romantic, [and therefore] he is strongly and personally committed to taking what comes from within our own desires or aspirations at least equally seriously. The resulting amalgam can readily offend most readers. His liberal critics among American philosophers do not care for the Catholicism, and believe that it leads him to espouse a potentially (or actually) oppressive relation between a society and its individual members. No doubt his Catholic critics are less enthusiastic about the Romantic elements, seeing these as licensing a *louche* and excessively aesthetic approach to the art of life, and a correspondingly enfeebled grasp of the requirements of God's Law. Either may well be partly right ...[10]

Again, Dunn writes elsewhere of Taylor: 'In the face of distressing choices he is apt to cling tenaciously to both horns of the dilemma, refusing, for what are often humanly excellent motives, to let either of them go.' In this passage, Dunn goes on to cite Taylor's simultaneous commitment to 'the modern post-Romantic project of self-exploration' and the premodern project of situating the self within an 'objective order of natural and social value.'[11] In these two commentaries, Dunn rightly identifies a crucial tension in Taylor's work between the enterprise of cultural interpretation that is contingent on the history of the modern self and, on the other hand, the intimation of a larger moral order that could furnish standards of transcultural judgment.[12] Taylor indeed seems inspired by the Hegelian impulse to combine somehow these two distinct endeavours; yet in the absence of Hegel's own philosophical commitment to a necessary coincidence of the larger rational order and the historically evolved articulation of selfhood, the tension persists.

This tension in Taylor's thought is directly relevant to my purpose in this essay, because I want to suggest that these two poles of intellectual endeavour – justification by appeal to self-understanding, and justification by appeal to a transcultural standard – are linked to the opposing conceptions of social theory that were presented earlier. Charles Taylor's main endeavour as a theorist, it seems to me, is to try to do the utmost interpretive justice to the aspirations of people in modern society both to express their individuality *and* to satisfy their longings for community. (In this sense, he is a communitarian *and* a liberal.) My own conception of theory, by contrast, is, I think, less geared to understanding and more geared to criticism: according to my conception, the main duty of the theorist is to expose both the excessive individualism of modern life *and* the sometimes excessive demands of communal belonging. (Therefore I think of myself as antiliberal and anticommunitarian!)[13] Yet it seems to me to go without saying that one cannot say in the abstract whether social practices demand interpretive generosity or severe critical scrutiny. Naturally, it all depends on the specific practices that present themselves for judgment. I don't propose to enter into this task in detail, since it would clearly be a vast undertaking. Instead, I want to make some very brief observations regarding three domains of human experience – family, religious commitment, and nationality – where Taylor's theoretical approach inclines him toward a rhetoric of understanding, whereas mine inclines me toward a rhetoric of criticism.

Family, Religion, Nationality

Let us start with the family. One of the leading intentions of *Sources of the Self* is to vindicate the move, certainly characteristic of the social experience of modernity, to focus human energies much more narrowly within the boundaries of domestic life. Taylor wants to argue that this transformation, relative to other epochs of Western experience, is not fortuitous or arbitrary, but is expressive of deep cultural currents in the evolving self-consciousness of the West, one of whose notable sources is, of course, the powerful legacy of Christianity.[14] But who is to say what the eventual cultural outcome will be of the historical evolution in attitudes toward domestic life? Suppose modern consciousness evolves in a way that privileges not the family unit in relation to larger structures of social life, but instead the individual unit in relation to the family. If the standard of theoretical judgment is simply the historically contingent evolution of identity, why shouldn't this too be vindicated in the way that the cherishing of domesticity is vindicated in *Sources of the Self?* Anyone acquainted with the facts of contemporary life will know that this suggestion is not an abstract hypothesis.

Taylor himself, at the margins of his narrative, makes sufficient acknowledgment of the fact that modern experiences of selfhood may well be evolving in directions that he would not be eager to vindicate. For instance, he sometimes refers to modern 'relationships' in quotation marks[15]; what the quotation marks signify is nicely conveyed in the following crack by Allan Bloom – although Taylor would never allow himself to make the point as bitingly as Bloom does: '"Relationships" are based on "commitments," as in "I'm not ready to make a commitment"'; or as Bloom elsewhere puts the same point: 'Commitment is a word invented in our abstract modernity to signify the absence of any real motives in the soul for moral dedication.'[16] At one point in the book, Taylor concedes that our situation in the late twentieth century is such that aspirations to family intimacy and individualism, previously in harmony, have begun to fall into conflict, to the extent that 'an ideology of "self-fulfilment" militates against family life.'[17] What this really amounts to is an acknowledgment that aspects of contemporary life are such that the moral sources have a tendency to unravel. So, again, if it is the case that the basic justification for the prominence that domestic life has in the lives of modern individuals is simply that this is in fact how individuals inhabiting the modern dispensation have come to understand themselves and articulate their self-identity, then what objection could be posed if individuals within some new dispensation come to understand themselves and define their identity in a way that requires radical liberation from the moral constraints and social obligations of family life? Taylor's own observations in this area offer some grounds for suspecting that this new dispensation may already be upon us. Now, without doubt, to say that Taylor himself would be rather uncomfortable with this outcome would be a massive understatement. But this merely confirms my point: that one requires a more robust standard than *Sources of the Self*'s appeal to historically evolved self-understanding can supply.

While on the subject of individualism, it would not be out of place to remark that Taylor goes nowhere near as far as one might expect in criticizing individualist tendencies in modern life. One sees this especially clearly in the work where Taylor's sympathy for Romantic individualism is most evident: namely, *The Malaise of Modernity*. In fact, I think that the basic theoretical thrust of that work is much better captured by its American title, *The Ethics of Authenticity*, for in the book Taylor devotes considerably more theoretical energies to trying to redeem the debased Existentialist idea of authenticity than he does to cataloguing the discontents of modernity. I think it should be obvious that 'authenticity' offers a very weak standard for making ambitious critical judgments concerning a way of life or the individual lives that are lived within that way of life – unless, as I mentioned earlier, one partakes of the Hegelian faith that the inner development of one's identity somehow coincides with a larger rational order that makes sense of the contingencies of one's psychic history. One may well concede that, say, the characters in Robert Altman's film *Short Cuts* are living lives that are authentically their own. But this is very far from giving one a basis for passing judgment on whether these are happy, flourishing, or attractive lives. I am, of course, well aware that Taylor's intention is to construct a radically reinterpreted and, so to speak, desubjectivized notion of authenticity; but it remains mysterious to me why a critic of individualism would want to salvage a theoretical category that has been so thoroughly compromised by radical subjectivism.

Let us now turn to religion, which is another sphere of cultural life that raises the same problem of understanding versus judgment. In *Sources of the Self*, Taylor consistently refers to the Enlightenment as the 'unbelieving Enlightenment.'[18] It is hard not to interpret this as a subtle reproach. The reproach becomes somewhat less subtle in a revealing little article Taylor wrote concerning the Salman Rushdie affair.[19] On the one hand, Taylor makes some concessions to Rushdie's defenders: he notes that there are certain indications of ambivalence in *The Satanic Verses*'s depiction of religious life; that the literature of unbelief doesn't merely perpetrate acts of cultural negation, but embodies a positive 'spiritual' stance of its own; and that one cannot ask writers within that literature to maintain a hands-off policy toward religiously charged symbols without requiring that they betray their own vision of the world. Yet symmetrical understanding really isn't a possibility in the Rushdie affair; as in war, one really does have to take sides. And Taylor *does* take sides, when he charges that the whole tradition of antireligious literature to which Rushdie belongs (Taylor cites also Joyce) 'has lost touch altogether with the possibility that religious symbols, stories, dogmas, might mean something very different to those who espouse them than they do to the rejecters ... Rushdie's book is comforting to the western liberal mind [because it confirms] the belief that there is nothing outside their world-view which needs deeper understanding.'[20] In other words, the onus of understanding falls predominantly on one side in this cultural struggle. For myself, I have trouble seeing why Rushdie is obliged to be fully understanding of how the faithful see the world, but the faithful are not obliged to understand how Rushdie sees the world.[21]

Salman Rushdie is a brilliant writer, and his book – contrary to the denunciations of it by guardians of the faith, many or most of whom haven't read it – is anything but a one-sided Western–secular mocking of the religious yearning for 'childlike security'[22] (as even Taylor to some extent concedes[23]). On the contrary, the novel is a rich and sensitive exploration of how both ancestral rootedness *and* Western cosmopolitanism offer limited horizons and less than fully satisfying experiences of life. Thus it's a little surprising to me that Taylor, whose trademark is after all the rhetoric of understanding, is quite unmoved by the literary power of Rushdie's novel – which just goes to prove that one cannot understand everything and everybody, and that one therefore needs some ultimate normative basis for distributing one's understanding in the way that one does.

The broader problem is this: If Taylor's ultimate standard is evolving historical self-understanding, why isn't the same principle of hermeneutical generosity applied to the rise of atheism within Western modernity? If, at least in the case of certain intellectual and cultural élites in the modern West, unbelief becomes integral to self-interpretation, why isn't this too treated as a moral source, as an 'epiphany,' and therefore favoured with understanding rather than (muted) criticism? This problem, I think, actually points back to the tension in Taylor's thought highlighted earlier – namely, theory as the effort to understand the historically evolving and self-articulated identity of the modern subject versus theory as a quest for quasi-objective good. Now in this particular case, I (as an 'unbeliever') would in fact be inclined to treat with more sympathy than Taylor that current of modern culture which is attempting to break free of theism. But my point here is not to challenge Taylor's theism, nor to try to mount an ambitious defence of the modern culture of unbelief. The point I'm trying to make is that theory can never be fully exhausted by the historicist enterprise of merely interpreting how modern selves come to conceive their emerging identity (which is – in its leading conception – what *Sources of the Self* suggests is the way to practise theory). Unlike Taylor, I would like to see theory defined much more unequivocally in terms of reflection on the good rather than in terms of interpretation of the modern self; but as his own guarded criticisms of modern individualism and modern unbelief, I think, disclose, Taylor himself cannot avoid being drawn away from his apparent privileging of the latter conception of theory.

My third focus of inquiry is the problem of nationality. Just as Taylor seeks to redeem the ideal of family intimacy in the midst of its current travails, buffeted by the winds of contemporary individualism, and just as he seeks to redeem the claims of religion (despite its potential for bigotry and fanaticism) in the face of modern unbelief, so he seeks to redeem the claims of the nation (again, despite its darker possibilities) in its quest for recognition of how nationhood constitutes identity. What 'authenticity' is for individuals in their efforts to assert their own uniqueness, 'recognition' is for nations in their efforts to assert *their* own uniqueness. Parallel to his affirmative stance toward religion in general, Taylor writes about nationalist aspirations without ever questioning the theoretical legitimacy of a people giving moral–political supremacy to the urge to affirm its own nationhood. But surely there are moral ambiguities here that deserve scrutiny. (Indeed, nationalism often generates something considerably more severe than mere 'moral ambiguities'; for despite whatever hopes one might have cherished for moral progress by the end of the twentieth century, what we have seen in various parts of Europe since 1989 reminds us that we have absolutely no guarantee that nationalism in its most virulent and illiberal forms will not re-emerge even in societies that had made heroic efforts to transcend ethnic particularism.) This can be illustrated by Taylor's writings concerning the political situation in Quebec. Let us consider, for a moment, a grammatical curiosity that is encountered in certain political texts by Taylor, notably his brief delivered on 19 December 1990 to the Bélanger–Campeau Commission: namely, his use of the possessive adjective 'our' when referring to the interests, claims, and sentiments of Québécois.[24] For a non-nationalist like myself, it may seem perfectly proper for Taylor to deploy the first person plural in addressing his fellow citizens in Quebec; but it is by no means obvious that (real) Québécois nationalists would grant Taylor a full entitlement to use this 'our.' This is because, for a true nationalist, no matter how much Taylor himself construes his identity in Québécois categories or identifies with the cause of a safeguarded Québécois nationhood, there is a dimension of ascriptive membership that (within some indeterminate range) objectively determines the degree of Taylor's possible participation in Québécois nationhood. The same kind of moral ambiguity is expressed in the fact that Canadian multiculturalism is considered more culturally threatening in Quebec than it is in English Canada – a fact to which Taylor refers in his essay 'Shared and Divergent Values,' but whose moral implications he tactfully doesn't highlight.[25] If this weren't so, Québécois nationalism really wouldn't be a form of *nationalism,* which it is – however much nationalists in Quebec may try to package it in 'civic' rather than 'ethnic' terms.

Again, Taylor's rhetoric is one of understanding rather than criticism, of deep description rather than wide justification. But the whole question of nationalism is one where deep description in no way suffices, and where the self-understanding of the collectivity needs emphatically to be challenged rather than merely understood. In December 1994, I went to

Cuba for a little holiday. At my hotel, one of my fellow tourists, a teenage
girl who was also a fellow Canadian, was wearing a T-shirt that read PROUD
TO BE SERBIAN. Now, wearing such a T-shirt in 1994 is probably not quite
as atrocious as wearing a T-shirt that reads PROUD TO BE GERMAN in the
1930s; still, there is sufficient moral proximity in this analogy for one very
much to prefer that she had been wearing a T-shirt that read, instead,
NOT PROUD TO BE SERBIAN. What is the function of theory in the face of
the phenomenon of 'Serbian pride'? Is it an exertion in the direction of
understanding, or rather, does theory require alienation and distanciation? Dilemmas of this kind apply with greater or lesser moral urgency to
all nationalisms; that is to say, they pose a problem with respect to nationalism as such.

As we saw in considering the problem of religion, the demand that we
accord deeper understanding to one side generally means that the opposite side gets less of a share of understanding. So, just as Taylor demands
deeper understanding of what moves religious communities while slighting the moral sensibilities of atheists, so in this debate, Taylor urges
greater understanding for the moral aspirations of Quebec nationalism
without making a comparable effort to understand those for whom
nationalism of any kind is a moral affront. I'm not suggesting that it is *ever*
possible to be perfectly symmetrical in granting understanding toward
opposing claims. My thesis is that the rhetoric of understanding presupposes that we've already established an independent basis for assigning
relative moral weight to these opposing claims (for example, one makes
more effort to understand nationalist aspirations in Quebec to the extent
that their case has objective moral weight). Again, Taylor's appeal to the
evolving articulation of historical identity, as if this sufficed, has the effect
of evading this ultimate theoretical reckoning.[26]

Identity and Recognition

I can restate my challenge in response to a more recent text of Taylor's,
'Identité et Reconnaissance,' a text in which he offers a wonderfully suc-
cinct summary of the themes of identity and recognition that have preoccupied him in his work of the last ten to twenty years.[27] In 'Identité et
Reconnaissance,' Taylor's aim is to contribute to answering the following
questions: What does it mean to be modern? What is the characteristic
phenomenology of modern experience? The implicit presumption is that
it is pointless to devote theoretical energies to asking whether modernity
as a global dispensation is a good thing or a bad thing. It is our fate, and

as such, to understand ourselves we need to understand how modernity reconstitutes or reshapes the task of defining our selfhood.

Prior to the arrival of modernity, it hardly makes sense to speak of 'the problem of identity,' since the boundaries of selfhood are more or less pre-established by structures of social, theological, and cosmological meaning. When all of these are swept aside by the intellectual revolutions of the sixteenth, seventeenth, and eighteenth centuries, 'the self' and its identity become uniquely problematical – the definition of identity becomes a *task* for the self whose identity is now at stake. Taylor refers to Erikson's account of the 'search for identity' of the young Luther, and makes the telling point that it is decidedly anachronistic to use the language of identity in reference to Luther: what was of concern to Luther was not mere problems of personal self-understanding, but rather, the objective character of humanity's condition in relation to universal issues of sin, grace, and salvation. The idea that what was at stake here was his own quest for identity would have made no sense at all to Luther himself; the question, rather, related to the objective adequacy of the structures of theological meaning embodied in the pre-Reformation Church. Today, on the other hand, the idea that this is a quest for identity is so familiar that we have trouble spotting the anachronism.

This way of characterizing what defines the modern horizon has direct implications for problems of contemporary social and political life, because (so Taylor argues) as modern selves pursue this quest for identity they are obliged to claim 'recognition' (one should really call this *Anerkennung* to flag its Hegelian ancestry) from other selves who are meanwhile pursuing alternative identities. This struggle for recognition and counter-recognition bestows an unprecedented complexity upon modern political life, since it is premised upon a quest for identity that lacks the stable ontological guideposts furnished by premodern cosmology and theology. Grasping this point, Taylor suggests, can help us come to a deeper understanding of the kinds of identity-preoccupations – including nationalisms of various kinds, gender politics, ethnic and racial politics, and the politics of sexual orientation – that grip people within the space of contemporary political culture. Nationality, gender, race, ethnicity, and sexual orientation come to be politicized because having lost the stable pillars of premodern existence, our identity becomes an open-ended *problem* for all of us modern selves, and resolving the problem in a secure way requires not just coming up with an identity that meets with our own satisfaction but, beyond that, securing for that identity a publicly sanctioned social recognition. If we fail to see how this whole modern predicament works, then – Taylor argues – we are condemned to find much of what unfolds within modern politics (with its intensely earnest politicizations of identity) simply baffling.

That, in brief summary, is Taylor's argument. The basic thrust of this enterprise, as I have just summarized it, is to *understand* some characteristic features of modern psychology and modern politics. Much less noticeable, on the other hand, is any attempt to submit this politics of identity, in its wide variety of instantiations, to rational criticism and moral judgment, which in my view are integral to the enterprise of political philosophy. That is to say, political philosophy must attempt to distinguish less reasonable and more reasonable definitions of human identity. What calls for critical scrutiny is the relationship between cultural history of the kind that Taylor sketches in 'Identité et Reconnaissance' and political philosophy as an enterprise that entails seeking ultimate grounds for normative judgment. That Taylor's categories of identity and recognition are descriptively quite useful for an understanding of what is actually going on in contemporary politics seems to me not very controversial; what is much less clear, however, is what *normative* mileage one can draw from these categories.

Taylor presents the quest for identity and recognition neither as something to be celebrated as such, nor as something to be condemned as such; it is simply a given – a natural outgrowth of modernity, of modern individualism and modern egalitarianism. It is presented, as it were, *neutrally*: to be neither affirmed nor repudiated, but simply to be understood by anyone who seeks insight into the givens of the modern condition – again, of what it means to be *modern*. But if the quest for identity is as it were neutral, neither to be applauded as such nor to be damned as such, then it is less than clear how tracing the phenomenology of modern identity-seeking can contribute to the political–philosophical interrogation of norms.

The interesting normative question here is not whether identity questions are relevant to modern politics (they obviously are), but rather, *which* identity? Or, what is the relative normative weight of conflicting identities? Consider, for instance, the mounting political battle between the Cree of Northern Quebec (and their anglophone supporters) and Québécois nationalists in the Parti Québécois and Bloc Québécois. It seems obviously true that the politics of identity is at play on both sides of this political argument. But political philosophy doesn't seem to carry us very far if it stops at the suggestion that this is a conflict of identity. What we want as political philosophers is a more ambitious probing of the claims of these two opposed identities with respect to principles of justice, calculations of aggregate welfare, conceptions of the human good, or whatever (depending on one's preferred vocabulary as a political philosopher). Taylor's phenomenology of identity politics, it might be said, places us in the moral space in which these identity conflicts are pursued, but offers little help in navigating within this space of normative contestation. The question for a political philosopher is not the relevance of identity, but how to assess the normative claims embodied in conflicting visions of identity.

The way in which Taylor elaborates the politics of identity and recognition – building on analogies of individuals struggling to define for themselves an authentic self-understanding – perhaps suggests that the quest for identity is basically an innocuous and inescapable aspect of modern experience. Inescapable it may well be, but nothing guarantees its innocuousness. Clearly, there are manifestations of identity politics that are *pure poison*. But in 'Identité et Reconnaissance' there is surprisingly little acknowledgment of the more pathological manifestations of identity politics. In Jerusalem today there are people who believe that they have been called to a divine mission to reconquer the Temple Mount so that they can commence rebuilding the Hebrew Temple. No doubt, these people are pursuing a project that is central to their own identity as they conceive it. But this is pure pathology, and its identity-constituting function does *nothing* to redeem this kind of politics; their need to understand their own identity on this basis does nothing to make the character of such an identity less pathological. Whether the number of people committed to this sort of identity is a tiny handful, or millions, is of no relevance to its normative authority. Either way, its claim to political 'recognition' is precisely zero – which proves that the mere fact that certain people are contingently committed to a certain identity furnishes no normative foundation for claims to recognition; whether the latter claims are valid or not depends on the substance of the identity to which those people are committed. For that matter, there is little acknowledgment in Taylor's argument of the pathologies one often encounters in the *individual* striving after identity. One symptom of the way that modernity complicates the search for identity is that, quite commonly, the very need that certain individuals feel to *find* their identity guarantees that the object of their strivings will always remain out of reach. A secure identity is an unproblematical given, whereas an identity that has to be *sought* is for that very reason often unachievable. Hence the need felt by so many individuals in modern society for psychotherapeutic guidance.

My purpose in this essay has been to try to clarify a persistent tension in Taylor's work between two opposing conceptions of what it is to do social theory. According to the first, the social theorist seeks to give as rich an account as possible of a society's own self-understanding or self-interpretation. According to the second, social theory involves *challenging* the society's self-understanding on the basis of a radical vision of ultimate standards of judgment. It is not hard to see why Taylor is reluctant to opt decisively for one of these conceptions to the exclusion of the other (though, as we have seen, Taylor does tend to privilege the former conception in his own practice of social theory). As John Dunn says in the commentary on Taylor cited earlier, the reason why Taylor is committed, for instance, both to the project of post-Romantic self-exploration and to the premodern quest for an objective human good is that both are in fact attractive visions of human experience, and it may well be that the richness of Taylor's own reflections on the human situation is connected precisely to his refusal to opt exclusively for one side at the expense of the other. However, as I tried to illustrate in the previous section by looking briefly at theoretical issues connected with the family, religion, and nationality, it is impossible to avoid ultimate theoretical judgments based on transcultural conceptions of the good. And however much we may deepen our understanding of the cultural history of the West as a result of this fruitful tension in Taylor's practice of theory, I strongly suspect (and believe I have good reasons for suspecting)[28] that in the final analysis, Taylor himself would not be averse to conceding that, as far as the decisive vocation of the theorist is concerned, transhistorical judgment must prevail over historicist understanding.[29]

17

Thin Ice

First come the disclaimers. Leszek Kolakowski professes to have no philosophy of modernity to offer, and claims to be at a loss to know even how to define modernity, let alone how to define such newfangled constructions as 'postmodernity.' Yet he has a sufficiently definite notion of modernity that he can understand very well why modern intellectuals are such a gloomy lot, and he has enough of a position of his own on the issue of modernity that he can share to quite a fair degree this mood of discomfort or unease. And while he would no doubt be put off by the faddish vocabulary, it might even be reasonable to say that his essays in *Modernity on Endless Trial* give evidence of a 'postmodern' sensibility.

The diverse pieces collected in his book were written over a period of thirteen years and for a wide variety of occasions and publications; even so, certain themes and preoccupations run through the collection as a whole: the conflict between science and religion; the disenchanting effects of secularization; the cultural malaise of modernity; the conceits of intellectuals (as well as their indispensability); the tendency of theoretical pretensions to turn into ideological pretensions, which in turn stifle political freedom (modern historicism is one example of the conversion of theory into ideology); the unattainability of perfection; the unavoidability of evil; and the irrationality of absolute rationality. One of the recurrent themes of the book is that whichever way one turns, whether toward faith or toward secular reason, toward modern science or toward theology, civilizing tendencies and barbarizing tendencies seem to intersect in

Review of Leszek Kolakowski, *Modernity on Endless Trial* (Chicago: University of Chicago Press, 1990); originally published in *History of the Human Sciences* 5, no. 3 (August 1992). Reprinted with the permission of Sage Publications Ltd.

unexpected ways, with the consequence that one is often drawn, willy-nilly, in a direction directly opposed to one's own best intentions. Yet this is offset by another of his themes: the persistence of hope and the unreasonableness of despair.

In the title essay, Kolakowski comes close to affirming Nietzsche's judgment on modernity: '"*Without the Christian faith*," Pascal thought, "you, no less than nature and history, will become for yourselves *un monstre et un chaos.*" This prophecy we have fulfilled, after the feeble-optimistic eighteenth century had prettified and rationalized man.'[1] Except that Kolakowski adds the necessary qualification of the good liberal: that attempts to enforce a political return to premodernity (or to leap out of modernity altogether) produce forms of barbarism at least equal to, and often much greater than, the barbarisms of modernity. In fact, modernity, however much it may be repudiated in word and intention, proves well-nigh irresistible in practice, as Kolakowski shows with the following example (p. 10). The Reformation, seeking to restore Christianity to an older and more authentic experience of faith, paradoxically and contrary to its own intentions gave further impetus to the inexorable rationalism of modern times. Or again (another of Kolakowski's examples), nationalistic movements in our own century, determined to resist or roll back modernity, have given rise to ghastly regimes that are not only devilish but also hypermodern. The more one aspires to resist modernity, the more it seems to hit back with a vengeance.

One might describe Kolakowski as an uneasy liberal. He insists that modern Europeans must summon up the self-confidence to celebrate the successes of Western civilization in promoting an attitude of scepticism and self-criticism relative to other less open, less tolerant societies. At the same time, he realizes all too clearly the price one must pay for the liberalizing achievements of the West:

Cultural influences act according to their own principles of selection, which are almost impossible to control. The first thing the rest of the world expects from European culture is military technology; civic freedoms, democratic institutions, and intellectual standards come last. Western technological expansion entails the destruction of dozens of small cultural units and languages, a process which really gives no cause for rejoicing. There is nothing uplifting in the fact that a great family of Indo-European languages, the Celtic branch, is dying out before our very eyes, despite all efforts to halt the process of its extinction. (p. 23)

Even worse, what is at stake is not merely the survival of the most vulnerable cultures, but rather, as Kolakowski acknowledges very openly, the possibility of cultural diversity as such in the face of Western dynamism: 'If our destiny were to annihilate cultural variety in the world in the name of a planetary civilization ... human civilization as a whole, not merely particular civilizations, would be in danger of extinction' (p. 23).

Kolakowski's concern here is with what one might call the paradox of openness and abrogation of openness. To its enormous credit, European civilization has opened vistas, expressed curiosity for other cultures, triumphed over parochialism, scrutinized its own assumptions with scientific detachment, and distinguished itself in relation to the closed societies of other traditions. Modernity represents the consolidation and consummation of this European legacy. Yet this same liberalizing civilization today threatens to sink all the diverse cultures that it has studied and appreciated into a homogeneous cultural void. Modernity seems to have taught us that there are moral limits to universalism. As Kolakowski acutely demonstrates, to be equally open to everything is to be left with nothing in terms of cultural and civilizational resources. If one carries liberalism too far one ends up with no traditions at all, neither one's own nor those of alien cultures, so what was initially an admirable openness to other cultures ends in a dissoloution or annulment of other cultures (or in gobbling them up with promises of technological marvels). For all that one celebrates the openness and tolerance of the West, too much openness does not liberate – rather, it casts one into the shapeless abyss of nihilism. Starting from a defence of European liberalism, Kolakowski again finds himself drawn into the gravitational field of Nietzschean insights.

Although Kolakowski begins the book by emphasizing his inability to define modernity, it is not long before he does present at least a rough definition (p. 13). To inhabit modernity is to live in a world without taboos (or in a world that is moving in the direction of the gradual lifting of all taboos). That is, a modern world is one that has increasing difficulty in conceiving a distinction between good and evil that is independent of human design, and hence, ultimately, in sustaining *any* distinction between good and evil. The supreme philosophical question for Kolakowski is whether the preservation of a moral universe requires appeal to revelation, or whether (as in Kant) secular morality can rescue the good/evil distinction from the taboo-destroying process of modernity. Expressed in religious terms, to live in a world without taboos is to live in a world that does not distinguish between the sacred and profane; and since it is impossible for the latter distinction to be generated out of secularity alone, we are left with the implication that we cannot contend with the challenges of modernity without some recourse to religious categories and religious experience. Out of this Kolakowski intimates that without religion, no barriers will be left to the most hubristic impulses of modern humanity.

Kolakowski looks to the Christian tradition for an antidote to modern hubris. But he understands that Christianity itself has been historically implicated in the process that has generated modern hubris. European modernity has in important respects been shaped by Christianity and Christian forms of consciousness. When Bacon articulated for the first time the aspiration to conquer nature and eliminate unnecessary human misery by establishing 'the empire of man over things,'[2] he was writing from within at least one version of the Christian consciousness. As noted above, the Reformation, while it sought to humble human reason, in fact contributed to the process whereby reason was liberated from the authority of tradition (pp. 30, 96, 147). And as Kolakowski also argues, the Enlightenment, which in appearance was an anti-Christian movement, had its roots in Western Christianity. In these and other respects, modernity and Christianity stand in a highly complex two-way relationship.

Kolakowski delights in the paradoxicality of the human condition, hence his fascination with tracing how, for instance, liberal cosmopolitanism is metamorphosed into cultural imperialism, the quest for faith promotes the total sovereignty of reason, myths of liberation become ideological pretexts for enslavement – in short, how what is supposed to civilize us often ends by helping to barbarize us. (Conversely, barbarism sometimes contributes to civilization, spurring the creative spirit by, for instance, driving the best minds into exile – the topic of Chapter 5.) Judging from these essays, Kolakowski's intellectual heroes are figures like Erasmus (a religious reformer who refused to join the Reformation), Pascal (a scientist who depreciated scientific reason), and Kant (a philosophical Jacobin who laid the foundations for contemporary liberalism). These are, like himself, thinkers for whom the fabric of human life is rent with self-stymying contradictions. As Kolakowski puts it in one place (p. 80), for every increment of moral progress there is a price to be paid, and it is always uncertain whether the gain outweighs the cost or vice versa. For instance, our modern culture prides itself on having put behind it doctrines of hell, the devil, and original sin. Yet for this accomplishment it pays the price of a belief in human perfectibility and the unreality of evil. Kolakowski is close enough to orthodox Christian theology in his judgments about human nature to be unsure of whether this represents a net progress.

Kolakowski is certainly not 'antimodern,' but he is (with good reason) concerned about some of the Promethean aspects of modernity, and he is particularly anxious about how Promethean human beings might be tempted to become in a decisively post-Christian modernity. All of us today must surely applaud the victory of the Enlightenment in liberating us from superstition and intolerance; and yet the legacy of the Enlightenment, in common with every historic human legacy, is a mixed one. Kolakowski's response to all of this is the usual liberal's refrain about the impossibility of utopia – the impossibility of combining all individual hopes and aspirations in the compass of a single individual life, or of combining all communal hopes and aspirations in the compass of a single political community. To this true but tiresome message Alan Ryan supplied a definitive rejoinder when he observed in a *London Times* obituary for *Encounter* magazine (for which several of the essays in Kolakowski's book were originally written): '*Encounter* set out to persuade the thinking classes never again to be tempted by totalitarianism; for 30 years they have not been tempted, and you can't go on for ever asserting what nobody wants to deny.' As Kolakowski himself acknowledges, the millenarian impulse seems to have lost its steam in recent years, certainly among intellectuals; and with the example of post-Gorbachev Russia before its eyes, the West hardly needs to be reminded of the delusions of utopian politics.

In a three-page credo, Kolakowski presents himself as a conservative-liberal-socialist. The essays bear out this credo. It is when he dons his Catholic theologian's cap that Kolakowski's conservatism comes most to the fore. (And who among us can really gainsay the pessimism about human nature that lies at the wellspring of conservative insights?) It is when he reflects on the longing for utopia that his liberalism is most evident. And it is when he thinks about the limits of conservatism and the limits of liberalism that Kolakowski's residual socialism shows itself.

According to Kolakowski, theoretical stances of pro-modernity and antimodernity can be equally productive of species of barbarism. Does this perhaps give us some grounds for thinking of him as a 'postmodern' theorist? According to one very influential definition, the postmodern condition signifies the renunciation of the kind of grand 'metanarratives' by which philosophers have hitherto sought to locate meaning in history.[3] This is why postmodern thinkers tend to prefer Heidegger to Hegel, and prefer Nietzsche to Marx. Put like this, Kolakowski is certainly close to being situated in the postmodern camp. Not that Kolakowski is eager to embrace Heidegger or Nietzsche! But Heidegger and Nietzsche at least preserve the sense of Pascalian *Angst* that Kolakowski associates with the best of the Christian tradition (as opposed to the optimism of the Enlightenment). Combining Lyotard and Kolakowski, one might say that what marks off postmodern from modern theory is that, having witnessed the horrors unleashed by the grand 'metanarratives' of modern philosophy, henceforth philosophers sufficiently temper the ambitions of their theorizing that they no longer help to spawn ideologies.

Kolakowski writes: 'It would be silly, of course, to be either "for" or "against" modernity *tout court*' (p. 12). This is certainly true. But the symmetry of this 'for' and 'against' is somewhat misleading. For in saying 'yes' to modernity (even with elaborate qualifications) we are saying 'yes' to what we are and whither we are going, while in saying 'no' (again with qualifications) we are questioning ourselves and keeping alive the scepticism and self-doubt that for Kolakowski mark the difference between civilization and barbarism. Kolakowski is right to remind us that a facile repudiation of modernity can be just as dangerous as a facile affirmation of it. Indeed, there are no ready 'solutions' for our predicaments, and any intellectual who promises to show us an escape hatch from the modern condition is a charlatan. Yet the assurance that modernity is for us an irresistible fate can breed complacency, or cowardly submission to its imperatives. This is a complacency that Kolakowski is least of all the sort of intellectual to encourage. For this reason we heirs of modernity are better off harkening to the foes of the modern age than to its partisans and cheerleaders. Better Nietzsche than Hegel. For Nietzsche never lets us forget that modernity, with all the blessings it brings and all the forms of liberation it secures, also leaves us in a spiritually precarious position. It is the critics of modernity like Nietzsche, not proponents of modernity like Hegel, who alert us to our lack of secure footing: 'Disintegration characterizes this time, and thus uncertainty: nothing stands firmly on its feet or on a hard faith in itself; one lives for tomorrow, as the day after tomorrow is dubious. Everything on our way is slippery and dangerous, and the ice that still supports us has become thin: all of us feel the warm, uncanny breath of the thawing wind; where we still walk, soon no one will be able to walk.'[4]

III POLITICAL JUDGMENT REVISITED

18

Practical Wisdom

In this collection of essays, Richard Bernstein offers an agreeable tour of some of the most interesting and controversial landmarks of recent philosophy and social theory. In his panorama of 'the current philosophic scene,' he surveys and criticizes leading contributions by thinkers at or near the centre of contemporary debate: Richard Rorty, Hans-Georg Gadamer, Jürgen Habermas, Alasdair MacIntyre, Charles Taylor, Herbert Marcuse, Martin Heidegger, Hannah Arendt, and John Dewey. Bernstein's insights and critical reflections are always stimulating and intelligent. His essays can be recommended as providing as good an introduction as any to the sorts of issues and concerns that have excited interest in the work of theorists like Rorty, MacIntyre, and Gadamer.

Bernstein is always seeking out the common ground shared by the authors he treats; always on the lookout for lines of convergence. There is certainly some virtue in this, confronted, as we are, with a highly fragmented intellectual culture. On the other hand, there is perhaps a price to be paid for this practice of philosophical diplomacy. To employ the metaphor shared by several of Bernstein's authors: the most engaging conversations are those where the differences of opinion are sharp and vigorous rather than muted or pacified. Bernstein, in his efforts to mediate the various disagreements, sometimes runs the risk of succeeding so well that the conversation terminates in the bland conclusion that conversation is a good thing.

The essays, diverse as they are, revolve around a common core. One

Review of Richard J. Bernstein, *Philosophical Profiles: Essays in a Pragmatic Mode* (Cambridge: Polity Press, 1986); originally published in *The Times Higher Education Supplement*, 16 May 1986. Reprinted with the permission of The Times Supplements Ltd.

might designate this core by referring to the idea of *phronesis*, or practical wisdom irreducible to rule or decision procedure. The classic exposition of *phronesis* is contained in Book Six of Aristotle's *Nicomachean Ethics*, but it has been resuscitated in contemporary thought, thanks to the philosophical efforts of Gadamer, MacIntyre, and Taylor, among others. Bernstein is committed to this revival of the Aristotelian idea, for it represents a 'type of practical reasoning ... which does not make any appeal to ultimate foundations, eternal standards, or algorithms.' Bernstein, in common with Rorty, sees this judgmental, nonalgorithmic reason as not confined to the domain of moral or political knowledge but extending also to the modes of natural scientific investigation. Here Bernstein appeals to the 'hermeneutical' turn of recent philosophy of science, beginning with Kuhn. Science and the humanities are less different than previously thought, not (as earlier generations imagined) because the latter can approximate to the methods of the former, but, on the contrary, because the former cannot help but have recourse to the ways of insight of the latter. As Charles Taylor has put the point: the natural sciences and the human sciences 'turn out to be methodologically at one, not for the positivist reason that there is no rational place for hermeneutics, but for the radically opposed reason that all sciences are equally hermeneutic.'

Since Gadamer, in his remarkable writings of the last twenty-five years, has done more than anyone to revive the theme of *phronesis*, Bernstein's theoretical encounter with his work is especially illuminating. It is with a certain note of surprise that Bernstein detects 'a latent *radical* strain' in Gadamer's thinking. But such radicalism should hardly be unexpected in a declared follower of Heidegger (unless one takes the term 'radical' in a very banal sense). According to Bernstein, Gadamer 'radicalizes' the traditional notion of *phronesis* by purging it of the élitist connotations that it has had 'from the time of Aristotle through Burke right up to the contemporary vogue of neo-Aristotelianism': 'Gadamer softens this élitist aura of *phronesis* by blending it with' Platonic and Hegelian motifs. Yet it seems to me somewhat off the mark to ask, as Bernstein does, what has greater weight in Gadamer's thought, his 'conservative strain' or his 'radical strain.' Bernstein offers no specific evidence of Gadamer's supposed conservatism, whereas the radicalism is very manifestly present in the incisiveness with which he questions the grounding assumptions of modernity.

Bernstein wishes to pose the challenge of whether the mere appeal to practical wisdom or prudence is sufficient if our contemporary moral and political situation is as conflict-ridden and fractured as MacIntyre, say, describes it. Here Bernstein cautiously takes sides with Habermas in his famous controversy with Gadamer. *Phronesis,* Bernstein states, presupposes a stable community of judgment that guides us in the appropriation of traditions. But it is just this context of 'shared *nomoi*' that is presently lacking. This statement of the problem is strongly indebted to MacIntyre's presentation of Aristotelian ethics. What Bernstein wishes to infer from this analysis is that a critical social theory like Habermas's is needed to make good the deficiencies of a *phronesis* no longer rooted in a unified ethical tradition. Gadamer's reply to this, I think, is that regardless of whether our moral and political predicament today is or is not as intractable as it appears in MacIntyre's account, a systematic social theory of the type that Habermas offers will in any case do little to surmount the problem. (Rorty makes the same point.) For the problem does not admit of *theoretical* solutions, but must be tackled at the level of shared experiences and solidarities of *praxis* in all their concreteness. As summed up by Gadamer in a very telling formulation (which I paraphrase): science may be disciplined by *phronesis,* but *phronesis* cannot be disciplined by science. At any rate, as Gadamer points out in a published letter in response to two of the essays in this collection, there is nothing unique about the conflict of traditions we are experiencing today: '*phronesis* is always the process of distinguishing and choosing what one considers to be right.'

As Bernstein says, the central problem of our civilization is that it tends to undermine 'the very possibility for the exercise of *phronesis.*' In light of this fact, diagnosed so acutely by Gadamer himself, Bernstein demands that attention be given to 'the question of how we can nurture and foster the types of community required for the exercise of *phronesis.*' To this Gadamer would answer that it is not for a philosopher or mere theorist to prescribe 'what is to be done.' The presumption of theorists that they might reconstitute the vanishing *ethos* of a society leads to, in his words, 'a terrible intellectual hubris.' Gadamer takes to heart Heidegger's statement at the end of the *Letter on Humanism:* 'It is time to break the habit of overestimating philosophy and of thereby asking too much of it.' It is this understanding of the limits of theory that ultimately defines the emphasis on *phronesis* that Bernstein both appeals to and criticizes.

19

Science and Wisdom

As Peter Steinberger points out in the opening pages of his new study, *The Concept of Political Judgment*, concern with the idea of practical *judgment* arises out of the common intuition that there is a natural and unbridgeable gap between theory and practice. Philosophers analyse concepts; scientists amass empirical knowledge; administrators and technicians apply rules; but no amount of scientific knowledge or command of abstract intelligence can guarantee that one will conduct oneself wisely or insightfully in navigating the demands of ordinary life. Great philosophers can be morally obtuse; learned scientists can put their knowledge in the service of evil; those who are superefficient in the application of rules can, all too often, be blind to common sense. To paraphrase Kant: not knowledge, not philosophy, but only good judgment offers a safeguard against stupidity.[1]

If theoretical understanding could offer unlimited guidance for its own application, judgment would be superfluous. But in fact there is an inescapable need for wisdom and discrimination in confronting a veritable infinity of concrete particulars; and happily, practice has its own independent integrity, and cognitive resources of its own upon which to draw. In this sense, the very enterprise of undertaking a theory of political judgment is a paradoxical one, for what it involves is an endeavour to theorize what is in principle untheorizable, or to theorize what lies outside the limits of theory. Borrowing a beautiful formulation from Montesquieu (in his 'Essai sur le goût'): judgment 'is not a matter of theoretical cognition;

Review of Peter J. Steinberger, *The Concept of Political Judgment* (Chicago and London: University of Chicago Press, 1993); originally published in *Political Theory* 22, no. 4 (November 1994). Reprinted by permission of Sage Publications, Inc.

it is a swift and exquisite application of the very rules that cannot be cognized.'

What is at stake here politically can be easily brought home to anyone who has seen the fine Merchant/Ivory film, *The Remains of the Day*, which is essentially concerned with the problem of what it means to exercise, or to abstain from exercising, political judgment. In the film, Mr Stevens (Lord Darlington's headbutler, the character played by Anthony Hopkins) steadfastly refuses to allow himself to be distracted in the performance of his domestic duties by presuming to exercise moral or political judgment. In this, he is in full accord with his employer and his employer's friends, who believe that lords and captains of industry are uniquely competent to render judgment upon public affairs, which requires a knowledge and experience beyond the ken of mere butlers and housemaids. Meanwhile, those who claim a monopoly of political competence for their own class demonstrate their great political acumen by very nearly selling out their country to the blackshirts.

Hence the interest in clarifying what it means to exercise political judgment, and it is just this worthy ambition that motivates Steinberger's book. Yet *The Concept of Political Judgment* gets off to a rather strange start. Much of Chapter 1 is devoted to a presentation of three radically different visions of political life: Machiavellian *virtù*, Tocquevillean participatory citizenship, and Nietzschean aestheticism. It is unclear why these three theorists in particular have been selected to exemplify the theme of political judgment. (Wouldn't Burke be a more suitable choice?) To make matters worse, these three different theoretical universes are collapsed by Steinberger into what he calls one 'iteration' of the political judgment 'thesis.' Machiavelli, Tocqueville, and Nietzsche constitute Iteration #2. Iteration #1 is a paragraph from an article by *New York Times* columnist Anthony Lewis. Steinberger writes: the 'Second Iteration has, I think, quite obvious advantages over the first' (pp. 42–3). Thus he seems to suggest that three major epochs in the history of political thought are to be evaluated on a par with a single paragraph from a newspaper column. This is a bit bizarre. Iteration #3 is again a conjunction of two very different political philosophies, those of Hannah Arendt and Michael Oakeshott. If there is a political judgment 'thesis' common to Machiavelli, Tocqueville, Nietzsche, Arendt, and Oakeshott, I'm afraid I am mystified as to what it is. Steinberger's aim is to provide clearer distinctions, a more perspicuous analysis, in our understanding of political judgment, but his procedure in Chapter 1 seems to do the opposite.

Things become considerably more focused in Chapter 2. Here Steinberger takes his point of departure from Plato's presentation in the *Gorgias* of the contrast between *techne* (a rationally governed craft) and *empeiria* (a mere 'knack'). For Plato, the relevant contrast here is between *logon* and *alogon*: the capacity or incapacity to offer a rational account of what one supposedly knows. As Steinberger explains, the Platonic contrast goes to the heart of the issue of judgment, for what concerns Plato is that which confers rational legitimacy upon the activity of judging particulars. At its most basic, the act of judgment is the subsumption of a particular under a universal: '*This* root canal is diseased'; '*This* bronze sculpture is magnificent.' Kant's indispensable distinction between determinant and reflective judgment identifies two ways of carrying out this act of subsumption: either there are pregiven rules or criteria that direct us toward the relevant universal (for example, the endodontist has at his or her disposal a science that establishes definite criteria for recognizing the diseased root canal); or the particular is appropriately characterized in some more mysterious way, without recourse to a science that affords ready criteria (as, perhaps, the connoisseur of fine art accomplishes a feat of judgment). In the former case, the mode of judgment is what Kant labels *determinant* judgment; in the latter, the act of judgment is *reflective*. Now, with the issues laid out in this way, it seems plausible to appeal to Plato as the archetypal representative of a rigorously rationalistic view concerning what is required for valid judgment – namely, the knower's grasp of rationally grounded criteria, or rules of subsumption. According to the teaching of the *Gorgias*, the mere knack of the cook, poet, or orator won't do.

Next, Steinberger turns, quite reasonably, to Aristotle, who clearly sought to redeem locally situated practical wisdom from the hyperrationalism of Plato. However, as becomes increasingly evident as the chapter unfolds, Steinberger is thoroughly sceptical of the distinction between *sophia* (theoretical wisdom) and *phronesis* (practical judgment) on the basis of which Aristotle challenges Plato. In this sense, the main thrust of the chapter appears to be a defence of Platonic rationalism against the Aristotelian challenge. But it seems to me that Steinberger has completely failed to grasp what Aristotle means by *phronesis*. Steinberger treats *phronesis* as the application of an antecedent moral knowledge to matters of practice, whereas I think it is clear that what Aristotle has in mind in his discussion of *phronesis* is the idea that real moral knowledge comes to life at the moment when the wise or virtuous person *concretizes* his or her abstract understanding of ethical requirements in particular situations; in that sense, there is no antecedent moral knowledge that awaits application. It is for this reason (which entirely escapes Steinberger) that *phronesis* cannot be thought of according to the model of a science put into practice.

Steinberger finds himself unable to fathom Aristotelian *phronesis*. Nor does Kantian *Urteilskraft* fare much better on his account; accordingly, he proceeds in the chapters that follow to construct his own conception of how one might better surmount the antinomy of science and wisdom. Having dismissed *phronesis* as 'ill-defined and elusive' and *Urteilskraft* as 'a will-'o-the-wisp,' Steinberger undertakes to supply the philosophical grounds that would allow us to recognize judgment as a mode of rationality that is 'at once noninferential and epistemologically compelling' (p. 157). In Chapter 3, Steinberger draws upon Wittgenstein, whose philosophy is indeed highly relevant to an appreciation of what Kant calls reflective judgment, and also upon other exponents of post-Wittgensteinian philosophy of language. As Steinberger rightly argues, the simple fact that we are able to interpret an utterance in a given pragmatic context confirms that the reality of reflective judgment extends throughout the fabric of our linguistic experience, since our utterances typically convey a pragmatic meaning (or give a pragmatic force to semantic contents) that relies on a tacit understanding of the context, and therefore far exceeds what one might infer from syntactic and semantic rules alone. Thus it is indeed true that 'the ability to use language is virtually a paradigm case of judgment' (p. 184).

This ubiquity of reflective judgment, as evidenced in our linguistic experience of the world, prompts Steinberger to criticize Kant for having failed to appreciate that this dimension of judgment 'is true not just of aesthetic endeavour; it applies equally to all other cognitive, knowledge-relevant activities' (pp. 197–8; cf. p. 238, note 25). Here Steinberger is certainly in the right, for Kant situates *Urteilskraft* uniquely in the province of aesthetic judgment (and teleology) on account of mistaken assumptions about what defines cognitive activity in general. As Hubert Dreyfus has pointed out, 'Kant explicitly analyzed all experience, even perception, in terms of rules,'[2] and therefore Kant regarded aesthetic   experience as quite *exceptional* in its transcendence of rule-governed understanding. In criticizing Kant for his blindness to the exercise of reflective judgment in realms of experience other than the aesthetic, Dreyfus is perfectly justified, and so is Steinberger.

It is only in Chapter 4 that one begins to apprehend the Hegelian aspiration of Steinberger's project; his ultimate aim is to draw together the two poles of judgment, determinant and reflective, into a kind of dialectical synthesis – an *Aufhebung* of subsumptive or rule-governed rationality and hermeneutic or interpretive rationality. Steinberger's basic solution is to distinguish between the spontaneous, intuitive act of arriving at a judgment, which, as the theorists of judgment insist, arises out of a tacit understanding of one's context, and the need for a subsequent justification, which conforms to the canons of more traditional rationality; and to claim that both moments – spontaneous judgment and *post festum* justification – are equally essential to the activity of judging. There is much that is interesting and important in this latter part of the book, but I have trouble seeing how Steinberger's own theory of judgment (or any theory for that matter) can escape the criticisms that he directs against Kant, Aristotle, and the other theorists earlier in the book: namely, that they fail to supply 'anything approaching a criterion on the basis of which we might reliably distinguish good from bad judgment' (pp. 75–6), and therefore fail to establish unimpeachable epistemological credentials. Indeed, more to the point, I have trouble seeing why these were reasonable criticisms in the first place, for they seem to ask more of a theory of political judgment than any such theory can possibly deliver. If prudential judgment is ultimately answerable to the standards of rule-governed reason, then praxis loses the autonomy that the political judgment thesis had accorded it, and theory is once again the final arbiter of rationality.

This is an ambitious book, impressively wide-ranging in its intellectual concerns and eclectic in its sources (although, as we saw already in reviewing Chapter 1, the eclecticism sometimes threatens to run out of control). My principal objection to Steinberger's argument is that having promised to 'sublate' reflective and determinant judgment, he annuls rather than preserves the distinctive character of wisdom vis-à-vis science. To demand rules, principles, criteria that vindicate a demonstrably valid judgment (whether prospectively or retrospectively), is to defeat the very insight that a 'theory' of political judgment is intended to communicate. Of course, it makes sense to expect people to be able to offer grounds or explanations that support the reasonableness of their judgments, but this is quite different from claiming that all real judgments presuppose a *theoretical* or quasi-theoretical account (a *logos*) that 'grounds,' 'validates,' or 'certifies' the original judgment.[3]

My own view, as I indicated at the beginning of this review, is that what a philosophy of judgment teaches is a kind of 'dualism' with respect to the demands of theory and the demands of practice: *qua* theorists, we should strive for philosophies of Platonic ambition; but *qua* citizens, we should temper our theorizing with Aristotelian modesty. In this respect, Oakeshott (although he is cited rather disapprovingly by Steinberger) seems to get it entirely right: 'It is not the clearsighted, not those who are fashioned for thought and the ardours of thought, who can lead the world. Great achievements are accomplished in the mental fog of practical experience. What is farthest from our needs is that kings should be philosophers' (p. 52; cf. p. 82, note 164).

20

Rereading Hannah Arendt's
Kant Lectures

I have to confess that, for me, there is something a little strange about my undertaking in this paper. For what I propose to do, really, is go back to some things I got interested in fifteen years ago, and try to give an account of why they seemed important to me then, and why they continue to seem important. Retracing one's steps along an intellectual path invites reflection in a more autobiographical mode than is usually appropriate in philosophy, and I hope I will be forgiven if I indulge myself a little in this autobiographical impulse.

I first started reading Hannah Arendt in my early twenties, and at the time I found it a liberating experience. Let me say briefly why reading Arendt was liberating for me. As an undergraduate, perhaps not unlike most undergraduates raised in a liberal society, I was basically committed to a set of beliefs and assumptions that one could describe roughly as 'radically individualist.' Reading Arendt's *The Human Condition* convinced me that my own radical individualism reflected certain grounding assumptions of the society in which I lived, and therefore represented an impediment to any more probing effort to reflect critically on that society; that is to say, these assumptions were a form of ideology. What *The Human Condition* teaches, as I understood it then and as I continue to understand it, is that the underlying dynamic that drives modernity is an ever-accelerating tendency to subjectivize human experience, with the consequence that human beings are deprived of their deepest needs. Our prime need as human beings is to be drawn out of ourselves, and to be inserted in a public world of shared experience, shared vocabulary,

Originally published in *Philosophy and Social Criticism* 23, no. 1 (January 1997). Reprinted with the permission of Sage Publications Ltd.

shared spectacles; for it is mutual involvement in the enacted stories that unfold in our public world that confers meaning upon an existence that might otherwise reduce to senseless drudgery or banality. Life in the modern epoch, by contrast, is radically privatizing, for the whole pressure of our civilization directs our energies as individuals into satisfying the productive imperatives of modern society and securing our material existence within the realm of private or domestic consumption. When our energies are displaced toward private concerns, our experience of a public universe of discourse and activity tends to get squeezed out, with the consequence that we become deprived of the most humanizing aspects of human life. Seen in this way, liberalism, with its emphasis on the safeguarding of a protected space of individual decision and choice of ends, functions more or less as a theoretical legitimation of the horizons that define life in a characteristically modern society.

It is not hard to see why the basic project of Hannah Arendt's Kant lectures is central to her fundamental endeavour to vindicate the idea of publicity, or of an intersubjective experience of life, in the face of the subjectivizing pressures of modernity. Even my brief sketch of the theoretical background should make it readily apparent why Kant's 'Critique of Aesthetic Judgment' would have such powerful appeal for Arendt, for the question Kant addresses there bears directly upon her central concerns: how to secure a publicly available realm of shared appearances and intersubjective judgments against the threat of subjectivization. Now, it might occur to us that there is a rather more straightforward antidote to the peril of subjectivism – namely, a philosophy that asserts an objectively shared structure of human needs, human desires, human interests. That is to say, a theory of objective human nature. But Arendt persuaded herself that an appeal to any fixed conception of human purposes having its foundation in nature posed an unacceptable limitation on the scope of human freedom. Again, this explains why she was so drawn to Kant: his transcendental inquiry into the grounds of our intersubjective experience of beauty and the sublime promises to redeem a shared realm of worldly appearances, and to do so without resorting to any foundational appeal to an objective ground in human nature in order to refute subjectivism. If one is unaware of the theoretical context laid out in *The Human Condition*, one is bound to be absolutely puzzled as to why Arendt is so insistent (on the face of it, in total disregard of Kant's own text) that the *Critique of Judgment*, and only the *Critique of Judgment*, is of immediate relevance to the leading questions of political philosophy.

It seems to me that any careful reader of Arendt's Kant lectures will be forced to confront a great bundle of puzzles and paradoxes in trying to figure out just what she's up to in this highly unusual set of lectures. The first and most obvious puzzle is this: If Arendt's basic project is to seize upon Kant's aesthetics as a way of vindicating the notion of a public realm of appearances, which is central to her own political philosophy, why does she take so long (not until the tenth of thirteen lectures, in fact) to commence a systematic encounter with the argument of the third *Critique*? Why does she devote so much time and space in the lectures to discussing precritical texts that have little relation to Kant's mature philosophy, as well as more directly political texts that, by her own account, fail to add up to an authentic Kantian political philosophy? If her aim is to reconstruct a novel political philosophy on the basis of Kantian aesthetics, why doesn't she proceed directly to the *Critique of Judgment* itself? The answer, I would suggest, is that all the themes aired in the long prelude (comprising Lectures 1 to 10) to Arendt's account of the *Critique of Judgment* – that all these themes have not very much to do with Kant's intellectual concerns but have everything to do with Arendt's intellectual concerns. For Kant, of course, our status as rational (that is, moral) beings is the ground for human dignity. Morality, too, is the Kantian answer to the arrogance of philosophers that their quest for truth is what exclusively confers cosmic seriousness upon human purposes.

Arendt rejects this core of Kantian philosophy, and therefore she draws upon marginal texts in the Kantian *oeuvre* in order to support her own conceptions of human dignity and meaningful purpose in human life. For Arendt, human dignity presupposes our implication in a shared public adventure that yields meaningful stories, historical narratives that give point to the cares and commitments of actors on the stage of human affairs (see p. 56, on Machiavelli's *Florentine Stories* – 'the last book that is written in this spirit').[1] These stories are situated in the polis, in the political community as a shared space of narrative action. For Arendt, political philosophy as Plato defined it – namely, as flight from the opinions of the cave – necessarily involves alienation from the polis, and therefore represents a mortal threat to this vision of human dignity. Throughout her work (including these lectures), Arendt remains obsessively preoccupied with the legacy of Platonically defined philosophy, since for her the whole philosophic tradition means a debunking of the polis as a site of meaningful stories, and therewith, as the privileged basis for human dignity. (In a profound sense, the centre of the Kant lectures is Arendt's citation of Pascal, who in § 331 of the *Pensées* presents the polis as a lunatic asylum, toward which the philosopher must preserve a stance of deliberate alienation [pp. 21–2].) Kant, as I mentioned earlier, had his own response to Plato, which consisted in a modest demotion of the whole cognitive enterprise, and a colossal elevation of the cosmic significance of the morality of ordinary moral agents. Arendt, because she rejects Kant's own challenge to Plato, places a great deal more weight on the philosophical outcome of the *Critique of Judgment* than Kant himself would ever have wished to place upon it.

Arendt is clearly dead wrong when she states in Lecture 10 that Kantian political philosophy must be reconstructed from the third *Critique* because his real political philosophy remained unwritten (p. 61: 'Since Kant did not write his political philosophy, the best way to find out what he thought about this matter is to turn to his "Critique of Aesthetic Judgment"'). Kant is of course a classic exponent of the liberalism that Arendt repudiates on account of its deliberately narrow and deliberately unambitious conception of the public sphere, and correspondingly, the exalted moral primacy it gives to the inviolable private sphere. Contrary to what Arendt suggests, Kant's politics are thoroughly shaped by his moral vision. For Kant, the ground of human dignity is our capacity for morally motivated conduct within the private sphere. Politics is decisively governed by the imperative to respect this capacity for moral choice by according individuals the maximum private liberty compatible with the liberty of other individuals. It seems astounding that Arendt could read Kant's *Rechtslehre* (*Doctrine of Right*) and yet fail to see that it offers an integral political philosophy that is authentically Kantian. It seems to me incontestable that the reason why Arendt fails to see this is because the political philosophy articulated in the *Rechtslehre* is not the political philosophy that Arendt wants Kant to give her.

Plato represents one major threat to this Arendtian vision of human dignity as grounded in the particular stories that human agents enact in the shared space of appearances; another major threat is modern historicism, which threatens to subsume the particular within a universal narrative of the march of progress. This is why Arendt, in the Kant lectures, is equally obsessed with various versions of the philosophy of history, which is a major theme of Kant's political texts (a theme in his work that seems very strongly to anticipate the philosophy of history enterprise pursued by Hegel and Marx in the nineteenth century). Again, it is easy to see why the *Critique of Judgment* would be received by Arendt as a kind of epiphany, and why *this* work would have vastly more appeal for her relative to Kant's conventionally political writings. For what one gets in the *Critique of Judgment* is the doctrine that there is no science of the beautiful, that

reflective judgment means attending to the unique qualities of the particular, to the particular *qua* particular, rather than simply subsuming
particulars under some universal formula. Or as Arendt would put it,
judgment involves attending to the particular as an end in itself -- that is,
as a singular locus of meaning that isn't reducible to universal causes or
universal consequences (see p. 56). When the Polish shipworkers hoisted
Lech Walesa over the fence of the Lenin Shipyard in Gdansk, this was a
miraculous moment, quite apart from the fact that it expressed factors
that could be given a sociological explanation, or the fact that it contributed to the end of communism within the space of one decade. To *judge*
this singular deed means appreciating it as a wondrous event, reflecting
on it in such a way that the judging spectator can derive disinterested
pleasure from the reflection. Again, following Kant's idea of reflective
judgment, this involves attending to the particular as a unique happening, irreducible to universals that would situate the wondrous event
within a larger vision of the historical process. Again, to acknowledge that
Kant already *had* a political philosophy would be to acknowledge that he
was thoroughly implicated in the modern enterprise of a philosophy of
history, and for Arendt this would mean having to forfeit Kant's real
contribution as a political philosopher, which consisted in his proto-
Arendtian appreciation of the particular *qua* particular. Arendt's solution
was to insist that the latter composed Kant's 'unwritten' political philosophy (that is, his anticipation of *her* political philosophy).

At the end of Lecture 1, Arendt rightly observes that whereas the precritical Kant had conflated moral philosophy and aesthetics, the postcriti-
cal Kant distinguished sharply between them. It is certainly true that for
the mature Kant, morality is situated firmly in the province of *reason*, not
in that of taste, and that here, Kant is proceeding in deliberate opposition
to the fusion of taste and morality found in the English moral sense philosophers, such as Shaftesbury. (Here one should consult Gadamer: in
Part I of *Truth and Method*, he argues that Kant's repudiation of the moral
sense tradition had eventually fatal consequences for the history of the
human sciences; whereas the traditional view had been that acquiring
social or political knowledge required immersion in a comprehensive
civic culture, Kant's compartmentalization of knowledge, morality, and
aesthetics established the view that one could attain knowledge of society
in abstraction from moral insights, and possess moral consciousness in
abstraction from taste.) From the fact that Kant had once thought in a
different way about the relation between morality and taste, Arendt draws
the surprising conclusion that Kant's aesthetics offers more promise than

his moral philosophy of furnishing what she calls, in the Postscriptum to *Thinking,* 'a halfway plausible theory of ethics' – as if the *Critique of Judgment* could remain untouched by the compartmentalization of faculties that characterizes the critical philosophy as a whole. Presumably, what she has in mind here is that the basic concepts elaborated in §§ 39–41 of the third *Critique* – communicability, enlarged mentality, common sense, imagination, disinterestedness – promise to do better justice to the inter-subjective fabric of moral life than the narrow moral vision of Kantian practical reason: that is, his conception of the moral subject, abstracted from the larger pattern of social life, confronting imperatives of duty that have been absolutely purified of non-deontological considerations.

Clearly, Arendt is of the opinion that Kant's *Critique of Practical Reason* fails to provide a plausible account of ethics; and I can certainly see why the basic categories of the third *Critique* would seem appealing, relative to the truncated horizons of Kant's moral philosophy. But I think that what she wants to draw from the third *Critique* is misleading, for two (related) reasons. First, she doesn't fully appreciate how both Kant's account of practical reason *and* his account of aesthetic judgment are shaped by the same supreme moral ideal, that of autonomy, and that this places constraints upon how much he can allow relations of community to enter into the formation of judgments. Secondly, she doesn't fully appreciate that all her favourite concepts from the third *Critique* (common sense, enlarged mentality, and so on) are *transcendental* categories: they don't connect judgments of taste to any empirical sociability (taste, as Kant construes it, is no more dependent on social relations than practical reason is), but merely specify conditions of intersubjective validity that are presumed when an individual subject presumes to judge something beautiful by reflecting on it *without* necessarily consulting the opinions or experiences of other judging individuals. We can see this mistake, for instance, in Lecture 13, where Arendt writes: 'One judges always as a member of a community, guided by one's community sense, one's *sensus communis.* But in the last analysis, one is a member of a world community by the sheer fact of being human.' What this passage suggests is member-ship in a variety of human communities that could be schematized as a set of expanding concentric circles, of which membership in humanity as a whole forms the largest circle. But this is not at all what Kant has in mind. In the *Critique of Judgment* he is concerned with what abstract human fac-ulties render it possible for a transcendental subject to posit valid judg-ments of taste; and for this purpose the only relevant community is the community of all human beings who possess the universal faculties that allow one to apprehend and reflect on the formal properties of, say, a beautiful crystal. The third *Critique*, no less than the second *Critique*, is based on the *purification* of the *a priori* from the *a posteriori*. In the same lecture (Lecture 13), Arendt appeals to §41's affirmation of sociability as a natural property of human beings. But Kant himself goes on to say: 'This interest, indirectly attached to the beautiful by the inclination towards society, and, consequently, empirical, is, however, of no importance for us here. For that to which we have alone to look is what can have a bearing *a priori*, even though indirect, upon the judgment of taste.' The *Critique of Judgment* as a work of transcendental philosophy is concerned exclusively with the question of the possible *validity* of our judgments, and to this validity, empirical sociability contributes nothing.

Hannah Arendt, one might say, wants to do for Kant's aesthetics what John Rawls did for Kant's moral philosophy: to detranscendentalize it, and to draw from it a political philosophy. Arendt pursues her strategy of detranscendentalizing Kant's aesthetic philosophy partly by playing up the continuity between the third *Critique*'s theme of communicability and the theme of sociability as found in some of the precritical writings. Now it is indeed true that the basic intention of the third *Critique* is to defeat the claims of subjectivity, and in that sense the book is a celebration of human sociability. But Kant is very far from wanting to rest the exercise of aesthetic judgment upon a social basis, and he wants to avoid resting it upon a social basis for the very same reason that he wants to avoid resting practical reason on a social basis: namely, because he thinks that to do so, in both cases, would be to do grave damage to human autonomy. This is expressed most clearly in §32 of the *Critique of Judgment*, where Kant writes: 'Every judgment which is to show the taste of the individual, is required to be an independent judgment of the individual himself. There must be no need of groping about among other people's judgments ... To make the judgments of others the determining ground of one's own would be heteronomy.' The illustration Kant offers of this necessary autonomy of taste is that of the 'youthful poet [who] refuses to allow himself to be dissuaded from the conviction that his poem is beautiful, either by the judgment of the public or of his friends.'

Here, in fact, the analogy between Arendt and Rawls may help us to appreciate the deep underlying affinities – which Arendt doesn't fully own up to – between the structure of Kant's *moral* thinking and the structure of his philosophy of aesthetic judgment. Let us start by recalling that the Kantian political philosophy elaborated by Rawls in *A Theory of Justice* doesn't involve an actual community of rational agents getting together to deliberate about the basic institutions of a just society; rather, the original position postulated by Rawls involves an experiment of moral reflection engaged in by one representative rational agent. This individual, who imagines himself or herself subject to a veil of ignorance, tries to think about social justice *as if* one's theory of justice were the outcome of an impartial consensus (therefore such an individual exemplifies the disinterested 'enlarged mentality' that Kant conceptualizes in the third *Critique*), but the resulting theory of justice is nonetheless the product of a singular individual's process of reasoning, not the product of a social process. To express this in Habermasian terms, the process of moral reflection that yields Rawls's hypothetical social contract is monological, not dialogical. But Kant's aesthetics, too, are monological, and *for the same reason.* Just as Kant would regard it as heteronomous to submit practical reason to the verdict of an actual dialogical community, so Kant would regard it as equally heteronomous to have questions of taste decided by dialogue within a society. The judgments that an individual may pronounce concerning the aesthetic qualities of a poem or sculpture may be blind or wrong-headed, but at least they will be genuine attempts to exercise taste, as opposed to a heteronomous forfeiture of judgment where one merely defers to the opinions of one's friends or neighbours.

This, I think, raises difficult questions about whether Kant's aesthetics offers a suitable model for thinking about *political* judgment, where one certainly does require *actual* dialogue between *real* (rather than hypothetical) interlocutors in communities shaped by a large range of 'heteronomous' factors (such as existing traditions, shared vocabulary, forms of rhetoric specific to those communities, and so on). But this is a set of questions that Arendt didn't pursue; her exclusive concern in the Kant lectures was to begin thinking about 'judging' as a distinct department of the life of the mind that might help to redeem the idea of human dignity, which she perceived as imperilled in ways discussed earlier.

A reader who comes to the *Lectures on Kant's Political Philosophy* without having read any of Arendt's other books, and who reads the book hoping to find out what Kant's political philosophy is about, is likely to end up quite puzzled and confused. If one reads it to get an exposition of the *Critique of Judgment*, one will probably come away with a rather misleading picture of Kant's aesthetics. But if one reads the book – as one should – as a crucial development of Arendt's own philosophical project, as an exploration of a set of political and intellectual preoccupations that really owe more to Jaspers than to Kant,[2] then the book turns out to be a richly illuminating expression of Arendtian thought. It is in fact Arendt's attempt to address the intellectual concerns that are at the very *centre* of her thought-world, and it expresses her determination to secure human dignity against a dual assault: the ancient Platonic disdain for the opinions of the cave, and the modern historicist tendency to reduce the particular stories enacted by human agents to a universal drama of historical progress.[3] One might say that what typically characterizes major thinkers is that everything they read gets shaped and appropriated by their own dominant driving concerns; and in precisely this sense, the vigour with which Kant's texts get appropriated by Arendt and reshaped according to her own preoccupations shows her to be a major thinker in her own right.

At the beginning of this paper I suggested that the central thrust of Arendt's political philosophy was a root-and-branch critique of political individualism, and correspondingly, a robust defence of the joys of collective action. But of course, Arendt herself did not devote her life to the life of action; her vocation was that of a solitary thinker and observer: someone whose purpose in life was to watch what was going on and to reflect on what it meant. I assume that what she was trying to do in the Kant lectures was to give some account of her own experience as a detached spectator rather than as an involved actor. This may help explain why it was specifically *Kant's* philosophy of judgment to which she appealed in trying to conceptualize this experience, rather than other possible sources of a theory of judgment: Aristotle's doctrine of *phronesis*, Burke's discussion of prudence, various other eighteenth-century accounts of taste, and so on. Kant, more than any of these other theoretical sources, is specifically concerned with how one addresses oneself to an ideal community of fellow judges – without forfeiting or qualifying one's own ultimate responsibility for the exercise of judgment. This issue of Kant's individualism connects up with the problems associated with Arendt's proposal to translate Kant's *allgemein* as 'general' rather than 'universal': for Kant's aesthetics no less than for his moral philosophy, the appeal to a universal community is intended to supply a foundation for the independence of the individual judging subject in his or her autonomy. I don't think Arendt appreciated how Kant's *universalism* goes hand in hand with his *individualism*; and her attempt to detranscendentalize Kant (therefore transposing his 'universal' community of judgment into a merely 'general' community of judgment) tends to muddle this issue.

This is the problem: how to transcend subjectivism, while emphasizing that individuals must take responsibility for their judgments without deferring to the authority of groups or communities. Hence, while

Arendt was resolutely anti-individualistic in her political philosophy (and therefore she ought to have been much more critical of Kant's political philosophy than she actually was in her Kant lectures), she was also resolutely anticommunitarian in her own praxis as a theoretical spectator and critic; and this, I surmise, was what gave the third *Critique* its appeal for her. Throughout her career as a theorist, she steadfastly opposed any group-based political ideologies – indeed, she opposed ideologies of any description, whether ideologies of the Left or ideologies of the Right or (one might say) ideologies of the Centre. And this, too, is crucial to Arendt's concern with conceptualizing the power of human judgment, for this is what judgment means: to size up the unique particular that stands before one, rather than trying to subsume it under some universal scheme of interpretation or pregiven set of categories. As someone who reflects on politics rather than practises it, the task of the observer of human affairs is to pass judgment on the discrete particulars that present themselves on the public stage without bowing to the demands of group ideologies or deferring to the verdict passed by others in society. And again, this is what Arendt sought ceaselessly to do throughout her career as a spectator of the human drama: to pass judgment in her own name, as someone who thought for herself, without submitting to the pressure of conformity exercised by any group or collectivity. Answering to the authentic demands of the power of judgment requires no less: namely, preserving one's undiminished independence of judgment.

In my own work on the idea of judgment in the early 1980s, I felt it necessary to turn to sources other than Kant, because I was convinced by my reading of Wittgenstein, Gadamer, Polanyi, and other twentieth-century philosophers that reflective judgment is not restricted to the Kantian domain of judgments of taste (nor is it restricted, as Arendt would have it, to the historian's task of retrospectively conferring meaning on what actors do). Rather, it pervades the whole fabric of human experience, including the efforts by engaged political actors to deliberate in common and to reach decisions collectively. But the fact that I felt required to look beyond Kant's third *Critique* in trying to conceptualize the power of judgment in its full breadth (what Gadamer calls 'the universal scope of hermeneutics') doesn't mean that I am insensitive to why Arendt was drawn to the third *Critique*, and why it seemed to her to articulate better than any other work her own experience as an independent observer of human affairs.

What was of concern to Arendt in the last phase of her work was what one might call the 'existential stance' of the theorist as a detached critical

observer, as opposed to the existential stance of the actors who enact
'words and deeds' in the practical realm. In order to be a theorist who
reflects critically on the 'doings' of an engaged citizenry, one really needs
to stand on one's own and to judge things for oneself (albeit in the context of a reflective dialogue with others who are trying to do the same
thing); whereas in the realm of political practice, one needs to join with
others in taking initiatives and deliberating about a suitable joint course
of action. Hence the attraction, for Arendt, of Kant's model of the person
of taste who passes judgment on what the artistic genius creates (see p.
62: the subordination of genius to taste = the subordination of the actor
to the spectator). Far from intending to criticize her for wanting to
appropriate Kant in this way, I think it should be pretty obvious that I
have great sympathy for Arendt's image of the theorist as judging critic.
Like her, I want to be able to engage in critical reflection on the world of
politics without feeling obliged to join some club of like-minded theorists, whether a club of Marxists or libertarians, communitarians or liberals, feminists or Straussians, or any other club for that matter – not even a
club of 'Arendtians'! (This is what Kant, in § 40 of the *Critique of Judgment*,
called *Selbstdenken*: see pp. 25, 32, 43.)[4] Rather, my criticism of her Kant
lectures is that *as an account of the power of judgment*, her exclusive attachment to Kant is partial and one-sided, for she failed to appreciate that the
capacity for making reasonable judgments, without reliance upon already
available rules or algorithms, and aiming at intersubjective validity, is not
restricted to one side (the spectator's side) of Arendt's distinction
between the doers who act and the critic who watches and reflects. The
retrospective observer holds no monopoly here; again, reflective judgment is a universal feature of human experience.

Notes

1: Liberalism in the Cross-Hairs of Theory

1 *Hans-Georg Gadamer on Education, Poetry, and History,* ed. Dieter Misgeld and Graeme Nicholson (Albany: State University of New York Press, 1992), 145

2 Charles Taylor, *Philosophical Papers,* vol. 2, *Philosophy and the Human Sciences* (Cambridge: Cambridge University Press, 1985); Michael Walzer, *Spheres of Justice* (New York: Basic Books, 1983); Alasdair MacIntyre, *After Virtue* (Notre Dame, IN: University of Notre Dame Press, 1981); Alasdair MacIntyre, *Whose Justice? Which Rationality?* (Notre Dame, IN: University of Notre Dame Press, 1988); Michael J. Sandel, *Liberalism and the Limits of Justice* (Cambridge: Cambridge University Press, 1982); Robert N. Bellah, Richard Madsen, William M. Sullivan, Ann Swidler, and Steven M. Tipton, *Habits of the Heart: Individualism and Commitment in American Life* (Berkeley: University of California Press, 1985); Christopher Lasch, *The Culture of Narcissism* (New York: W.W. Norton, 1979)

3 John Rawls, *A Theory of Justice* (Oxford: Oxford University Press, 1971); John Rawls, *Political Liberalism* (New York: Columbia University Press, 1993); Ronald Dworkin, *Taking Rights Seriously* (London: Duckworth, 1977); Ronald Dworkin, *A Matter of Principle* (Cambridge: Harvard University Press, 1985); Bruce A. Ackerman, *Social Justice in the Liberal State* (New Haven: Yale University Press, 1980); Charles Larmore, *Patterns of Moral Complexity* (Cambridge: Cambridge University Press, 1987); Will Kymlicka, *Liberalism, Community, and Culture* (Oxford: Clarendon Press, 1989)

4 Friedrich A. Hayek, *The Constitution of Liberty* (Chicago: University of Chicago Press, 1960); Robert Nozick, *Anarchy, State, and Utopia* (New York: Basic Books, 1974); Michael Oakeshott, *On Human Conduct* (Oxford: Clarendon Press, 1975)

5 It must be noted that not all contemporary liberals are 'neutralist' liberals; indeed, the axiom of 'neutralism' has been strongly contested by a group of authors who have come to be called 'perfectionist' liberals. Among the important works in this category, see Joseph Raz, *The Morality of Freedom* (Oxford: Clarendon Press, 1986); Stephen Macedo, *Liberal Virtues: Citizenship, Virtue, and Community in Liberal Constitutionalism* (Oxford: Clarendon Press, 1990); William A. Galston, *Liberal Purposes: Goods, Virtues, and Diversity in the Liberal State* (Cambridge: Cambridge University Press, 1991); Amy Gutmann, *Democratic Education* (Princeton, NJ: Princeton University Press, 1987). Needless to say, I have much greater sympathy for the antineutralist version of liberalism common to these works, although they still fall short of the horizon of critical reflection that I am demanding. It seems fair to say that perfectionist liberalism is situated somewhere midway between the liberal neutralism that is the primary focus of my critique, and the more ambitious vision of social criticism that is being defended in this essay. (Cf. Galston, *Liberal Purposes*, 43–4.)

6 Ronald Beiner, *What's the Matter with Liberalism?* (Berkeley: University of California Press, 1992), 8 n. 4

7 Alasdair MacIntyre, 'The Privatization of Good: An Inaugural Lecture,' *Review of Politics* 52, no. 3 (Summer 1990): 344–61

8 I owe this formulation to Stephen Newman.

9 An extreme illustration of this point is the fact that the prime agent of the Islamic persecution of Salman Rushdie is (at least officially) not the Iranian state, but an institution within 'civil society,' namely the 15 Khordad Foundation, which put up the bounty for Rushdie's execution. For Mill's views, see, for instance, John Stuart Mill, *On Liberty*, ed. David Spitz (New York: W.W. Norton, 1975), 15, where he writes that what concerns him is the 'disposition of mankind, whether as rulers *or as fellow-citizens*, to impose their own opinions and inclinations as a rule of conduct on others' (my italics). The tendency that worries Mill is advanced, he says, both by legislation and 'by the force of opinion.'

10 The 'fact of pluralism' is John Rawls's phrase: see Rawls, 'The Priority of Right and Ideas of the Good,' *Philosophy and Public Affairs* 17, no. 4 (Fall 1988): 259, 275.

11 Isaiah Berlin, *Four Essays on Liberty* (London: Oxford University Press, 1969), 165

12 Ibid., 153 n

13 It is not uncommon for liberals to argue that the philosophical rationale for the market economy is a moral conception, namely, a certain kind of egalitarianism that sees market society as having emancipated individuals from the hierarchical ascriptive roles and relationships characteristic of a preliberal,

premodern social order. One such argument is offered in William James Booth, *Households: On the Moral Architecture of the Economy* (Ithaca: Cornell University Press, 1993), pt. 2. This is consistent with my argument above in regard to the logical priority of liberalism as a moral vision to capitalism as a vision of the economy.

14 This is the basic structure of argument in Rawls, *Political Liberalism*; Larmore, *Patterns of Moral Complexity*; and Charles Larmore, 'Political Liberalism,' *Political Theory* 18, no. 3 (August 1990): 339–60. However, Rawls insists that his 'overlapping consensus' theory is not a *modus vivendi* conception, and to this extent would want to distance himself somewhat from Larmore's version of liberalism.

15 Richard Rorty, *Contingency, Irony, and Solidarity* (Cambridge: Cambridge University Press, 1989); Richard Rorty, 'The Priority of Democracy to Philosophy' in Rorty, *Philosophical Papers*, vol. 1, *Objectivity, Relativism, and Truth* (Cambridge: Cambridge University Press, 1991), 175–96. See the criticisms of Rorty's political philosophy elaborated in Chapter 8 of this volume.

16 George Grant, *Lament for a Nation: The Defeat of Canadian Nationalism* (Toronto: McClelland and Stewart, 1965). Grant's book was a major theoretical manifesto for Canadian nationalism in the 1960s. Although Grant himself conceived his argument on behalf of nationalism as an expression of his commitment to conservatism, or more strictly Anglo-Canadian Toryism, the book also had a great impact upon Canadian nationalists on the Left, who of course had their own reasons for hostility to the imperialistic thrust of Americanism.

17 Consider, here, Leszek Kolakowski's acute remarks concerning the looming extinction of the Celtic languages: *Modernity on Endless Trial* (Chicago: University of Chicago Press, 1990), 23. See also my commentary on Kolakowski in Chapter 17 of this volume, where I discuss the complexities of judgment concerning modernity and antimodernity.

18 'Is Nothing Sacred?' in Salman Rushdie, *Imaginary Homelands* (New York: Penguin, 1991), 415

19 Cf. ibid., 261 (Rushdie quoting Italo Calvino): 'Nobody these days holds the written word in such high esteem as police states do.'

20 As concerns sexual life: in an unpublished essay, 'Borrowed Truths: Sexuality, Authenticity, and Modernity,' Leslie Green argues that it is to the credit of liberal society that it takes sex 'off the high-tension wires,' and turns decisions about sexual life into matters of taste and mere preference, stripping them of any 'cosmic' meaning. Here too, it may be replied, one pays a price for this banalization of sexuality.

21 Macedo, *Liberal Virtues*, 278

22 John Gray, *Liberalism* (Minneapolis: University of Minnesota Press, 1986), 82

23 Rorty, *Objectivity, Relativism, and Truth*, 190

24 Here I can actually cite the authority of John Stuart Mill, who *agrees* that this is the proper function of theory: 'The first question in respect to any political institutions is, how far they tend to foster in the members of the community the various desirable qualities, moral and intellectual.' *Considerations on Representative Government*, chap. 2.

25 My source for biographical information concerning the painting is Peter Webb, *Portrait of David Hockney* (New York: E.P. Dutton, 1988), 109–10. For reproductions of the painting and preliminary studies, see plates 87–90 and 112. The inclusion in the painting of one of Hockney's works (a print from his 'A Rake's Progress' series) strikes me as a self-parody. Hockney seems to be saying: these people are in real trouble, spiritually speaking, if a *Hockney* is all that they have available to them to furnish their world.

26 It is a central aspect of my argument in this essay that the decisive measure of one's liberalism is the extent of one's philosophical commitment to modernity. This will have what many will see as a paradoxical consequence (but one that I willingly embrace) – namely, that authors such as Charles Taylor and Jürgen Habermas who offer strong defences of modernity in their recent work are to that extent to be categorized as liberals, in contrast with, say, Hannah Arendt and Alasdair MacIntyre, who throughout their work are consistent critics of modernity.

27 For a cinematic version of the same depiction of contemporary existence, see Todd Haynes's film, *Safe*.

28 For notable examples of works representing this tendency, see Rawls, *Political Liberalism*; Ronald Dworkin, *Law's Empire* (Cambridge, MA: Belknap Press, 1986), chap. 6; Ronald Dworkin, 'Liberal Community,' *California Law Review* 77, no. 3 (May 1989): 479–504; Rorty, *Contingency, Irony, and Solidarity*; Rorty, 'The Priority of Democracy to Philosophy.'

29 The communitarian critique of liberalism in its least penetrating version seems to issue in the suggestion that the failings of liberalism can be remedied by a heightened collectivist consciousness; for me, the demand for a heightened collectivist consciousness does not pose a sufficiently radical challenge to liberalism. Hannah Arendt once remarked that 'just as socialism is no remedy for capitalism, capitalism cannot be a remedy or an alternative for socialism' (*Crises of the Republic* [New York: Harcourt Brace Jovanovich, 1972], 220), and I am tempted to say that the same applies to the quarrel between liberals and communitarians.

30 Beiner, *What's the Matter with Liberalism?*, 15. In Chapters 1 and 7 of that book, I try to make the case that it is not the chief purpose of theorists to offer immediate guidance on questions of policy. Rather, the aim of theory at its best is to

offer grand visions of moral and political order in the light of which we can engage in ambitiously critical self-reflection about the character of our society. It is *not* the purpose of this essay to argue that the standard by which contemporary political philosophies should be judged is the ambitiousness with which they presume to legislate political practice from the heights of philosophical insight; the purpose, rather, is to argue that they should be judged according to their ambitiousness in enlarging the space of critical reflection (which is certainly not the same thing as presuming to direct political practice). Therefore I cannot agree with John Dunn that 'The purpose of political theory is to diagnose practical predicaments and to show us how best to confront them': *Interpreting Political Responsibility* (Princeton, NJ: Princeton University Press, 1990), 193. I do agree with him, however, that political philosophy as it is dominantly practised today reflects 'its radical domestication, its complete subordination to the dynamics of an existing ideological field' (ibid., 195).

31 To cite one example: In 'Do We Have a Right to Pornography?' (in *A Matter of Principle*, 335–72), Ronald Dworkin severely criticizes Bernard Williams's philosophical premises, yet he has no desire at all to contest the validity of the practical recommendations Williams seeks to draw from these premises.

32 An instructive case is Judith Shklar's 'liberalism of fear' (see, for instance, her article of that title in *Liberalism and the Moral Life*, ed. Nancy L. Rosenblum [Cambridge: Harvard University Press, 1989], 21–38), since Shklar's liberalism, even though it is richer and more interesting than the neo-Kantian liberalisms that have been so influential, shares the decisive flaw common to all contemporary liberalisms. For Shklar, a society that doesn't torture, maim, oppress, degrade, or humiliate its members, or particular groups within it, meets the only relevant standard of political desirability. It is true that even this minimalist standard offers some scope for criticizing existing liberal regimes; yet it is very easy to think of societies that meet this standard and nonetheless embody in their social order a pretty crummy way of life. Shklar's conception of what it is to do political theory discourages her from passing judgment on these 'cultural' concerns. Exactly the same considerations apply to Isaiah Berlin.

7: Liberalism, Pluralism, and Religion

1 John Rawls, *Political Liberalism* (New York: Columbia University Press, 1993), 243

2 Ibid., 243 n. 32

3 As Peter Berkowitz argues in a forthcoming book (*Virtue and the Making of Modern Liberalism*, to be published by the Princeton University Press), the

neutralist conception of liberalism that recommended itself so powerfully to many important defenders of liberalism in the 1970s and 1980s was not simply a perverse invention of these thinkers (though it did help to establish a quite one-sided rendering of the liberal idea). Rather, there is something in the very logic of liberalism that draws it in the direction of a neutralist self-understanding. Berkowitz argues forcefully, as does Macedo, that this must be resisted.

4 William A. Galston, 'Two Concepts of Liberalism,' *Ethics* 105 (April 1995): 517

8: Richard Rorty's Liberalism

1 Henry S. Kariel, 'Nietzsche's Preface to Constitutionalism,' *Journal of Politics* 25, no. 2 (May 1963): 211–25. For a more recent attempt to 'postmodernize' liberalism, turning both Nietzsche and Foucault into the sources of an improved liberal pluralism, see William E. Connolly, 'Identity and Difference in Liberalism' in *Liberalism and the Good*, ed. R. Bruce Douglass, Gerald M. Mara, and Henry S. Richardson (New York: Routledge, 1990), 59–85.

2 For good examples of some standard lines of critique, see the chapters by Tom Sorell, Bernard Williams, and Charles Taylor in *Reading Rorty*, ed. Alan R. Malachowski (Oxford: Basil Blackwell, 1990), 11–25, 26–37, and 257–75 respectively. It is a matter of some irritation in Rorty that even one of his ostensible allies in the war against 'representationalism,' namely Hilary Putnam, submits Rorty to a realist critique. See *ORT*, 24, and Putnam, *Reason, Truth, and History* (Cambridge: Cambridge University Press, 1981), 216. This would seem to indicate that Rorty's antirealist rhetoric carries him rather farther than he realizes, or farther than he is prepared to acknowledge.

3 Rorty himself is emphatic in denying that he is a relativist: *ORT*, 23–30, 38–9, 42–3, 49–51, 59, 66–7, 89, 202. My own view is that the problem of Rorty's 'relativism' lies more in his use of a certain provocative rhetoric than in the substance of his views; however, he is sometimes willing to press this rhetoric far enough (e.g., *ORT*, 176–7, 187–8, 199–200, 207–8; *EOH*, 74–7, 168) that he trips himself up in needlessly counterproductive ways.

4 Late Rorty (as opposed to early Rorty) thinks that he can do without a substantive account of truth, so he drops his pragmatist truth-theory (*ORT*, 150 n 61), as he had been urged to do by Donald Davidson (*Reading Rorty*, 136–8); but it is doubtful whether Rorty can avoid letting his pragmatist interpretation of truth sneak back in.

5 'The true' = 'the expedient,' according to a formula cited favourably by Rorty: *ORT*, 127. Cf. *EOH*, 2.

6 A typical Rortyan formulation is 'success or failure' in 'solving life's problems' (*ORT*, 66, 68).

7 So, for instance, in hermeneutics we have the seemingly self-evident view that interpretations are addressed to a text, whereas in deconstructionism we have the paradoxical view that interpretation is so all-pervasive that there is no separate 'text' that constitutes a standard for weighing the plausibility of interpretations. Here, as one would expect, Rorty tends to side with the deconstructionists against the hermeneuticists: *ORT*, 88–9; *EOH*, 59 n 21, 115–16 ('regress of interpretation,' 'the endlessness of interpretation'), 125 ('endless sequence of recontextualizations'). The 'aboutness' relation, whether for texts or for anything else, is precisely what Rorty has to find some way of circumventing: see *ORT*, 97–8; *EOH*, 38.

8 If what hangs upon the distinction is the idea that 'we have to start from where we are,' as he puts it in *ORT*, 29, well, it is hard to see that *anyone* has ever thought otherwise, *including Plato.*

9 Cf. *EOH*, 110, 113. Oddly enough, some of the points I make against Rorty in this essay are quite similar to points Rorty himself makes against Derrida in Part 2 of *EOH.*

10 See, for instance, *ORT*, 46–62, 109–10, 116.

11 Rorty vigorously resists this opposing strategy in *ORT*, 162–3.

12 Rorty is aware that there is an army of critics lying in wait longing to catch him in a 'self-referential paradox' (*ORT*, 192), and that he has to keep hopping if he is to avoid getting caught in one (Cf. *EOH*, 94).

13 Cf. *EOH*, 154, 193–8

14 Tom Sorell, 'The World from Its Own Point of View' in *Reading Rorty*, 22

15 For a very insightful exploration of such tensions in Rorty's political thought, see Nancy Fraser, 'Solidarity or Singularity?' in *Reading Rorty*, 303–21.

16 Rorty, *Contingency, Irony, and Solidarity* (Cambridge: Cambridge University Press, 1989), xv, 74, 146. For a good summary of Shklar's liberalism, see Judith N. Shklar, 'The Liberalism of Fear' in *Liberalism and the Moral Life*, ed. Nancy L. Rosenblum (Cambridge: Harvard University Press, 1989), 21–38.

17 *The New Republic*, 4 April 1988, 28–33

18 I should emphasize that I regard complaints from those on the left about Rorty's 'conservatism' as entirely unfair, for as his political writings in response to those complaints have made amply clear, his basic contentment with bourgeois liberalism as a way of life has not blunted his sense of the urgent need for egalitarian reforms. Politically, he seems strongly committed to a left-liberal or social-democratic agenda for pursuing such reforms. Satisfaction with the general shape of a social order does not preclude being sharply critical of the specific practices of that social order's ruling class. The 'liberal complacency' at issue here refers to a spiritual-philosophical stance toward modern life, not to a full endorsement of the status quo. (What I mean by 'a spiritual-philosophical

stance' toward modernity comes out clearly enough in Rorty's response to MacIntyre in *EOH*, 158–61.) In 'For a More Banal Politics,' *Harper's Magazine*, May 1992, 16–21, Rorty classifies himself as a leftist intellectual.

19 But note Rorty's disclaimer in *EOH*, 1–2.

20 J.G.A. Pocock, 'The Ideal of Citizenship Since Classical Times,' *Queen's Quarterly* 99, no. 1 (Spring 1992): 51

21 Ibid.

22 For a comprehensive elaboration of this view of the self, see 'Freud and Moral Reflection,' *EOH*, 143–63 – perhaps the most important piece in these two volumes of philosophical papers. While Rorty claims that maturity of the self consists 'in an ability to seek out new redescriptions,' he offers no hint as to how the never-ending process of revising vocabularies will help to produce, as he also claims, 'a genuinely stable character in an unstable time' (ibid., 152–3).

23 Thomas L. Pangle, *The Ennobling of Democracy: The Challenge of the Postmodern Age* (Baltimore: Johns Hopkins University Press, 1992), 58

24 As discussed above, Rorty wishes to keep sharply distinct the rules of public justice relevant to the citizen and the intellectual's unruly quest for self-perfection, which is to be rigorously privatized. But since postmodernism excels at subverting boundaries, why shouldn't some of the aestheticism proper to the cultural sphere seep over the boundary into the political sphere? For Rorty's answer to this worry, see *ORT*, 193–4.

25 In *ORT*, 44, Rorty tries to reorient the purpose of intellectual activity from 'getting it right' to 'making it new.' But if novelty is the supreme standard, enemies of liberalism, provided that their versions of illiberalism are sufficiently novel, would count as exemplars of Rorty's new intellectual culture.

26 See *EOH*, 160.

27 Generally speaking, Rorty tends to portray postmodernism as a fairly innocuous cultural tendency – a badge that a political liberal can without much hesitation pin to his or her lapel. Within Rorty's theoretical landscape, pragmatism and postmodernism approach synonymity; thus, he refers to Dewey as 'a postmodernist before his time' (*ORT*, 201). Yet it is interesting that when he comes face to face with a real postmodernist – namely, in his debate with Lyotard (*ORT*, 211–22) – Rorty suddenly begins to sound surprisingly like Habermas, emphasizing universal consensus, and trading in his proudly advertised ethnocentrism for cosmopolitanism. This might suggest that Rorty phrases his liberalism in terms borrowed from an illiberal quarter, with an eye to rhetorical impact.

28 For a similar analysis, see Charles G. Guignon and David R. Hiley's critique of Rorty in *Reading Rorty*, 355–61.

29 Stephen Macedo, *Liberal Virtues: Citizenship, Virtue, and Community in Liberal Constitutionalism* (Oxford: Claredon Press, 1990), 278

30 To bring out the contrast between the older self-developmental liberalism and modern, lowest-common-denominator liberalism, one might compare T.H. Green's statement (*Lectures on the Principles of Political Obligation* [London: Longmans, Green, 1941], 177–8) that 'the better organisation of the state means freer scope to the individual (not necessarily to do as he likes, e.g. in the buying and selling of alcohol, but in such development of activity as is good on the whole)' with Isaiah Berlin's statement that liberals 'wish the frontiers between individuals or groups of men to be drawn solely with a view to preventing collisions between human purposes, all of which must be considered to be equally ultimate, uncriticizable ends in themselves' (*Four Essays on Liberty* [London: Oxford University Press, 1969], 153 n).

31 For an excellent statement of how little philosophers have to contribute, politically speaking, see *EOH*, 24–6. See also *EOH*, 120, 133–7, 190–2, as well as Rorty's marvellous essay, 'Thugs and Theorists,' *Political Theory* 15, no. 4 (November 1987): 564–80. For a more recent challenge to the self-inflation of intellectuals, see Rorty, 'The End of Leninism and History as Comic Frame' in *History and the Idea of Progress*, ed. Arthur M. Melzer, Jerry Weinberger, and M. Richard Zinman (Ithaca: Cornell University Press, 1995), 211–26.

32 In *Contingency, Irony, and Solidarity* (141–68), Rorty offers a chapter on Nabokov (a writer who supposedly prides himself on his aestheticism) that is actually a critique of aestheticism. His argument is that Nabokov cannot be a consistent aesthete because his art serves moral purposes that are inseparable from the artistic effect he is seeking to achieve with his novels. Rorty also argues, contrary to what most philosophers have assumed, that what the novelist does serves a more public (social and political) function than what the philosopher does (which is more geared to self-creation or self-perfection). Therefore, it is easier for the philosopher to be a pure aesthete, because what he or she does is more private than what novelists do. This argument is continued in a lively essay on 'Heidegger, Kundera, and Dickens' in *EOH*, 66–82.

33 See *What's the Matter with Liberalism?* (Berkeley: University of California Press, 1992)

9: Foucault's Hyper-Liberalism

1 See, for instance, Michel Foucault, 'History of Systems of Thought, 1979,' *Philosophy and Social Criticism* 8, no. 3 (Fall 1981): 353–9. For a very thorough account of Foucault's complex stance toward liberalism in his lectures of the late 1970s, see Colin Gordon, 'Governmental Rationality: An Introduction' in

The Foucault Effect: Studies in Governmentality, ed. Graham Burchell, Colin Gordon, and Peter Miller (Chicago: University of Chicago Press, 1991), 1–51, esp. 1–8 and 41–8.

2 Colin Gordon, in his introduction to *The Foucault Effect*, 6, in fact sees something deliberately Weberian in Foucault's 'serene and ... exemplary abstention from value judgments.' Gordon is referring specifically to Foucault's lectures on governmentality of 1978 and 1979; but he concedes that elsewhere in his work, 'Foucault's Nietzschean affiliations' often lead readers to hear an 'implicit pejorative sarcasm.'

3 Michel Foucault, *Discipline and Punish: The Birth of the Prison*, trans. Alan Sheridan (New York: Vintage Books, 1979), 292. See his discussion of the Fourierists, 288–92.

4 Ibid., 140–1, 146, 169. See also 187, 216, 217.

5 See, especially, ibid., 293–308 (chapter on 'The Carceral').

6 For a good example of this mode of analysis, see Michel Foucault, *The History of Sexuality*, vol. 1, *An Introduction*, trans. Robert Hurley (New York: Vintage Books, 1980), 40–1.

7 For a fairly clear statement of Foucault's antipathy toward the modern state, see Michel Foucault, 'Omnes et Singulatim: Towards a Criticism of "Political Reason"' in *The Tanner Lectures on Human Values*, vol. 2, (Salt Lake City: University of Utah Press, 1981), 235–9, 242–54. As Foucault declares at the very conclusion of his second Tanner Lecture, his study of govermentality is motivated by a concern for liberation from political rationality (that is, rationality exercised on behalf of the power of the state), and therefore his aim is to attack political rationality at its very roots.

8 Foucault himself once offered the following encapsulation of this aspect of his politics: 'my position leads not to apathy but to a hyper- and pessimistic activism' (*The Foucault Reader*, ed. Paul Rabinow [New York: Pantheon Books, 1984], 343). What is so tantalizing about this formulation is the implied distinction, which is left unspecified, between 'activism' and '*hyper*-activism.' Why doesn't activism that isn't so qualified suffice, and what constitutes its character as 'hyper'? I believe that it was questions of this sort that prompted Michael Walzer to relegate Foucault's politics to the category of 'infantile leftism' ('The Politics of Michel Foucualt' in *Foucault: A Critical Reader*, ed. David Couzens Hoy [Oxford: Basil Blackwell, 1986], 51).

9 To be sure, this isn't a conception of contemporary society that is unique to Foucault. Compare, for instance, Theodor W. Adorno, *Prisms*, trans. Samuel Weber and Shierry Weber (Cambridge: MIT Press, 1981), 34: 'the open-air prison which the world is becoming.'

10 Cf. Lawrence Stone, in *Critical Essays on Michel Foucault*, ed. Peter Burke

(Aldershot, UK: Scolar Press, 1992), 67: 'Since man is a social animal, and since all of social life involves some form of influence, molding, direction, or compulsion, the reduction of all social relationships to issues of power renders it almost impossible to make the fine intellectual, moral, and material distinctions necessary for any serious evaluation of change in history.'

11 Michel Foucault, *Politics, Philosophy, Culture: Interviews and Other Writings, 1977–1984*, ed. Lawrence D. Kritzman (New York: Routledge, 1988), 271–85

12 Ibid., 201

13 I think it is only fair to acknowledge that many feminists have argued in a similar direction for various reasons. The point that concerns me here is what I take to be Foucault's underlying motive in pursuing this line – namely, that all sexual activities, *qua* sexual activities, are in themselves legitimate forms of self-expression, and therefore deserve to be absolutely unregulated (and beyond moral approbation or disapprobation). If this is indeed what is driving Foucault to deny that rape is a *sexual* crime, then what is entailed is a more permissive attitude toward, for instance, practices of sexual bondage than would be acceptable to, one hopes, most feminists.

14 See Foucault, *Politics, Philosophy, Culture*, 200.

15 Ibid., 205

16 *The History of Sexuality*, vol. 1, 131

17 Foucault, *Politics, Philosophy, Culture*, 211–24

18 Ibid., 14–15. Cf. P.N. Furbank, 'Unhappy Man,' *London Review of Books*, 22 July 1993, 13: 'For happiness (only possible if you posit a "true self") the substitute in Foucault's system is pleasure.'

19 Foucault, *Politics, Philosophy, Culture*, 11. Cf. Michel Foucault, *Power/Knowledge: Selected Interviews and Other Writings, 1972–1977*, ed. Colin Gordon (New York: Pantheon Books, 1980), 213: The history of sexuality begins 'from the day when it was said to man, "You shall not merely make yourself pleasure with your sex, you will make yourself truth."'

20 Cf. Charles Taylor, 'Comments and Replies,' *Inquiry* 34, no. 2 (June 1991): 238–9

21 Foucault, *Politics, Philosophy, Culture*, 245–6

22 I myself think Foucault is wrong about this. In someone like Marcus Aurelius, morality is much *more* closely bound up with cosmological and theological views than it is in, say, Aristotle's *Nicomachean Ethics*. Stoic morality *is* metaphysical. But I obviously don't have the space to pursue these issues in this essay. Cf. Beiner, *What's the Matter with Liberalism?* (Berkeley: University of California Press, 1992), 54–5

23 Foucault, *Politics, Philosophy, Culture*, 247

24 Ibid., 253

25 Ibid., 253–4
26 Ibid., 49
27 Ibid., 50
28 Ibid. On Foucault's urging Hayek and Von Mises upon his students, see James Miller, *The Passion of Michel Foucault* (New York: Anchor Books, 1993), 310. See also note 1 above.
29 See Foucault, *Politics, Philosophy, Culture*, 12: 'I think that the kind of pleasure I would consider as *the* real pleasure would be so deep, so intense, so overwhelming that I couldn't survive it ... There is also the fact that some drugs are really important for me because they are the mediation to those incredibly intense joys that I am looking for ... A pleasure must be something incredibly intense.' Although he doesn't refer to it in this context, Foucault's fascination with S/M is clearly relevant here. One might say that Foucault's spiritual universe is that of Liliana Cavani's *The Night Porter* or Roman Polanski's *Bitter Moon* – that is to say, a world of erotic extremity achieved through an equilibrium of sexual terror. Accordingly, I would suggest that the reader of Foucault for whom the word 'nihilism' never comes to mind is perhaps missing something. For similar intimations of the darker side of Foucault's vision, see Vincent Descombes, 'Je m'en Foucault,' *London Review of Books*, 5 March 1987, 20–1, and the references to Foucault in the following texts by Charles Taylor: *The Malaise of Modernity* (Concord, ON: Anansi, 1991), 65–9, and *Philosophy in an Age of Pluralism*, ed. James Tully (Cambridge: Cambridge University Press, 1994), 232–3.
30 Foucault, *Politics, Philosophy, Culture*, 15; Michel Foucault, *The History of Sexuality*, vol. 2, *The Use of Pleasure*, trans. Robert Hurley (New York: Pantheon Books, 1985), 90–1
31 No less paradoxical in the thought of late Foucault is the appeal, in some of his last texts, to Kant and to the Kantian idea of Enlightenment (Foucault, *Politics, Philosophy, Culture*, 86–95; Rabinow, ed., *The Foucault Reader*, 32–50); stranger still is his attempt to align Kant with the modernist ideal of the dandy as depicted by Baudelaire (*The Foucault Reader*, 39–42). Admittedly, one isn't quite sure what to make of Foucault's claims, since he himself, in *Power/ Knowledge*, characterizes his whole enterprise as a set of 'fictions' (193), a 'game' (209), a 'fabrication' (212). All one can say is that anyone who can present the Stoics as exemplifying an art of aesthetic self-creation geared to the intensification of pleasure is equally capable of construing Kant as a progenitor of Baudelairean dandyism.
32 Foucault, *Use of Pleasure*, 89–93; Michel Foucault, *The History of Sexuality*, vol. 3, *The Care of the Self*, trans. Robert Hurley (New York: Pantheon Books, 1986), 44
33 Foucault, *Care of the Self*, 41, 43

34 Ibid., 40–41
35 Foucault, *Use of Pleasure*, 10–12. Cf. Rabinow, ed., *The Foucault Reader*, 362, 370
36 Foucault, *Care of the Self*, 95
37 Rabinow, ed., *The Foucault Reader*, 340–72
38 Ibid., 341
39 Ibid., 343
40 Ibid., 348
41 Ibid.
42 Ibid.
43 Ibid., 349
44 Ibid., 350
45 Ibid., 350–1
46 I would be inclined to reverse Rorty's formula: 'The citizens of my liberal uto-
    pia would be liberal ironists ... [By contrast] Michel Foucault is an ironist who
    is unwilling to be a liberal' (Richard Rorty, *Contingency, Irony, and Solidarity*
    [Cambridge: Cambridge University Press, 1989], 61). It is precisely because
    Foucault is a Rortyan 'ironist' that he turns out to be a *hyper*-liberal.
47 Rabinow, ed., *The Foucault Reader*, 351. The reference here is to *The Gay Science*,
    § 290. For a presentation of Nietzsche that almost compels one to see
    Nietzsche as the source of many of these conceptions, see Alexander Neha-
    mas, *Nietzsche: Life as Literature* (Cambridge: Harvard University Press, 1985).
    Of particular relevance here is Nehamas's citation, on p. 195, of Nietzsche's
    slogan (*The Gay Science*, § 299), 'we want to be the poets of our life'; cf. *The Gay
    Science*, § 301.
48 Rabinow, ed., *The Foucault Reader*, 361
49 Ibid., 362
50 Ibid. A similar challenge is posed by Alasdair MacIntyre: 'We have good rea-
    son to be suspicious of any contemporary ethics of free choice, according to
    which each individual makes of her or his life a work of art. For something
    very like this aestheticization of the moral, which places the choices of each
    individual at the core of her or his moral life and represents these choices as
    an expression of that individual's creativity, is characteristic of advanced capi-
    talistic modernity.' 'Miller's Foucault, Foucault's Foucault,' *Salmagundi*, no. 97
    (Winter 1993): 60
51 Rabinow, ed., *The Foucault Reader*, 362
52 This is by no means the only oddity that one encounters in the last phase of
    Foucault's thought. See note 31 above.
53 Rabinow, ed., *The Foucault Reader*, 362
54 Foucault, *Care of the Self*, 44
55 Ibid., 45. There is another brief discussion of the dialogue in *Technologies of the*

Self: A Seminar With Michel Foucault, ed. Luther H. Martin, Huck Gutman, Patrick H. Hutton (Amherst: University of Massachusetts Press, 1988), 23–6, 30–1

56 As Foucault acknowledges in 'The Ethic of Care for the Self as a Practice of Freedom' (*Philosophy and Social Criticism* 12, nos. 2–3 [Summer 1987]: 112–31), for Plato there can be no care of the self in abstraction from the possibility of self-knowledge. Posed within the terms of Foucault's distinctly un-Platonic formulation: 'That is where ethics is linked to the game of truth' (116).

57 Jürgen Habermas, 'Taking Aim at the Heart of the Present' in Hoy, ed., *Foucault*, 103

58 I am grateful to Edward Andrew for his critical responses to an earlier draft of this essay. I also want to thank Shadia Drury for inviting me to deliver a version of this essay to a meeting of the Institute of Human Values in Calgary, June 1994; her own contribution to the gathering in Calgary, 'The Roots of Post-modern Politics: Bataille and Foucault,' sheds important light on some of the problems explored above. Finally, my thanks to Jeffrey Friedman, whose suggestions prompted this revised version.

10: Do We Need a Philosophical Ethics? Theory, Prudence, and the Primacy of *Ethos*

1 Jürgen Habermas, 'Legitimation Problems in the Modern State' in *Communication and the Evolution of Society*, trans. T. McCarthy (Boston: Beacon Press, 1979), 201

2 Ibid. Cf. Habermas's combative references to neo-Aristotelianism in 'Discourse Ethics: Notes on a Program of Philosophical Justification' in Habermas, *Moral Consciousness and Communicative Action*, trans. Christian Lenhardt and Shierry Weber Nicholsen (Cambridge: MIT Press, 1990), 44, 98–9.

3 Leo Strauss, one of the targets of Habermas's critique, admits as much in *Natural Right and History* (Chicago: University of Chicago Press, 1974), 7–8

4 Alasdair MacIntyre, 'Bernstein's Distorting Mirrors,' *Soundings* 67, no. 1 (1984): 38–9

5 Hans-Georg Gadamer, 'Gibt es auf Erden ein Maß?' *Philosophische Rundschau* 32, no. 1/2 (1985): 18. Cf. Gadamer, *Truth and Method* (New York: Seabury Press, 1975), 278: 'By placing limits on the intellectualism of Socrates and Plato in his enquiry into the good, Aristotle became the founder of ethics as a discipline independent of metaphysics.' See also Gadamer, *Reason in the Age of Science*, trans. F.G. Lawrence (Cambridge: MIT Press, 1981), 117: 'The expression *practical philosophy* intends precisely to say that it makes no determinate use of arguments of a cosmological, ontological, or metaphysical sort for practical problems.'

6 Habermas, 'Legitimation Problems in the Modern State,' 202, my italics

7 Ibid., 202–3. Habermas alludes in this context to the experience of National Socialism, where the participation in a shared ethical consciousness provided absolutely no bulwark against political evil.

8 Gadamer, *Truth and Method*, 21, my italics

9 For a discussion of similar themes, cf. MacIntyre, 'Bernstein's Distorting Mirrors,' 39–40. For a more direct statement by Gadamer, see also his letter to Richard J. Bernstein, published as an appendix to Bernstein's book *Beyond Objectivism and Relativism* (Philadelphia: University of Pennsylvania Press, 1983), 264, where he states that the aspiration to universal freedom 'has been self-evident to any European since the French Revolution, since Hegel and Kant.'

10 Martin Heidegger, *Basic Writings*, ed. D.F. Krell (New York: Harper and Row, 1977), 232–3

11 Gadamer describes the cultural drama of this ebbing of the *ethos* in the context of his commentary on Book X of *The Republic* in 'Plato and the Poets' in *Dialogue and Dialectic*, trans. P.C. Smith (New Haven: Yale University Press, 1980), 39–72

12 That the fear of relativism remains Habermas's chief objection to hermeneutic philosophy can be seen from his more recent essay, 'Philosophy as Stand-In and Interpreter' in *After Philosophy: End or Transformation?* ed. K. Baynes, J. Bohman, and T. McCarthy (Cambridge: MIT Press, 1987), 304, 307–9, 314. See also Habermas, 'Interpretive Social Science vs. Hermeneuticism' in *Social Science as Moral Inquiry*, ed. N. Haan, R. Bellah, P. Rabinow, and W. Sullivan (Berkeley: University of California Press, 1983), 258

13 Gadamer, *Truth and Method*, 22

14 Ibid., 20

15 Ibid., 21

16 Cf. Gadamer, *Reason in the Age of Science*, 112, 133–4; also, Gadamer, *Truth and Method*, 286; Gadamer, 'On the Possibility of a Philosophical Ethics' in *Kant and Political Philosophy: The Contemporary Legacy*, ed. Ronald Beiner and William James Booth (New Haven: Yale University Press, 1993), 369

17 Gadamer, *Reason in the Age of Science*, 135

18 Gadamer, 'On the Possibility of a Philosophical Ethics,' 363

19 Immanuel Kant, *Critique of Practical Reason*, trans. L.W. Beck, 3rd ed. (New York: Macmillan, 1993), 8n

20 Gadamer, 'On the Possibility of a Philosophical Ethics,' 371: 'The recipient of Aristotle's lectures on ethics must be immune to the peril of wanting to theorize simply in order to extricate himself from the demands of the situation. It seems to me that the abiding validity of Aristotle consists in his holding this peril constantly in view. As Kant did with his formalism, Aristotle too expelled all false claims from the notion of a philosophical ethics.'

21 Bernstein, *Beyond Objectivism and Relativism*, appendix, 263, my italics

22 In 'Discourse Ethics' (43–5, 98–102), Habermas conceives only deontological ethics as cognitivist, and therefore totally misreads MacIntyre as a noncognitivist 'sceptic.' The acknowledgment that Aristotelians like Gadamer and MacIntyre *are* moral cognitivists would force Habermas to rethink his strange assumption that one must be a Kantian in order to avoid moral scepticism. The same misapprehension arises in Habermas's debate with Charles Taylor in *Kommunikatives Handeln*, ed. Axel Honneth and Hans Joas (Frankfurt: Suhrkamp, 1986), 35–52, 328–37. Seeking to repulse Taylor's critique, Habermas replies on behalf of 'a formal *and cognitivist* ethics' (333, my italics) – as if to suggest that these terms are synonymous, or as if Taylor's Aristotelian perspective were any the less cognitivist.

23 Habermas, 'Questions and Counterquestions' in *Habermas and Modernity*, ed. R.J. Bernstein (Cambridge: MIT Press, 1985), 195 (quoting Herbert Schnädelbach)

24 Cf. Gadamer, 'On the Possibility of a Philosophical Ethics,' 369: 'What is meant by *hexis* [habit] is not a possibility of this or that, as with capability and knowledge, but rather a naturelike state of being, a "thus and not otherwise."'

25 Gadamer, 'The Heritage of Hegel' in *Reason in the Age of Science*, 58–9

26 Habermas, *Autonomy and Solidarity*, ed. P. Dews (London: Verso, 1986), 160–1, 170–1, 204 ff

27 In this respect, Gadamer and Habermas stand together in opposition to French postmodernists, such as Derrida and Lyotard, and their American followers, such as Rorty. For a critical response by Gadamer to French 'deconstructionism,' see Gadamer, 'Reply to Jacques Derrida' in *Dialogue and Deconstruction: The Gadamer–Derrida Encounter*, ed. Diane P. Michelfelder and Richard E. Palmer (Albany: State University of New York Press, 1989), 55–7. It bears observation that Gadamer, in his letter to Bernstein (see note 9 above), at least implicitly sides with Habermas in criticism of Rorty, just as he sides with Rorty in criticism of Habermas. Habermas typically conflates Gadamer's hermeneutics and Rorty's pragmatism (see 'Philosophy as Stand-In and Interpreter,' 299, 304–5, 309, 314). In my view, the critique of Rorty as a relativist is somewhat easier to sustain, at least insofar as Rorty plays up relativist themes in order to give added bite to his antifoundationalist rhetoric.

28 Cf. 'Gadamer on Strauss: An Interview,' *Interpretation* 12, no. 1 (January 1984): 10: 'As you know, we are formed between the ages of fourteen and eighteen. Academic teachers always come too late. In the best instance, they can train young scholars, but their function is not to build up character. After the war, I was invited to give a lecture in Frankfurt on what the German professor thinks of his role as an educator. The point that I made was that professors have no

role to play in that regard. Implied in the question at hand is a certain overestimation of the possible impact of the theoretical man. That is the thought behind my attitude.'

29 Habermas, *Autonomy and Solidarity*, 171

30 Ibid., 207–8

31 Cf. Gadamer, 'On the Possibility of a Philosophical Ethics,' 370: 'Ethical practice ... depends so much more on our being than on our explicit consciousness.' Hence Gadamer's attempt to redeem the pre-Enlightenment sense of 'prejudice': *Truth and Method*, 235 ff.

32 For a more radical challenge to Habermas's 'universalism,' cf. Richard Rorty, 'Habermas and Lyotard on Postmodernity' in *Habermas and Modernity*, 165–6. As if to underline the irony, Rorty seeks to enlist Habermas's affirmations of modernity in Rorty's own frankly historicist cause.

33 Albrecht Wellmer, 'Reason, Utopia, and the *Dialectic of Enlightenment*' in *Habermas and Modernity*, 59

34 Ibid., 60–1

35 That the latter possibility is still entertained by Habermas is evident in 'Questions and Counterquestions,' 197, when he asks, 'Does it not remain an open question whether or not the social integrative powers of the religious tradition shaken by enlightenment can find an equivalent in the unifying, consensus-creating power of reason?' (Cf. *Habermas and Modernity*, 92.) I believe that Gadamer would view this unwavering commitment to the Enlightenment idea of reason as a symptom of the 'intellectualism' to which Gadamer's Aristotelianism is opposed. (See *Truth and Method*, 278, and 'On the Possibility of a Philosophical Ethics,' 367.)

36 Habermas, *Autonomy and Solidarity*, 171, 204–5, 207. Habermas wrestles with these questions in 'Discourse Ethics,' 98–109

37 Habermas, 'Philosophy as Stand-In and Interpreter,' 314

38 Habermas, *Autonomy and Solidarity*, 160–1; 'Discourse Ethics,' 98

39 Gadamer's antifoundationalism is clearly expressed in the Foreword to the second edition of *Truth and Method*, where he concedes that his hermeneutical philosophy 'does not satisfy the demand for reflective self-grounding.' 'But is the dialogue with the whole of our philosophical tradition, in which we stand and which, as philosophers, we are, groundless? Does what already supports us require any grounding?' *After Philosophy: End or Transformation?* ed. Baynes, Bohman, and McCarthy, 349. Also, see the exchange between Gadamer and Karl-Otto Apel in *Rationality To-day*, ed. Theodore F. Geraets (Ottawa: University of Ottawa Press, 1979), 348–9. For Habermas's own disavowal of foundationalism, see 'Discourse Ethics,' 94–8, 'Interpretive Social Science vs. Hermeneuticism,' 260–1.

40 Bernstein, *Beyond Objectivism and Relativism*, appendix, 262–3
41 This was Rousseau's grim insight: that intellectuals or theorists can do much
   to *undo* the *ethos* of a sound political community, but they can do little to
   restore it once it is lost. For a similar line of thought, cf. Heidegger, 'Why Do I
   Stay in the Provinces?' in *Heidegger: The Man and the Thinker*, ed. T. Sheehan
   (Chicago: Precedent, 1981), 29.
42 Bernstein, *Beyond Objectivism and Relativism*, appendix, 264. Cf. 'Gadamer on
   Strauss,' 9–11; Strauss and Gadamer, 'Correspondence Concerning *Wahrheit
   und Methode*,' *Independent Journal of Philosophy* 2 (1978): 8, 10; *Truth and Method*,
   xxv

13: Hannah Arendt and Leo Strauss: The Uncommenced Dialogue

1 Elisabeth Young-Bruehl, *Hannah Arendt: For Love of the World* (New Haven: Yale
   University Press, 1982), 98
2 Hannah Arendt, *Lectures on Kant's Political Philosophy*, ed. R. Beiner (Chicago:
   University of Chicago Press, 1982), 23, 28, 37–9
3 Friedrich Nietzsche, *Early Greek Philosophy and Other Essays*, trans. M.A. Mügge
   (London: T.N. Foulis, 1911), 11
4 Martin Heidegger, *Basic Writings*, ed. D.F. Krell (New York: Harper and Row,
   1977), 232–3. See also Heidegger, *An Introduction to Metaphysics*, trans. R. Man-
   heim (New Haven: Yale University Press, 1959), 16
5 Heidegger, *An Introduction to Metaphysics*, 103. Also, Heidegger, *Poetry, Language, Thought* (New York: Harper and Row, 1971), 62
6 Aristotle, *Nicomachean Ethics*, trans. M. Oswald (Indianapolis: Bobbs-Merrill,
   1962), 153, 157
7 Arendt, *Lectures on Kant's Political Philosophy*, 28–9
8 Michael Oakeshott, 'Introduction,' Thomas Hobbes, *Leviathan*, ed. M. Oakeshott (Oxford: Basil Blackwell, 1960), lxiv
9 Arendt, *Lectures on Kant's Political Philosophy*, 29
10 Allan Bloom, *The Closing of the American Mind* (New York: Simon and Schuster,
   1987), 85, 125
11 See ibid., 188
12 See the discussion below of the correspondence with Löwith.
13 On the danger of 'doctrinaire' naturalism, see Hans-Georg Gadamer, *Truth
   and Method* (New York: Seabury Press, 1975), 490. For a statement of Strauss's
   own repudiation of dogmatism, see Strauss, *Natural Right and History* (Chicago:
   University of Chicago Press, 1953), 163–4.
14 Arendt's anti-historicism is expressed most sharply in her motto from Cato,

Lectures on Kant's Political Philosophy, 5 (and commentary, 126–7). Significantly, Strauss makes allusion to the same motto, *Natural Right and History*, 318.

15 M.A. Hill, ed., *Hannah Arendt: The Recovery of the Public World* (New York: St Martin's Press, 1979), 308

16 Strauss, *The City and Man* (Chicago: University of Chicago Press, 1964), 11

17 Karl Löwith and Leo Strauss, 'Correspondence Concerning Modernity,' *Independent Journal of Philosophy* 4 (1983): 107–8

18 Ibid., 113

19 W. Kaufman, ed., *The Portable Nietzsche* (New York: Viking Press, 1968), 558–9. It may well seem surprising that I align Heidegger so closely to Strauss, who often passes judgment so scathingly on Heidegger (whereas Arendt is placed at a greater distance, although she seems, at least on the face of it, much more sympathetic to Heidegger). On my reading, both Strauss *and* Heidegger are ultimately committed to Nietzsche's notion that the best philosophers are 'commanders and legislators' (*Beyond Good and Evil*, § 211) – that is, founders of historical epochs. This, despite Heidegger's many disclaimers to the effect that 'thinking does not endow us directly with the power to act' (*What is Called Thinking?* trans. J.G. Gray [New York: Harper and Row, 1968], 159). What Heidegger and Strauss share is the idea that, again in Nietzsche's words, 'It is the stillest words that bring on the storm. Thoughts that come on doves' feet guide the world' (*Thus Spoke Zarathustra*, Second Part, 'The Stillest Hour'). In other words, the world revolves around philosophy (cf. *Thus Spoke Zarathustra*, Second Part, 'On Great Events': 'The greatest events – they are not our loudest but our stillest hours. Not around the inventors of new noise, but around the inventors of new values does the world revolve; it revolves *inaudibly*'). This, I take it, is the notion that Arendt resolutely disavows.

20 Richard Rorty, 'That Old-Time Philosophy,' *The New Republic*, 4 April 1988, 32. For a statement of Strauss's view, see Strauss, *Spinoza's Critique of Religion* (New York: Schocken Books, 1965), 1–2. See also Nathan Tarcov and Thomas L. Pangle, 'Epilogue: Leo Strauss and the History of Political Philosophy' in *History of Political Philosophy*, 3rd ed., ed. L. Strauss and J. Cropsey (Chicago: University of Chicago Press, 1987), 913.

21 Rorty, 'That Old-Time Philosophy,' 32–3

22 The Arendt–Voegelin exchange is published in *Review of Politics* 15 (1953): 68–85. The quotation is from 80.

23 See Tarcov and Pangle, 'Epilogue,' 908–9, 911–12, and 917–18

24 Thomas L. Pangle, 'Classical Political Philosophy and the Study of the American Founding' (manuscript), 23. For a counterstatement, one that has much

influenced me in the response that follows, see Hans-Georg Gadamer, *Reason in the Age of Science* (Cambridge: MIT Press, 1981), 58–9.

25 See Hans-Georg Gadamer, 'Plato and the Poets' in Gadamer, *Dialogue and Dialectic*, trans. P.C. Smith (New Haven: Yale University Press, 1980), 39–72. The *opposite* argument is offered by Heidegger in the *Letter on Humanism*, where Sophoclean drama is said to 'preserve the ethos' more authentically than Aristotelian philosophy. By the time it reaches philosophical expression in an 'ethics,' the *ethos* has already basically exhausted itself. See note 4 above.

26 M. Cranston and R.S. Peters, eds., *Hobbes and Rousseau* (Garden City, NY: Anchor Books, 1972), 288

27 Bloom, *Closing of the American Mind*, 250

28 Cranston and Peters, eds., *Hobbes and Rousseau*, 289

29 Richard Rorty, 'Thugs and Theorists,' *Political Theory* 15 (November 1987): 579, n. 27. For a more detailed discussion of Heidegger, see Rorty, 'Taking Philosophy Seriously,' *The New Republic*, 11 April 1988, 31–4

30 Young-Bruehl, *Hannah Arendt*, 338

31 Rorty, 'Taking Philosophy Seriously,' 32

32 Conor Cruise O'Brien, 'Patriotism and *The Need for Roots*' in *Simone Weil: Interpretations of a Life*, ed. G.A. White (Amherst: University of Massachusetts Press, 1981), 98–9

33 See Bloom, *Closing of the American Mind*, 276–7. Needless to say, this rendition of ancient political philosophy owes a great deal to the Islamic philosophers of the Middle Ages; see, especially, Alfarabi, 'The Attainment of Happiness' in *Medieval Political Philosophy*, ed. R. Lerner and M. Mahdi (Ithaca: Cornell University Press, 1963), 58–82. As Strauss formulates this Farabian perspective, 'The way of Plato combines the way of Socrates, which is appropriate for the philosopher's relations to the elite, with the way of Thrasymachus, which is appropriate for the philosopher's relations to the vulgar.' Strauss, *What Is Political Philosophy?* (Chicago: University of Chicago Press, 1988), 153.

34 Strauss, *Liberalism Ancient and Modern* (New York: Basic Books, 1968), 14

35 Ibid., 12, 14

36 Interestingly, the other 'hero' of the Kant lectures is Socrates (Arendt, *Lectures on Kant's Political Philosophy*, 33, 36–9, 41–2). It is, of course, significant that both Rousseau and Kant invoke the figure of Socrates as the model of their philosophical egalitarianism. See Rousseau, *First Discourse*; Kant, *Critique of Pure Reason*, Bxxxxi; Kant, *Foundations of the Metaphysics of Morals*, trans. L.W. Beck (Indianapolis: Bobbs-Merrill, 1959), 20. Arendt, too, invokes precisely this Rousseauian–Kantian (or egalitarian) Socrates. For discussion of the opposition between Kantian Socratism and Platonic Socratism, see Richard L.

Velkley, 'On Kant's Socratism' in *The Philosophy of Immanuel Kant,* ed. R. Kennington (Washington, DC: Catholic University of America Press, 1985), 102.

37 Arendt, *Lectures on Kant's Political Philosophy,* 29: 'If there is a distinctive line between the few and the many in Kant it is much rather a question of morality: the "foul spot" in the human species is lying, interpreted as a kind of self-deception. The "few" are those who are honest with themselves.' See also Judith N. Shklar, *Ordinary Vices* (Cambridge, MA: Belknap Press, 1984), 233: the exemplary Kantian character 'above all else ... must not lie.' That this represents a real inversion of the traditional hierarchy can be gathered from reflecting that, according to Strauss, what defines philosophers as a class, at least politically speaking, is that they are liars – that they must practice deception (although not self-deception) to ensure their own survival. See Bloom, *Closing of the American Mind,* 266–79.

38 Arendt, *Lectures on Kant's Political Philosophy,* 28. The crucial Kantian text in this context is the passage from *Critique of Pure Reason* (B859) quoted by Arendt on the same page: 'In matters which concern all men [viz., philosophers and nonphilosophers alike] without distinction nature is not guilty of any partial distribution of her gifts.' One may reasonably assume that these matters are from Kant's point of view the most important matters ('the essential ends of human nature').

39 Arendt, *Lectures on Kant's Political Philosophy,* 21–2, 29; Strauss, *The City and Man,* 18

40 Strauss, *Liberalism Ancient and Modern,* 14

41 Arendt, *Lectures on Kant's Political Philosophy,* 29

42 'A Giving of Accounts: Jacob Klein and Leo Strauss,' *The College* 22 (April 1970): 4

43 This point is reaffirmed in the Löwith correspondence, 113. See also Tarcov and Pangle, 'Epilogue,' 924. See also the reference to philosophers' exemption from categorical imperatives in Strauss's account of the *Crito*: *What is Political Philosophy?* 33.

44 Strauss, *Liberalism Ancient and Modern,* 8

45 Arendt, *On Revolution* (New York: Viking Press, 1965), 23. Also, Arendt, *The Human Condition* (Chicago: University of Chicago Press, 1958), 32–3

46 Arendt, *On Revolution,* 23. Arendt borrows the term 'isonomy' from the speech of Otanes in the 'Debate on Government' in Herodotus's *History* (III.80, 83). It is, of course, open to doubt whether Herodotus himself intended to celebrate the isonomic or democratic regime, as Arendt seems to imply; for as Arendt acknowledges in *On Revolution,* 289, n. 11, a defence of democracy according to its 'fairest name' suggests that there are aspects of democracy that the fair name obscures.

47 Hill, ed., *Hannah Arendt: The Recovery of the Public World*, 317–18
48 Arendt, *The Human Condition*, 5. Strauss offers a matching disclaimer of his own in *The City and Man*, 11.
49 *Hannah Arendt: The Recovery of the Public World*, 331
50 *Natural Right and History* culminates in a critique of Burke. Harvey Mansfield, Jr's contribution to the third edition of Strauss and Cropsey's *History of Political Philosophy* likewise adopts a fundamentally critical stance toward Burke. One might even read Arendt's critique of Plato in Chapter 31 of *The Human Condition* as a direct answer to Strauss's critique of Burke in *Natural Right and History*, 313–14. An excellent statement of this anti-Platonism is to be found in the motto from Burke that is at the head of volume 1 of Karl Popper's *The Open Society and its Enemies*, 5th ed. (Princeton, NJ: Princeton University Press, 1966), vi.
51 Tarcov and Pangle, 'Epilogue,' 928

14: Eros and the Bourgeoisie

1 Allan Bloom, *Giants and Dwarfs: Essays, 1960–1990* (New York: Simon and Schuster, 1990), 17 ('My teachers – Socrates, Machiavelli, Rousseau, and Nietzsche – could hardly be called conservatives'). Bloom clearly understood himself to be a Socratic gadfly trying to sting the complacency of students and readers for whom liberal dogmas had become a matter of automatic reflex. Reflection on the character of Bloom's 'conservatism' may call to mind something Jacob Burckhardt once confided in a letter to his sister: '[For once] I had the courage to be conservative and not to give in. (The easiest thing of all is to be liberal)' (*The Letters of Jacob Burckhardt*, ed. Alexander Dru [New York: Pantheon Books, 1955], 60 [letter to Louise Burckhardt, 5 April 1841]). But there is an important difference: Burckhardt was speaking of summoning up the courage to be the conservative he *really was*.
2 I don't think one can mitigate the severity of what I take to be Bloom's ultimate teaching: namely, that the claims of love are, in the final reckoning, shallow as compared with those of friendship. It certainly seems impressive, but perhaps also dismaying, that Bloom does not shirk from carrying his thinking to this radical conclusion.
3 How far does theory really shape practice? One must decide between two opposing positions. On the one hand is Keynes's famous statement: 'The ideas of economists and political philosophers, both when they are right and when they are wrong, are more powerful than is commonly understood. Indeed the world is ruled by little else. Practical men, who believe themselves to be quite exempt from any intellectual influences, are usually the slaves of some defunct

economist' (John Maynard Keynes, *The General Theory of Employment Interest and Money* [London: Macmillan, 1973], 383; cf. J.S. Mill, *On Bentham and Coleridge* [New York: Harper and Brothers, 1962], 39). Opposed to this is Freud's depiction of philosophy as a contemporary form of animism – he calls it 'an animism without magical practices' – on account of its 'overestimation of the magic of words and the belief that real processes in the external world follow the lines laid down by our thoughts' (Sigmund Freud, *New Introductory Lectures on Psycho-Analysis*, trans. W.J.H. Sprott [New York: W.W. Norton, 1933], 226). Clearly, Bloom is much closer to Keynes's view; Freud's position seems to me closer to the truth of the matter.

15: Left-Wing Conservatism: The Legacy of Christopher Lasch

1 Christopher Lasch, *The True and Only Heaven: Progress and Its Critics* (New York: W.W. Norton, 1991)
2 Christopher Lasch, *The Revolt of the Elites and the Betrayal of Democracy* (New York: W.W. Norton, 1995)
3 For an eloquent summary of Lasch's view of contemporary America, see Christopher Lasch, 'The I's Have It for Another Decade,' *New York Times*, 27 December 1989, A23; see also Lasch, 'The Age of Limits' in *History and the Idea of Progress*, ed. A.M. Melzer, J. Weinberger, and M.R. Zinman (Ithaca: Cornell University Press, 1995), 227–40.
4 Stephen Holmes, *The Anatomy of Antiliberalism* (Cambridge: Harvard University Press, 1993), 135. For a very fair-minded defence of Lasch in the face of Holmes's intemperate critique, see Stephen L. Newman's review of Holmes's book: *Journal of Legal Education* 44, no. 2 (June 1994): 293–6. See also (for a sympathetic account of Lasch) John Gray, 'Does Democracy Have a Future?' *The New York Times Book Review*, 22 January 1995, 1, 24–5.
5 *The True and Only Heaven*, 29
6 Ibid., 241
7 Ibid.
8 Ibid., 180
9 Ibid., 178
10 Ibid.
11 Ibid., 191
12 Ibid., 192
13 Ibid., 196. Cf. 233: 'Nineteenth-century populism meant something quite specific: producerism; a defense of endangered crafts (including the craft of farming); opposition to the new class of public creditors and to the whole machinery of modern finance; opposition to wage labor.'

14 Ibid., 198–201

15 Ibid., 316: syndicalism, for Sorel, was a response to the quasi-religious intuition 'that life can be lived on a higher plane.' Church and army had once disclosed the meaning of 'strenuous ideals' (314) – an 'epic state of mind' (314, 315); what Sorel sought in syndicalism was a new antidote to contemporary 'moral fatigue' (314). 'Moral heroism and the restoration of craftsmanship [were] the two great objectives of the syndicalist movement, as Sorel understood it' (315).

16 Lasch himself emphasizes that Chapter 6, on Carlyle and Emerson – and Emerson in particular – constitutes the core of the book: ibid., 546. I must confess that I find this claim puzzling.

17 Ibid., 203–25, esp. 205, 207, 209–11, 213. Also, 154, 157; and 335: '[syndicalism's] radicalism made Marxism look tame by comparison.'

18 Ibid., 315: 'Marxists ... shared the liberal view of nature as so much raw material to be turned to the purpose of human convenience.' See also 319 n, 335, 457–8.

19 Ibid., 116; Karl Marx and Frederick Engels, *Selected Works* (New York: International Publishers, 1968), 99 ('The Eighteenth Brumaire of Louis Bonaparte'); *The Gospel According to St. Matthew* 8: 21–2; *The Gospel According to St. Luke* 9: 59–62

20 Marx and Engels, *Selected Works*, 99. For a quasi-Marxist challenge to Marxian progressivism, see Walter Benjamin, 'Theses on the Philosophy of History' in Benjamin, *Illuminations*, ed. Hannah Arendt (London: Fontana, 1973), 255–66; and for related discussion, see Christian Lenhardt, 'Anamnestic Solidarity: The Proletariat and its *Manes*,' *Telos* 25 (Fall 1975): 133–54, and my essay, 'Walter Benjamin's Philosophy of History,' *Political Theory* 12, no. 3 (August 1984): 423–34. Cf. *The True and Only Heaven*, 150: Marxists 'wasted no time in mourning the past'; 354: 'the dependence of progress on amnesia'; and 221–2 n: 'May we never weep over the defeated?' – a question that Lasch quotes from one of his intellectual heroes (Orestes Brownson), and that reads as if it were a direct reply to the progressivist injunction to let the dead bury their dead.

21 Seamus Murphy, *Stone Mad* (London: Routledge and Kegan Paul, 1966), 87

22 *The True and Only Heaven*, 112–13: 'Once nostalgia became conscious of itself, the term rapidly entered the vocabulary of political abuse. In societies that clung to the dogma of progress, no other term was more effective in deflating ideological opponents'; and 116: 'By the early sixties, denunciations of nostalgia had become a ritual, performed, like all rituals, with a minimum of critical reflection.'

23 Holmes regards the antinostalgia theme in the book as a clever but unconvinc-

ing 'ploy': *The Anatomy of Antiliberalism*, 137. Lasch tends to associate communitarianism with the seductions of nostalgia. For examples of his animadversions on the rhetoric of community, see *The True and Only Heaven*, 16, 119, 166–7, 172, 303, 328; also, see *The Revolt of the Elites*, chap. 5.

24 *The True and Only Heaven*, 118; cf. 92: 'Progress implied nostalgia as its mirror image.'

25 Ibid., 17

26 Ibid.

27 Ibid.

28 Ibid.

29 Ibid.

30 Ibid., 377–8, 387

31 This is the general thrust of *The True and Only Heaven*, 512–22; but see, especially, 516 n.

32 Ibid., 33–4. After reading this passage, it doesn't seem at all surprising that Lasch refers appreciatively to Allan Bloom's *The Closing of the American Mind*: see *The Revolt of the Elites*, 248.

33 Holmes, *The Anatomy of Antiliberalism*, 125

34 As discussed above, Lasch clearly wants to do for the American left what E.P. Thompson and Raymond Williams in the 1950s sought to do for the British left: to incorporate within leftist thought, conservative themes of attachment to locality and tradition, solidarity with the past, and appreciation of the nobility of ancient crafts; see *The True and Only Heaven*, 29, 328.

35 For instance, he writes that the modern welfare state represents 'the negation of everything the old republican tradition stood for' (*The True and Only Heaven*, 554). Cf. *The Revolt of the Elites*, 105–6.

36 Holmes, *The Anatomy of Antiliberalism*, 125. For another instance of the kind of 'guilt by association' argument commonly employed against Lasch, see Stanley Aronowitz, *The Death of American Radicalism* (New York: Routledge, 1996), 158–63.

37 *The True and Only Heaven*, 170. Cf. 163, where Lasch makes the case that the triumph of large-scale production was *not* an ineluctable fatality. Other courses of social evolution were possible.

38 On cultural infrastructure, cf. *The Revolt of the Elites*, 98–101.

39 *The True and Only Heaven*, 359 n

40 Ibid., 385

41 Ibid., 208–9 n. Cf. 33, 522.

42 Cf. ibid., 532: 'The populist tradition offers no panacea for all the ills that afflict the modern world. It asks the right questions, but it does not provide a ready-made set of answers.'

43 See, for instance, *The Revolt of the Elites*, 71.

44 Ibid., 5: 'The new elites ... are far more cosmopolitan, or at least more restless and migratory, than their predecessors ... Success has never been so closely associated with mobility ... Ambitious people understand ... that a migratory way of life is the price of getting ahead.'

45 Ibid., 6. Lasch is hostile to the multiculturalist impulse of the left in recent years, not just because of its pseudo-cosmopolitanism, but, I think more importantly, because it represents a distraction from the older left's indivertible preoccupation with *class*: see *The Revolt of the Elites*, chap. 5, 7, 10; for instance, 113–14: 'If we can surmount the false polarizations now generated by the politics of gender and race, we may find that the real divisions are still those of class. "Back to basics" could mean a return to class warfare ... or at least to a politics in which class became the overriding issue'; also, 139–40, endorsing 'a politics that will emphasize class divisions instead of racial ones.' One finds the same thought expressed in Michael Lind, *The Next American Nation* (New York: Free Press, 1995), 182: 'As Nixon realized, the greatest beneficiary of the demise of transracial class politics has been the white overclass. Since the 1960s, the effect – and, in the minds of at least some cynical conservative politicians, the purpose – of racial preference and the multicultural ideology that justifies it has been to divert attention from the class divisions in American society and focus it on racial/cultural squabbles.' For another important statement of this theme, see Eric Hobsbawm, 'Identity Politics and the Left,' *New Left Review*, no. 217 (May/June 1996): 38–47.

46 *The Revolt of the Elites*, 76–7: 'the concept of social mobility [is] by no means inconsistent with a system of stratification that concentrates power and privilege in a ruling elite. Indeed, the circulation of elites strengthens the principle of hierarchy.'

47 Ibid., 74–5, 79

48 Ibid., 5

49 Ibid., 64. 'The Democratic Malaise' is the subtitle of the book's introductory chapter.

50 Ibid., 78–9

51 Ibid., 79

52 Ibid., 96–8, 103–4. For a similar line of argument, see Benjamin R. Barber, 'An American Civic Forum: Civil Society between Market Individuals and the Political Community,' *Social Philosophy and Policy* 13, no. 1 (Winter 1996): 269–83.

53 *The Revolt of the Elites*, 101

54 This is particularly evident in his hostile references to liberal norms concerning abortion and divorce: see, for instance, *The True and Only Heaven*, 34, 166, 488–92; and *The Revolt of the Elites*, 95, 107–8, 111, 180–1.

55 *The True and Only Heaven*, 38

56 Ibid., 22

57 Ibid., 16

58 Ibid., 279

59 Ibid., 518

60 Ibid., 34, 35

61 It seems clear that Lasch's frequent use of phrases of this kind contributes a lot to Holmes's animus: see *The Anatomy of Antiliberalism*, 125.

62 Richard Rorty, 'Two Cheers for Élitism,' *The New Yorker*, 30 January 1995, 87. Cf. Holmes, *The Anatomy of Antiliberalism*, 182: 'As diagnosticians of liberal self-deceit, [communitarians] claim to be the midwifes of our spiritual rebirth.'

63 A similar question animates the writings of Michael Sandel: see, for instance, 'Easy Virtue,' *The New Republic*, 2 September 1996, 23: 'Democrats ... resisted the politics of virtue, not by disputing conservatives' particular moral judgments but by rejecting the idea that moral judgments have a place in the public realm ... the Democrats' rejection of the politics of virtue carried a high price, for it left conservatives with a monopoly on moral discourse in politics.' For a book-length elaboration of this thesis, see Michael J. Sandel, *Democracy's Discontent: America in Search of a Public Philosophy* (Cambridge: Harvard University Press, 1996). Although Sandel refers only once in his book to Lasch (313), the philosophic affinity between *The True and Only Heaven* and *Democracy's Discontent* is unmistakable.

64 *The True and Only Heaven*, 420

65 Ibid., 356–9

66 Ibid., 421–4

67 I'm referring, of course, to the famous 'malaise' speech of 15 July 1979: *Public Papers of the Presidents of the United States: Jimmy Carter, 1979*, Book 2 (Washington, DC: United States Government Printing Office, 1980), 1235–42; see Sandel, *Democracy's Discontent*, 307–8. Concerning Lasch's influence on the Carter speech, the source on which I'm relying is Jackson Lears, 'The Man Who Knew too Much,' *The New Republic*, 2 October 1995, 43. On 22, 38, and 515–16 of *The True and Only Heaven*, Lasch alludes to Reagan's manipulation of the 'malaise' theme; and implies that although, in the Reagan/Carter confrontation, it was Reagan who was the immediate political winner, it was Carter's more enduring philosophical insight that ultimately prevailed. (To bring Lasch's survey of political history up to date, it might be added that Bill Clinton's impressive success seems to reside in his having forged an unlikely synthesis of Lasch and Reagan: the Laschian insight that the Democratic Party could never restore its political fortunes without embracing – and rooting its

liberal politics in – the traditionalism of Middle America is combined by Clinton with his own version of the feel-good optimism of Reagan.)

68 Cf. *The True and Only Heaven*, 416, where Lasch cites approvingly Herbert Croly's view that what political activists and program makers need from intellectuals are not 'propagandists, high-level strategists, or ideological masterminds,' but rather, 'disinterested chroniclers and historians of their exploits.'

69 The idea of writing this essay on Christopher Lasch was suggested to me by Jeffrey Friedman; for this, I owe him not a little thanks.

16: Hermeneutical Generosity and Social Criticism

1 Charles Taylor, 'The Motivation behind a Procedural Ethics' in *Kant and Political Philosophy: The Contemporary Legacy*, ed. Ronald Beiner and William James Booth (New Haven: Yale University Press, 1993), 351–4

2 Ibid., 352

3 Ibid., 354. If one prefers modern philosophical exemplars, one could substitute Nietzsche for Plato as the exemplary 'revisionist' theorist and substitute Hegel for Aristotle as the exemplary 'comprehensive' theorist. On Nietzsche's explicit repudiation of any aspirations towards comprehensiveness on the part of the moral philosopher, cf. Hans-Georg Gadamer, 'On the Possibility of a Philosophical Ethics' in *Kant and Political Philosophy*, 367, and the accompanying references, 373, n. 6.

4 Charles Taylor, *Sources of the Self: The Making of the Modern Identity* (Cambridge: Harvard University Press, 1989), 342

5 William A. Galston, *Liberal Purposes: Goods, Virtues, and Diversity in the Liberal State* (Cambridge: Cambridge University Press, 1981), 16

6 See Michael Walzer, *Interpretation and Social Criticism* (Cambridge: Harvard University Press, 1987). In a recent restatement of his argument (*Thick and Thin: Moral Argument at Home and Abroad* [Notre Dame, IN: University of Notre Dame Press, 1994], chap. 3), Walzer makes more explicit his challenge to philosophy as a form of social criticism: see, in particular, 50–2.

7 Among contemporary theorists, Walzer is certainly the one who has done the most to highlight the problem of the appropriate location of the theorist as social critic in relation to the political community that is being criticized. Thus he writes: 'When someone says "our country," emphasizing the possessive pronoun ... the possessive pronoun is a problem. The more closely we identify with the country, so we are commonly told, the harder it is for us to recognize or acknowledge its wrongs. Criticism requires critical distance. It is not clear, though, how much distance critical distance is. Where do we have to stand to be social critics?' (*Interpretation and Social Criticism*, 35–6). Walzer's own answer

to this question is that the appropriate location of social criticism is firmly in the bosom of a shared culture rather than outside its boundaries. Or as he later puts the point: 'critical distance is measured in inches' (ibid., 61). Again, it must be observed that a critical distance measured in inches appears to leave little scope for philosophy as a form of social criticism.

8 Walzer, of course, is explicit in insisting that the social theorist must forgo the aspiration to ascend from the cave: see Michael Walzer, *Spheres of Justice: A Defense of Pluralism and Equality* (New York: Basic Books, 1983), xiv; see also *Thick and Thin*, 59. On Rorty and Taylor, see the exchange between them in *Philosophy in an Age of Pluralism: The Philosophy of Charles Taylor in Question*, ed. James Tully (Cambridge: Cambridge University Press, 1994), 20–33 and 219–22. In fairness to Walzer, it should be added that Rorty is a more radical inside-the-caver than Walzer is. In *Thick and Thin*, in contrast to what seemed to be the ultracommunitarian position in *Spheres of Justice*, Walzer embraces a dual-sided view of theory: namely, thin universalism and thick particularism. Any community must pass a moral threshold of minimalist universal morality, but once it is past that threshold, the only relevant moral standards are, again, its own historically evolved self-understanding. (Taylor's view is very similar.) So this means that there *is* something outside the cave: namely, universal human rights. Rorty's view, by contrast, is more radically 'communitarian': even human rights are just an ethnocentric particularism posing as a universalism.

9 I cannot go along with Quentin Skinner's judgment, in 'Who Are "We"? Ambiguities of the Modern Self' (*Inquiry* 34, no. 2 [June 1991]: 145), that Taylor offers a 'gloomy and vehement' critique of our contemporary age. I don't think Taylor would recognize himself in this characterization. But it surely says something about the character of Taylor's rhetoric that his work can present itself as a kind of Wittgensteinian duck-rabbit, seen as a vehement critique of modernity by readers like Skinner and seen as a defence (albeit a qualified defence) of modernity by readers like myself.

10 John Dunn, 'Pursuing the Personal by Way of the Communal,' *Times Higher Education Supplement*, 22 January 1993, 20. Dunn is quoting Taylor, *The Malaise of Modernity* (Concord, ON: Anansi, 1991), 58.

11 John Dunn, *Interpreting Political Responsibility* (Princeton, NJ: Princeton University Press, 1990), 186. With the basic duality of his thought characterized in this way, Taylor's debt to Hegel seems unmistakable. The difference, of course, is that Hegel thought he had an assured way of surmounting the duality.

12 This tension can obviously be resolved in two different ways: Taylor can drop the appeal to binding conceptions of the human good, and simply tell a story about the vicissitudes of the modern identity. Or, as I prefer, he can talk less

about being true to our authentically modern identity and place more emphasis on objectively desirable configurations of human life. But what he cannot
do, in my view, is go on equating conceptions of the good with conceptions of
how we have come to be the particular selves that we presently are. (This is a
paraphrase of Skinner's formulation: see 'Who Are "We"?' 137; Skinner cites
Sources of the Self, 105. There, Taylor writes that 'our visions of the good are tied
up with our understanding of the self.' In a sense, the whole of the book is
intended to elaborate the meaning of this claim.) My sense is that it is the
determination to align 'the Good' with 'the (modern) self' that accounts for a
certain lack of theoretical radicalism in Taylor's work, notwithstanding its
astonishing breadth and intelligence.

13 Let me suggest an illustration of how one can be, as a social theorist, simulta-
neously anti-individualist and anticommunitarian. It seems to me that one can
be critical of those tendencies in liberal society which are at the furthest
extremity from the quiet simplicity and nobility of the Amish way of life, and at
the same time critical of the constriction of individual personality that the
Amish way of life enforces. Moreover, I don't see why one is, as a social critic,
precluded from offering these opposing criticisms by the fact that one doesn't
have ready-to-hand some ideal image of social arrangements that would constitute a golden mean between liberal dynamism and Amish conformity.

14 More specifically, it is, as Skinner emphasizes ('Who Are "We"?' 134, 138), the
legacy of *Protestant* Christianity. This has the odd consequence that much of
Sources of the Self, qua vindication of modern identity, reads like a defence of
the *Protestant* experience of life! Perhaps this should not be so surprising,
given the intimate causal relationship (which Taylor fully acknowledges)
between Protestantism and the evolution of modernity. But in other respects,
of course, it *is* surprising. In any case, it is hard to square with Skinner's
suggestion (147) that *Sources of the Self* is a work of Catholic philosophy
(cf. Bernard Williams, 'Republican and Galilean,' *New York Review of Books,*
8 November 1990, 45–8).

15 *Sources of the Self,* 106, 293, 305

16 Allan Bloom, *Love and Friendship* (New York: Simon and Schuster, 1993), 14;
Bloom, *The Closing of the American Mind* (New York: Simon and Schuster,
1987), 122

17 *Sources of the Self,* 561, n. 13. Cf. Galston, *Liberal Purposes,* 293: 'the core liberal
notions of free choice and contractual relations ... have permeated the previously sacramental understanding of marriage and the family. The notion of an
irreversible, constitutive commitment has been undermined by notions of liberation and autonomy: "Till death do us part" has been replaced by "till dis-
taste drive us apart."'

18 See, for instance, *Sources of the Self,* 265, 308, and 319; for examples of some passages in which Taylor hints at his sense of alienation from the mainstream of post-Enlightenment intellectual life, see 17, 158, 234–5, 237, and 241.

19 Charles Taylor, 'The Rushdie Controversy,' *Public Culture* 2, no. 1 (Fall 1989): 118–22

20 Ibid., 122

21 For a point of view similar to Taylor's, although the antisecular animus is expressed much more stridently, see Michael Dummett, 'An Open Letter,' *The Independent on Sunday,* 11 February 1990. For the most part, my differences with Taylor have to do with choices of rhetoric and styles of theorizing rather than with the substance of our sympathies and practical judgments. However, his unsympathetic response to *The Satanic Verses* offers at least one instance where I think there is a genuinely substantive difference in our respective points of view. It is surely no coincidence that this disagreement is provoked by one of the rare texts in which Taylor drops his usual reserve in giving a public display of his theistic commitments.

22 Taylor, 'The Rushdie Controversy,' 122

23 Ibid., 119

24 Charles Taylor, 'The Stakes of Constitutional Reform' in *Reconciling the Solitudes: Essays on Canadian Federalism and Nationalism,* ed. Guy Laforest (Montreal: McGill-Queen's University Press, 1993), 140–54; but see also 'Shared and Divergent Values,' *Reconciling the Solitudes,* 167, 171, 175. It is worth noting that Taylor *also* uses 'our' to signal his membership in the *Canadian* political community: see, for instance, 'Shared and Divergent Values,' 156, 158, 160, 170, 172, 173, 183; but see also 'The Stakes of Constitutional Reform,' 143, 144. I would be inclined to say that this dual usage is a sign of Taylor's failure to engage at the deepest theoretical level with the nationalist claim that one cannot have it both ways: one's deepest existential commitment is *either* to *la nation québécoise or* to a political community that is something other than the vehicle of national self-expression. (I'm not saying that one should *accept* this nationalist claim; I'm saying one shouldn't fudge its intended force.)

25 Taylor, 'Shared and Divergent Values,' 161, 162. Cf. 'The Stakes of Constitutional Reform,' 153–4. In the latter text, Taylor urges Quebec to 'move towards a more multi-ethnic model,' right after insisting that the top priority is to establish political instruments by which to promote the uniqueness of Québécois identity. Taylor omits to note the tension between these two political objectives.

26 Taylor, 'Shared and Divergent Values,' 176: 'Quebeckers ... tend to opt for a rather different model of a liberal society [than that articulated in the procedural liberalism of Dworkin and Rawls]. On this view, a society can be orga-

nized around a definition of the good life.' I agree with Taylor that public definitions of the good life are not in principle illegitimate; in fact, my view is that *all* societies define the good life, whether they own up to this or not. But nevertheless, I think a separate argument needs to be made (which Taylor doesn't supply) as to why it is commitment to the *nation* that is worthy of this public undertaking. I would also add the point that some Quebeckers have in mind a less liberal model of political community than other Quebeckers. (But there is greater acknowledgment of this latter point in *Philosophy in an Age of Pluralism*, ed. Tully, 254, 256 [Taylor's reply to Laforest].)

27 Charles Taylor, 'Identité et Reconnaissance,' unpublished manuscript. For a published version of most of this text, see Taylor, 'Les sources de l'identité moderne' in *Les frontières de l'identité: Modernité et postmodernisme au Québec*, ed. M. Elbaz, A. Fortin, and G. Laforest (Paris: L'Harmattan, 1996), 347–54.

28 Consider, for instance, *Philosophy in an Age of Pluralism*, ed. Tully, 224: 'What moral realism requires is that one be able to identify certain changes [associated with the arrival of modernity] as gains or losses. I think we can, and also that there have been significant gains. I also think there have been losses' (Taylor's reply to Skinner). Presumably, these judgments concerning gains and losses appeal to a vision of what's good for human beings that is distinct from the historically evolved articulation of modern identity. In 'Must We Return to Moral Realism?' (*Inquiry* 34, no. 2 [June 1991]: 183–94), Michael Rosen tries to nudge Taylor away from his self-conception as a moral realist. My purpose in this essay is to nudge Taylor in the opposite direction.

29 I am grateful to Guy Laforest for having solicited this essay, and to Julie Bernier for several very fine suggestions. Thanks are also owed to Edward Andrew for having prompted the clarification of Walzer's position in note 8.

17: Thin Ice

1 Friedrich Nietzsche, *The Will to Power*, ed. Walter Kaufmann, trans. W. Kaufmann and R.J. Hollingdale (New York: Vintage, 1968), 51–2 (section 83)

2 Francis Bacon, *The New Organon*, ed. Fulton H. Anderson (New York: Macmillan, 1960), 118

3 Jean-François Lyotard, *The Postmodern Condition: A Report on Knowledge*, trans. Geoff Bennington and Brian Massumi (Minneapolis: University of Minnesota Press, 1984), xxiv: 'I define *postmodern* as incredulity toward metanarratives.'

4 Nietzsche, *The Will to Power*, 40 (section 57)

19: Science and Widsom

1 Immanuel Kant, *Anthropology from a Pragmatic Point of View*, trans. M.J. Gregor (The Hague: Martinus Nijhoff, 1974), 76, 81 (§§ 46, 49); Kant, *Critique of Pure Reason*, trans. N.K. Smith (London: Macmillan, 1980) 178 (B 172, note a)
2 Hubert Dreyfus, *What Computers Can't Do*, rev. ed. (New York: Harper and Row, 1979), 176
3 Consider, here, Chaïm Perelman's helpful distinction between the 'rational' and the 'reasonable': see *Rationality To-day/La Rationalité aujourd'hui*, ed. Theodore F. Geraets (Ottawa: University of Ottawa Press, 1979), 213–24.

20: Rereading Hannah Arendt's Kant Lectures

1 All page references in this essay refer to Hannah Arendt, *Lectures on Kant's Political Philosophy*, ed. R. Beiner (Chicago: University of Chicago Press, 1982).
2 As we know from Arendt's letter to Jaspers of 29 August 1957, she arrived at her distinctive reading of the third *Critique* (as the book in which 'Kant's real political philosophy is hidden') at exactly the same moment that she was reading the part of Jaspers's *The Great Philosophers* devoted to Kant. As that letter and the subsequent exchange between Arendt and Jaspers in Letters 210 and 211 in the published correspondence show beyond any possible doubt, what Arendt found so inspiring in the third *Critique* was entirely mediated by Jaspers; see Hannah Arendt/Karl Jaspers, *Correspondence, 1926–1969*, ed. L. Kohler and H. Saner, trans R. Kimber and R. Kimber (New York: Harcourt Brace Jovanovich, 1992), 318, 320–1. (Jaspers is referred to on the very first page of the Kant Lectures.)
3 Summarized thus, it is tempting to interpret Arendt's Kant lectures as an implicit response to the famous Strauss–Kojève debate (Leo Strauss, *On Tyranny*, ed. Victor Gourevitch and Michael S. Roth [New York: The Free Press, 1991]), with Arendt offering Kant as a preferred third alternative to Strauss's Xenophon/Plato and Kojève's Hegel.
4 Cf. Hannah Arendt, 'On Humanity in Dark Times: Thoughts about Lessing' in her *Men in Dark Times* (Harmondsworth: Penguin, 1973), 11–38, esp. 16.

Index